BURNLEY "ROCKY" JONES
REVOLUTIONARY

BURNLEY "ROCKY" JONES REVOLUTIONARY

AN AUTOBIOGRAPHY BY

Burnley "Rocky" Jones & James W. St.G. Walker

FOREWORD BY

James W. St.G. Walker & George Elliott Clarke

AFTERWORD BY

George Elliott Clarke

ROSEWAY PUBLISHING
an imprint of Fernwood Publishing
HALIFAX & WINNIPEG

Editing: Brenda Conroy
Cover design: John van der Woude
Photos courtesy of Joan Jones and Sharon Jones
Printed and bound in Canada

A Draft Elegy for B.A. Rocky Jones is reprinted with permission from Gaspereau Press.
This book is based on a true story.

Published in Canada by Roseway Publishing
an imprint of Fernwood Publishing
32 Oceanvista Lane, Black Point, Nova Scotia, B0J 1B0
and 748 Broadway Avenue, Winnipeg, Manitoba, R3G 0X3
www.fernwoodpublishing.ca/roseway

Fernwood Publishing Company Limited gratefully acknowledges the financial support of
the Government of Canada through the Canada Book Fund, the Manitoba Department
of Culture, Heritage and Tourism under the Manitoba Publishers Marketing Assistance
Program and the Province of Manitoba, through the Book Publishing Tax Credit, for
our publishing program. We are pleased to work in partnership with the Province of
Nova Scotia to develop and promote our creative industries for the benefit of all Nova
Scotians. We acknowledge the support of the Canada Council for the Arts, which last
year invested $153 million to bring the arts to Canadians throughout the country.

Library and Archives Canada Cataloguing in Publication

Jones, Burnley, 1941-2013, author
Burnley "Rocky" Jones : revolutionary : an autobiography
/ by Burnley "Rocky" Jones and James W. St.G. Walker.

Issued in print and electronic formats.
ISBN 978-1-55266-828-3 (paperback).--ISBN 978-1-55266-858-0
(epub).--ISBN 978-1-55266-859-7 (kindle)

1. Jones, Burnley, 1941-2013. 2. Human rights workers--Nova
Scotia--Biography. 3. Lawyers--Nova Scotia--Biography.
4. Blacks--Nova Scotia--Biography. 5. Nova Scotia--Race relations.
6. Nova Scotia--Biography. I. Walker, James W. St. G., 1940-, author
II. Title.

FC2326.1.J65A3 2016   323.092   C2016-903187-X
                             C2016-903188-8

CONTENTS

ABOUT THIS BOOK

by James W. St. G. Walker & George Elliott Clarke

The Subject

This is more than one man's autobiography or memoir. The personal and community activities of B.A. "Rocky" Jones intersected with the most compelling moments of African Nova Scotian history. His experience of growing up on the Marsh, in Truro, reflects the self-sufficient and supportive community developed over generations by Nova Scotia's African-descended people. His later disillusionment with the broader mainstream population and its racist attitudes was surely a typical event in the coming-of-age of the Black teen in Canada, and as such it is instructive and moving. Launched as a spokesperson for the Canadian civil rights movement beginning in 1965, Rocky engaged with the people and events associated with the radical sixties: with the student movement through the Student Union for Peace Action, with the emerging women's movement through the Voice of Women, with the civil rights movement both in the United States and in Canada through the Student Non-Violent Coordinating Committee, with Black Power through the Black Panthers, with a novel experiment in affirmative action through the Transition Year Program at Dalhousie University and with the decade's most dramatic protest through the events at Sir George Williams University in Montreal.

There's an old joke that goes: "If you can remember the sixties, you weren't really there." But that was only a certain sixties, the hang-out, tune-in, drop-out version. There was another one, intensely memorable and deeply

1

involved in social issues, that accomplished the disruption of some of the fundamental notions in Canadian (and global) society. Rocky is an exemplar of those memorable sixties. Yet his contribution did not end in 1970. His initiatives in the 1960s and his continuing engagement with the Black and mainstream communities resonate still in many of the institutions promoting human rights and social equality in Canada. Journalists dubbed him "Rocky the Revolutionary" because of his association with the Black Panthers and other supposed radicals, but perhaps his most revolutionary innovation was the introduction into Canadian public discourse of his insight that racism is systemic in nature, rather than the product of a few racist individuals. This led him to campaign for remedial programs that would change the system itself and promote equality for all oppressed people in Canada. What was once "revolutionary" has become commonplace today, both in the public mind and in the programs and policies of human rights commissions and social agencies, and this is a vital part of Rocky's legacy.

Genesis

The story of how our book came to be written is an adventure worthy of its subject, and its history goes back a long way. Rocky and Jim first met in Toronto during a demonstration in support of the American civil rights movement in 1965. They reconnected later when Jim moved to Halifax to undertake graduate studies on the history of Blacks in Nova Scotia at Dalhousie University. Their friendship grew as they conducted speaking tours in schools and community associations in the Halifax region, with Jim giving a historical analysis and Rocky expounding on what it meant for Black people in the present. They were both involved in the founding of the Transition Year Program at Dalhousie, and they taught there together until Jim moved to the University of Waterloo in 1971. Over the years they remained in close touch, during Jim's frequent visits to Halifax, occasionally speaking together at conferences across Canada and abroad, and through lengthy telephone conversations, emails and Skype.

As an impressionable young lad George delivered the daily newspaper to the Jones's household, and gradually he worked his way inside the house, where Rocky encouraged him to absorb Black literature and music. In effect Rocky became a mentor to George, introducing him to concepts that expanded his understanding of his own African Nova Scotian heritage. It was on Rocky's recommendation that George attended the University of Waterloo, where he and Jim became friends.

When Rocky's friend and associate Gilbert Daye was planning a community celebration of Rocky's achievements in November 2004, as a fundraiser for the Buddy Daye Foundation's education programs, he turned to the two of us as invited speakers for the event. Rocky was apparently impressed by all the good things we said about him, for the next day he suggested that "we three" should write a book together about "The Movement" and, in particular, his own prominent role in it. We enthusiastically agreed.

Teamwork

Together we decided to base our story substantially on a set of interviews with Rocky, along with our own analytical interjections. For several years Jim had been conducting archival research on the period in Black Canadian history that encompassed Rocky's adult career. He distilled some of that research into a 40-page summary that was intended to serve as an outline to follow in our oral sessions. It was not until December 2006 that we managed to get together for a full week at the Algonquin Hotel in Saint Andrew's-by-the-Sea in New Brunswick. It was a lively and fruitful occasion, resulting in a recording of about 26 hours of enthralling reminiscences from Rocky, prodded by our questions and comments and informed by our combined understanding of African Canadian history. This original session covered most of Rocky's early life and into the "heroic" period of the 1960s.

Our next opportunity to spend a full week together was in February 2007, in Rocky's basement. This session took our story into the 1990s. Jim returned to Halifax for a week in May 2007, when he and Rocky "back-filled" details missed in our earlier discussions. By chance, all three of us were invited to a conference, "The Sixties and the Shaping of Global Consciousness," at Queen's University in June that year. We arrived in Kingston a few days early to continue our recorded exchanges before proceeding to the conference. Our recording efforts reached Rocky's colossal 1997 victory at the Supreme Court of Canada in the case of *R v RDS*. What turned out to be our final three-way recording session occurred in March 2008, again at the Jones residence, when we carried Rocky's account into the twenty-first century.

New Directions

We now had close to 90 hours of taping. We had hoped that a grant from the Social Sciences and Humanities Research Council (SSHRC) would enable us to engage in further archival research, to conduct interviews with some of the other personalities who were important in the story, to attend more conferences to try out our research conclusions and, not least, to meet in some interesting location (Cuba was the number one choice) for more taping and back-filling. Jim prepared our grant application, with the expert assistance of Angela Roorda at the University of Waterloo. The external references were extremely positive, but to our astonishment the sshrc officials rated us "4A," which meant "project approved but no funding." *No funding.* Instead of writing a broader account of The Movement using Rocky's leadership role as our focal point, we decided we would have to make the tapes themselves the basis for our manuscript. Fortunately, the University of Waterloo gave us a consolation grant, which we transferred to Rocky's brother Roger B. Jones as token payment for his efforts in transcribing our tapes.

Rocky and Jim did get to Cuba, though not courtesy of sshrc. We were invited to give a joint keynote address to an international conference at the University of Matanzas, all expenses paid, in February 2012. While lounging at our resort in Varadero we did some strategizing about our book, but our technological limitations prevented us from doing any taping. Meanwhile Roger was undertaking the Herculean task of transcribing our rambling tapes. He would listen to our conversation, repeat it into his voice-recognition equipment, and print out the result. Hundreds of pages came forth, sometimes idiosyncratic in spelling and syntax. As a second-guess, Jim listened to all the tapes again and made up a set of "Notes from Tapes," which he used to monitor Roger's transcripts.

We selected Fernwood to publish the book, and came to an arrangement with Errol Sharpe during an exploratory meeting in May 2007. Then in February 2013 we all got together in Rocky's basement to discuss the format and a contract. The three collaborators decided that we would spend two more weeks together that summer to go over the transcripts, determine what further information was required, make choices about which parts of the massive body of information to include in the book and come to some conclusions about the format and writing responsibilities. Arrangements were made to meet at Jim's in-law's cottage in Muskoka, Ontario, to do this work. On the very day Rocky was to fly to Toronto he called us from the waiting room of the hospital: he would not be coming. Sadly, he died there less than two weeks later. It was July 29, 2013.

Preparing the Manuscript

As a result, our narrative only got to the year 2003. Nevertheless, by prior arrangement, Jim began shaping the notes into a sustained history in the summer of 2014 and then, during a term away from teaching beginning in January 2015, he continued to write the manuscript. Chapters were sculpted from the transcripts, occasionally enhanced by archival or newspaper accounts of the events described. Sometimes one episode would have relevant material in 15 or more taped sessions. It had been decided early on that the book would be in Rocky's voice, a surreal experience for the writer but by no means an unpleasant one. It kept Rocky constantly in Jim's thoughts, and in any case he had Rocky's own words on the tapes. In order to sketch the final decade in Rocky's life not covered in the tapes, Jim travelled to Halifax in May 2015 to interview Rocky's friends and family, view several videotaped speeches Rocky had delivered in recent years, and consult the newspaper collection at the Halifax Public Library. He also went to Truro to get further information about the Jones family and Rocky's early years. As a result the final chapter is written in Jim's own voice; the further material on the Marsh was incorporated into an enriched Chapter 1. The draft was completed, symbolically and deliberately, on July 29, 2015, the second anniversary of Rocky's death.

Revisions followed, based primarily on comments from Errol and from Lynn and Roger Jones and Marie Jones Francis, who read the entire draft manuscript. Rocky made mistakes — he even got the birth order of his family wrong — and he gave some extreme opinions from time to time about people and events. He did not have an opportunity to edit the manuscript, make corrections or revise judgments made in the heated atmosphere of our recording sessions. His own perspective in his own voice rings true, but the content of this book is not Gospel. It is an oral history, adapted from only partially structured conversations. An oral discussion cannot be transferred directly to the printed page: it must be "translated," and this is what has been done with our recordings.

The result is an important story about an important Canadian, revealing that the idealism of the sixties was not a passing phenomenon but a factor that continues to influence the lives of many Canadians and our institutions. It will encourage Canadians to consider the implications of citizen engagement with the policies that affect them, and it will be of value to lawyers, human rights professionals and non-government organizations. For historians, both academic and public, there will be new insights. We deliberately aim our message at those Canadians who wish to understand the history of race relations and human rights in our country. We expect, we hope, that Rocky's life will be particularly inspiring to young African Canadians, but assuredly every Canadian deserves to be reminded of how our rights are established and enhanced. Rocky's story does more than relate one person's impact on our recent history, though indeed it does that; it reveals how that impact was achieved and the process by which advances can be made in our journey toward social justice. And above all, it is an intensely engaging and entertaining read.

Acknowledgments

Our heartfelt thanks go to those who helped with the research, with information on Rocky's life, with comments on the draft manuscript, and with hospitality in Truro and Halifax. They include, especially, Rocky's siblings Roger, Lynn and Marie, family members Sharon, Shalyn (Folami) and Joan Jones, friends and associates Bruce "Bookie" Wood, Bill Yarn, Carolann Wright-Parks, Gilbert Daye, Lenore Zann, Joy Woolfrey, Shawna Hoyte, Errol Sharpe and, in Waterloo, Stephanie Kirkwood Walker.

The full documentation of this evolving project will be located in the Special Collections and Archives of the Dana Porter Library at the University of Waterloo. This will include reams of primary research notes used to produce the working outline for our three-way discussions, several proposed outlines for the book, Roger's transcripts and Jim's "Notes from Tapes," the sshrc application and the comments by the anonymous referees, drafting notes and chapter arrangements. They will be open to researchers, once indexed, and digital copies will be available over the internet.

Chapter One

ON THE MARSH

Itook my first sense of identity from my family. I was a Jones. I was Jerry Jones's grandson, decorated World War I hero. I was Elmer Jones's son, World War II hero, wounded in the service. I was Willena Jones's son, a powerful force in our community who told me "You are just as good as anybody. Never let anybody do anything or say anything to demean you." My family was well-known and well-respected. It automatically gave me built-in protection and acceptance wherever I went in my community. As much as you define yourself, the community defines you. Because of the family I was born into there were certain expectations, and people would voice it: "Listen, you are not supposed to do this. You are Elmer's son or Jerry's grandson and *you should know better*." I've always thought my protection is my family and the extended family of my community. They looked after me, they made it possible for me to develop. I give full credit everywhere I go to my family and the Marsh in Truro — wherever I speak, whatever I do — because they made it possible.

I was in awe of my grandfather. During the Battle of Vimy Ridge he single-handedly captured a German machine-gun nest which had his unit pinned down under deadly fire. His commanding officer recommended him for a medal, but allegedly because of racial discrimination he never received it during his lifetime. Many years later, in 2010, the army made up for this by awarding him the Distinguished Service Medal posthumously. He was a huge man. By the time I was born he was stooped a bit. When I was little we would walk together along the road. It was uneven, and he would stumble from time to time. I was terrified that he would fall on me and crush me. But I really loved to be with him. His hands were so huge, when he took my hand his whole hand went right over mine. He was a monster of a man, yet he was so gentle. He never raised his voice.

Strange thing about Jones men: they didn't talk. Now, what happened to me I don't know. They never carried on conversations, ever. I don't remember a single conversation that I ever heard that my grandfather had. One of his good friends was Mr. Leamont, a white man who lived two doors away. They were about the same age, and they would sit on a bench in the sun with their jack-knives and stones, and they would spit on the stone and sharpen the knives and whittle pieces of wood. And never talk. I would sit by them while they just sat there for what would seem to me like hours. They both chewed tobacco, and they would sit there and chew tobacco and spit and whittle. And it seemed to me that they didn't make anything, that they just had a piece of wood and cut the wood and spat.

We lived at 71 Ford Street, and my grandfather lived at number 30, right across the road. We called it the "Old House." He lived alone, as my grand-mother died before I was born. When that house burned down he moved in with us. In his younger days he had been a farm hand, and after that he became a teamster and worked in the woods until coming to Truro. Every year he would take me to the Exhibition on my birthday, August 26. He'd take me into the barns, where he knew all the farmers. We would look at the horses. I loved to go, as it was a time for just the two of us. When I was a bit older he would take me fishing, travelling all over, to Guysborough County, to differ-ent places. I could spend an entire day fishing with him and never talk about anything. He might say "Try to use this boy, you might catch more fish," a little advice here and there. It would be the same with my father. We'd go off to a trout brook and just sit, just put your line in and get a fish, not saying anything. These guys were patient, they could wait and wait and wait. Or I'd go rabbit hunting with my father or grandfather. We'd sit and wait and I'd think "Man, what is going on!" Eventually a rabbit would come. They might say "This is a good spot, we'll get a rabbit here boy." I learned to recognize a good rabbit trail because there is nothing else to do but look. No talking.

Jerry Jones seldom cashed a cheque. He would get his old age pension in the mail, and he'd stick the cheque in his pocket and never cash it. When he did cash them he always had a lot of money in his pocket because he never spent anything. He would lend people money, and he kept a record in a little notebook. Wherever he went people just gave him things, meals, whatever. He would take off, up to New Glasgow or Pictou or Halifax, and just disappear for a few days. Everyone knew him, so they would take him in. While on his way to Halifax one time, he drowned in the North West Arm. It was in winter, and it took months for his body to be found. Meanwhile he was just missing. There was a suggestion that he had been rolled and robbed, as he'd left home with money and none was found on the body, but this was never followed up officially. I was only nine years old, and his loss left a great hole in my life.

My father Elmer shared a lot of his father's characteristics, both physical and temperamental. He served in the forestry corps in France during World War II, and he was wounded, just like his father. Neither of them made a big deal out of that, but there was a certain pride in their military contribution. Grandfather, father, older brother Alvin, all were huge men, over six feet tall, and all were extremely gentle. You would never ever hear of any of the Jones men being in a physical fight. One time one of the neighbours came by and he was drunk. It was a Sunday night and my parents were going to church, but this guy was determined to stay. My father said, "You can't stay in the house because we are going to church." This neighbour got quite belligerent, he wasn't leaving. My father was so gentle. He reached down and picked up the chair this guy was sitting on, just like he was cradling a baby, and carried him outdoors and set him down out in the yard and said, "Okay Sandford, I'll be back after church." And that was the end of it. He had the strength and the power to be able to do that, to be able to pick up a grown full-sized man. Another time I saw my father pick up the back end of a car, by our house. The boys were playing with a ball, and it got stuck under the car. He just picked up the car so they could get it.

My father was quite a famous hockey player in the Black community. If you would speak to anyone who was around in those days, they would know, you couldn't knock Elmer Jones down. He was a great defence man. People said if it hadn't been for racism he'd likely have been an NHL player. He never got into a fight playing hockey. Nobody would pick on him, that's for sure. My sister Marie remembers that when she was little our father would play games with the children, Chinese checkers maybe, and read stories to them. I remember we would all play horseshoes together, with the family and neighbours.

My father had a steady job, what was later called a stationary engineer. He looked after the boilers for the Lewis Eastern Hat and Felt Company, and later on he worked at the post office looking after their boilers. A steady job gave a lot of prestige in the community. He carried a lunch pail to work, depending on his shift, came home, went to sleep, got up and did his chores, and went back to work. At the end of the week he handed his pay envelope over to my mother, who looked after all the family expenses. He must have kept a little aside for himself, because on special occasions he would invite his men friends over for a drink. Our parents had an agreement that there would be no drinking of alcohol in the house, so he had to take his friends out to the barn. And even in the barn they couldn't be obvious. The rum was always hidden in the feed barrel. There is no question our mother knew he bought alcohol. She grew up in a situation where there was a lot of drinking, and there was never going to be any drinking in her house. My father had a stash in the house, in a little cubbyhole in the hallway over top of the door. That was the little tiny bottles. He could sneak in there and have a drink by himself. The quarts were always hidden out in the barn. Everybody knew. Some friend might say "Well Elmer, I think we better go out and see them chickens, how they're doing." If you came to our house, you got your drink out in the barn.

My mother was the one who articulated values. She was emotional, so she could cry. If something went wrong, as tough as she was, she could cry. And my mother made it possible for even us as men to be able to cry. It wasn't wrong for us to do that. My mother was the one who really instilled in us the sense of pride that we should have, being who we were. And my mother was the one who taught us that you can't lord it over anybody, you can't take advantage of anybody, you must always be fair. She would find opportunities to say that. Whereas my father rarely said anything, my mother could talk. If something happened at the school my mother would assess it, and she'd say, "We are going right back to that school," and she would be the one who would either have you by the ear or holding your hand, whichever was appropriate. She was the one to deal with it. She provided that kind of strength, in terms of any of the problems we encountered growing up.

I've wondered at times who made the decisions and how much. I know she made immediate decisions. They never argued in front of us. They believed that they should shelter the children from any kind of conflict. She was certainly in charge of our discipline. If we were behaving particularly badly she'd say, "Wait until your father gets home, you are getting a beating." You'd go all day, hoping she forgets, but she never forgets. Now that I think back at it, it must have been tough for my father to come home — he hasn't been there all day and now he is supposed to be the one to administer this beating. It was an awful thing. I saw many times my father came home and I'd be doing stuff, kind of hoping to stay out of the way, and I'd go to bed and then I'd hear him coming and I'd get down on my knees saying my prayers. I could pray a long time. I'd be there and he'd be getting ready for bed, and I'd be praying, praying that I could outlast him. And then he'd have to come in and give me a beating. I never got a beating I didn't deserve, but as a father you look back at it and think "Gee whiz."

My mother's family, the Gabriels, were in Springhill while we were children. She would go there to visit, maybe for a weekend or even for a week, and sometimes as a special treat some of us kids would go along. For us that was total freedom, going to our grandparents' place where you could get away with a lot. It was in Springhill where my mother developed her incredible values and her wisdom. When I was going to get married to Sharon, a couple of my sisters were not in favour of it because Sharon was white, or at least that's the way I understood it. I said, "If that is the way you feel, then you are not welcome and don't bother coming to the wedding." I felt the position they were taking was unfair. Well, my mother had a little talk with me. She said, "You go back and apologize." I said, "ME? Why should I go back and apologize? I didn't do anything wrong, they are wrong." She said, "No, you go back because you can handle this, it is okay, you are bigger than that. You will go back, and you will make things right." At the time I couldn't understand it, really. I'm thinking gee whiz, I'm not wrong. But she was right. It worked out just as she said. Today my sisters and wife are all friends and get along and respect each other. Because I was so pig headed, that without her telling me to do the right thing, I might have spoiled everything. The family wasn't broken up. My mother had enough knowledge of her own children and enough insight to take a look at that situation and see the resolution. And she had enough power within the family unit to enforce it.

Willena Jones ran the house with an iron fist. You did not step out of line without facing the consequences. Many a day I had to go out and cut down a switch. "Go out and cut the switch, and I'm going to use it to tan your hide." All the way you are going out thinking about getting this switch, and that is punishment, serious serious punishment. You've got to cut a switch. You don't want to cut a switch that is too good because it is going to hurt too much and if you get a switch that is not strong enough, you know it is going to take a couple little licks and it will break and you'll be sent out for another one, so you can't get it too small. And you don't want it too whippy. You had to make sure exactly which switch you cut, that would give the least amount of pain on your legs, last as long as it had to but not too long, because the beating is over when the switch breaks. You had to do some serious thinking to get that switch. The beating with the switch didn't hurt nearly as much as the going to get it and thinking about it, and she would be saying, "You think about what you did," but I'd be thinking, "Oh man if only I hadn't done this. If I hadn't done it, I wouldn't be out here getting the switch."

And I could cry, oh I could cry. I got in trouble so much. Mom would be coming up the road to get me. You see your mother coming and you know you are in trouble because you know what you did and you know somebody phoned her and told her what you did. There is no getting away from it, because how are you going to say, "Mrs. Clyke is lying to you Mom." There's no way you can do that. I can see Mom now, she is coming up the road. There was always something in her hand, a switch or a belt or whatever. You can see her coming up the road, and you know you've got to go down the road and go by her. And you start crying. "Ohhh Mom I didn't mean it." "Get over here!" "Ohhh Mom Mommm, I don't want to get hit. Oh Mom I won't do it again." I'd be crying and she hasn't laid one on me yet. You couldn't run, but you tried to stay as far away so that when she swings the belt it just glances you. You've got that measure pretty good in your mind. She'd be coming down the street and you'd be dancing along, people would think you were being killed. I've got tears running down my cheeks just remembering this!

My mother set us all an inspiring example. She scrubbed floors all the time; my whole young life she was a domestic. She would come home with her feet swollen over her shoes, and then she'd do laundry and sewing that she took in from people in town. Then she'd spend the rest of her evenings studying. She was always doing courses: sewing, home nursing and academic subjects too. She only had a grade 5 education, but she went back to night school and she completed high school, and then she attended the Teachers' College full-time. This was from 1972 to 1974, long after I had left home. At age 60 she got a job in the junior high school, teaching history and serving as counsellor to Black students. She held this job for ten years, until after our father died in 1983. From her I learned that with dedication you can overcome anything.

My grandfather had a sister, Aunt Martha, known to one and all as Big Foot Martha Jones. She was a school teacher and was apparently the first or one of the first African Canadians to graduate from the Nova Scotia Normal College. She was an itinerant teacher, who taught all around Nova Scotia — in the Prestons, Weymouth Falls, Dartmouth. Years later I would hear stories about this woman who had such an impact on education in Nova Scotia. When I was growing up, this fact that we had a famous teacher in our family was a source of pride.

In our own house our family structure was very clear. My older sister Elaine ran the younger children. Until I was five I was the baby of the family. In that sense I had a special place because they had to cater to me, being the youngest, and I also had a special position because I was born on Elaine's birthday, so I was her birthday present. That's what she always said. It was five years later that Wilma was born, when my father came home from the War. My mother went off to work in the morning and sometimes she came home at lunch but sometimes she didn't. While she was away Elaine was in charge and Elaine didn't take any fooling. Elaine would tell you to do something and you had to do it, there was no question, whatever she said you had to do you had to do. She'd think nothing of smacking you upside of the head in a minute. We grew up in an era where corporal punishment was just a part of the way you were raised.

We were a family of ten children altogether: Elaine came first, then Alvin, then Marie, and then I came along. Then five years after me came Wilma, then Janis, Luella, Lynn and Debby, the little kids. So our family was structured in two groups: the "pre-war kids" and the "after-war kids," and then Roger was born after I left home, almost at the same time as my own daughter Tracey. He was called "the after-thought."

My brother Alvin was always happy go lucky. Alvin didn't take things too seriously and if he could get out of work, he would. He was a big guy, very athletic. He could ride a bike, sitting on the handle bars, facing the back seat. Alvin was three years older than me, and never let me travel with him. The only way I travelled with him was if I followed him and showed up someplace. When we were teenagers, I'd be 13 and he'd be 16, and that was just a "no no" for him to hang around with me. He joined the air force as soon as he was eligible. My sister Marie was more my age. Marie could fight, and I could use Marie for protection against the older and bigger guys. We were really a tight, close family. Elaine had a little closet bedroom to herself, and the other girls shared a bedroom. There was another one for Alvin and me. There was a wood stove downstairs in the dining room area, with a hole cut in the ceiling to let the heat go upstairs. No central heating or furnace. Mostly it was Alvin and me who kept the stove with firewood.

Only two of the houses on the Marsh had basements. The others were all built maybe a foot and a half or two feet off the ground. In preparation for winter you'd have to insulate all the area around the house, in what we called a "bank." It was just like a flower box that went all around the house, and you filled it with ashes or sawdust. So all of our houses had to be banked every fall, and that stopped the wind from coming in. When our house was constructed, they put up the tar paper on the outside walls and then over the tar paper we had a fire board, small chips of stone, and that was the siding. It was a little thicker than sandpaper. But when they nailed the tar paper on the walls the nails would go right straight through into the house. So upstairs we put cardboard on the inside, pieces of cardboard boxes, to try and keep the cold out. That was our upstairs insulation. The nails would come through and they would turn to frost. There would be half an inch or an inch of nail sticking into the house, and all through the winter they would be white because they were frozen. Downstairs was insulated with store-bought slabs of pink wool-like material. This was on the inside of the house.

Out in the back yard we had an outhouse, that is until we were connected to the water and sewers, and we had a huge vegetable garden. Each year a guy came with a horse to plough the garden, and then we had to plant and cultivate it all summer. We also had pigs in the back, and chickens and ducks. Inside the house we had a radio, like everybody else, and mostly around supper time we'd all gather to listen to certain programs together. We also had an organ. Don't ask me how we had an organ when we couldn't even have insulation in our house. Mrs. Clyke next door also had an organ. Perhaps a smooth-talking salesman came along and said "I have this organ for you." I'm assuming we were paying for it for years and years.

Music was a part of everything we did. There were lots of people who could play guitars in the community, a couple of organs, my father's brother Uncle Vic with his bugle, Sam Wood was a fiddler. My grandfather in Springhill played the mandolin; in fact all the Gabriels played stringed instruments. My father was a famous bass singer, and Uncle Vic was a tenor. They were part of a group called the Four Flames. Often when we got together for a singsong it would be to play and sing country and western music, and this is what we would listen to on the radio too. But church music, of course, dominated. Everyone learned all the spirituals and hymns, and they were sung at every occasion, everywhere all the time.

Besides our own family members, it was quite common that people would come and stay. Sometimes it would be our relatives from Springhill, or family friends. If they stayed for a day or for much longer, it was never discussed; somehow people were accommodated. I remember as an example after my brother joined the air cadets, he would have been maybe 14, he met some guys from Sydney who had never been in our part of the province. So he invited them to come to Truro and they just came and they stayed any time they wanted to after that. If they came for the weekend or the week it didn't make any difference. The Collins family next door always had people staying with them, and so did most of the families. There was no place a Black person could rent a room in Truro, so people from the Marsh would offer Black strangers a place to stay with them while they were in town. It was strange that it was such a benevolent society. I may be romanticizing it a bit in retrospect, but people didn't seem to focus on the negative things that happened to people, they just seemed to accept that there were hard times and you just deal with it. Occasionally we would have boarders, foreign students who were at the agricultural college in Truro. Often they would be Africans, and they were the first people I ever met who came from Africa. We knew Africa was our homeland; in fact there was a family tradition that we were descended from kings in West Africa. We had a book about Africa in our home called *Flaming Torch in Darkest Africa*, written by an African American missionary bishop, but our knowledge was very limited until we had a chance to talk with some of these students.

We knew we were poor, but we didn't know how poor. I had no idea how tough things were until after I left the community. My parents were raising 10 kids, but because the whole community was in the same boat it just seemed normal. There were certain things you did without but that was no big deal. You ate and you were warm. I used to take a pair of wool socks and darn them, and then when you couldn't darn them anymore you just cut the tops of the socks into a pair of mittens. So that was as warm as all get out. You didn't suffer and you didn't care. You went out to play hockey and you had a pair of warm mitts and that was good.

Our mother made clothes for all of us, and we also got clothing, what we called "boxes," from outside the community. A lot of it was through families where my mother did domestic work. The Camerons was one of those families. They had a son who was just a little older than me and a little bigger. So I'd get a box, and it would be all his sweaters or shirts or whatever. They also had a girl in that family, and we'd get a box of things for my sisters. It was a big thing to get a box.

Both my parents worked, but we had to supplement our family income. When I was as young as five years old I would go out into the marsh to collect mushrooms. I knew exactly where to find them, and I knew which ones to pick and which ones not to pick because they could make you sick. We ate some of them in the family, but mostly we sold them to people in the town. We would go door to door with little baskets, and we would place some in the stores around town. We did the same with blueberries. That was the earliest way I ever made money, because I was able to keep some of it for myself. We also sold eggs and chickens from our back yard and some of the fish we caught that we didn't eat ourselves. We also gathered wood on the marsh fields. I would go with my brother Alvin. By the time I was about 10, and he would be 13, we had a big sleigh, almost as big as one that would be pulled by a horse, and we used it to haul the wood that we would find on the frozen marsh. Alvin, big Alvin, had to pull the sleigh. I remember one day when we were out getting wood I got so cold I was just crying, and Alvin had to put me on top of the load and pull me as well as the wood all the way home. When we got it home we would have to cross-cut the wood because we had no power saw. I couldn't keep up to him cross-cutting the wood so it was easier for him to use the saw without my help. He could easily cut a cord of wood all by himself with the cross-cut or bucksaw, and then it was my job to stack it or carry it into the house. The other thing that we had to do in terms of raising money was we gathered beer bottles, and we had what we called the beer bottle bushes. What used to happen was the men would buy their beer and they had certain places where they would park with their girlfriends, and drink and throw the bottles out, and we knew all those spots. In the morning, bright and early, we'd go looking for beer bottles, and I suppose we would check places within a three or four mile radius. My sister Lynn tells the story of walking to church with my father on a Sunday morning. If he discovered some useful piece of junk, something salvageable, he would hide it in the bushes beside the road. Then on their way home from church he would pick it up, either to use or to sell.

Our diet was enriched by things we raised, grew or gathered. Then at supper time, if I was home, my mother would say "Get them in the house for dinner." So I'd go outside and yell "Alvin, Marie, Elaine, you're wanted." That was the call, and you'd hear it all over the community. Somebody else can pick up the call down the street. Suppose somebody knew Alvin was over at Hector Hill's, at the barns. They'd pass along the call: "Alvin, your mother wants you." Then around the dinner table was the time to involve Mom in anything you wanted her to deal with. "Elaine did this to me... Alvin took my that... The teacher did this..." I'd say that was most of our conversations, a chance to recap what was going on during the day. We didn't discuss politics or world events, just close to the family stuff. There were a lot of things I suppose that were happening, that grown-ups didn't think were the business of children. Anyway my father didn't usually participate in our dinnertime chatter. My faithful companion Chubby, the dog, wasn't allowed around the table, so you couldn't pass off scraps of food you didn't like. You ate what was put in front of you. There was no such thing as "I don't like this or I don't like that." Like porridge, I would get porridge in the morning and fool with it and not eat.

"Don't worry about it," Mom would say, "it will be here when you get home at lunch time." It was like a basketball, you could bounce it off the floor and it is there waiting for you. We had a lot of fresh produce from the garden, potatoes, carrots, turnips, squash, pumpkins, and our own chickens and eggs, like a normal truck farm would have. We gathered dandelion greens and lamb's quarters, and we had whatever berries were in season. They made preserves, so we always had preserved berries and fruit. We ate a lot of fish that we caught in the river and rabbits that we hunted. We often had a side of beef in the house, used mostly for beef stew, but we never had steak. I think I had my first steak, other than deer steak, after I left home. We just couldn't afford it. We had a lot of bologna, some wieners. We used molasses and you weren't allowed to have butter and molasses on the same piece of bread, you either had to have butter or molasses. That was the time when that awful white margarine came that looked like lard and tasted like lard. For the first margarine, the colouring was in a piece of paper. You sprinkled it over and mixed it all up. It was awful orange, tasted awful. You wouldn't believe how bad this stuff tasted. Then it came in a bag, with a little button and you busted the button and the colouring went in and you manipulated the bag and that was the next generation of margarine. And then the next generation of margarine was when you bought coloured margarine, but that was years later. Oh it was terrible. My thing was that I would always be able to have butter on my table when I grew up.

For Christmas in our family we were allowed to ask for one thing for a present. We were told what we were allowed to spend, like $2 or $3 or whatever, and we could look in the Simpson's catalogue and the Eaton's catalogue. I would spend half the summer going through the catalogues trying to find what it was that I wanted for my one big present. In addition to that, every year I got a piece of hockey equipment. As a rule, what I got was a hockey stick and a puck, because my hockey stick would be gone from last year. My most memorable Christmas I think was the year I got a pair of shin pads, instead of cardboard or just pieces of stick that didn't cover the knee. This special year I had a real pair of shin pads that had the cup over the knee and the pad below and that was pretty awesome. That was really something to get that. And another year I got a sled. That was very exciting, though we didn't have that many hills in Truro. But I got a good coasting sled.

In our community there was a lot of visiting at Christmas. Everyone visited everyone else's house, so it couldn't all happen in one day. The visiting would start a few days earlier and the men always had a drink for the other men. Christmas was exciting because there was so much visiting with family and relatives and they still do it to this day. Everybody came to our house to sing. If you go to Truro today, somebody will say, "Let's go down to the Joneses and we'll have a singsong." After the singsong we'd sneak outside where the men were having their drink, and we'd watch them; that was really exciting. Plus there were always gifts exchanged between the different families. You exchange gifts with your special friends. It's not like every family gave to every family, but I'd always give my friend up the road a gift and he'd give me one. And my sisters would give to certain people up the road and back and forth. You had these gifts that were not only your ten brothers and sisters and your mother and father, and your uncles and aunts but you also had these gifts coming from other people. It was a real good time. And eating. If anybody was there of course they were forced to stay, and it always happened to you if you were at someone else's house. On Christmas you ended up eating two or three dinners. We'd kill some of our chickens. Women prided themselves on fruit cake; everybody wanted to try everyone else's fruit cake. I don't know how my mother dealt with this, but she would put rum in her fruit cake. Those fruit cakes were a really big thing.

There were three Black communities in Truro, the Island, the Hill and the Marsh, with something over a mile between each of them. The Island, which was the largest, was located at the west end of Prince Street, near the town dump, where the Islanders could scavenge. The Hill was more spread out, but centred along Young Street off Prince Street. Some Black people on the Hill were Anglicans, descended from Black Loyalists who migrated down from Guysborough, where they had settled after the American Revolution. The rest of us all attended Zion Baptist Church, and it was understood that we descended from the Black Refugees, who came to Nova Scotia after the War of 1812. We lived on the Marsh, which basically consisted of two streets, Ford and Cross, on the marshland near the Salmon River. I always loved the Marsh. Obviously our houses weren't grand, but they weren't one-room shacks. Some outsiders might have called them six-room shacks. Most people built onto their houses as their families grew over the years. I didn't see anything wrong with our houses. My friend Bruce Wood, always known as "Bookie," met a friend who lived over the other side of town, and Bookie says, "I'll never forget the day I invited him over to my house, and the friend said, oh, you live in a shack." And Bookie said, "I don't live in a shack," and the guy says "Yeah, you live in one of these shacks along here." And Bookie says to this day, "I didn't know I lived in a shack and this guy told me I lived in a shack and it really upset me." Bookie was very talented as a kid. He could draw anything.

He has become a famous sculptor, painter and designer, and he still identifies completely with the community of the Marsh.

Uptown there were beautiful homes on Smith Avenue, big stately buildings in the town of Truro, but I didn't see any contradiction or I had no envy to want to move into those houses, because I was so happy living where I lived. I did get into a couple of those houses when I went to visit friends who went to Willow Street School. I never thought that their place was a better place to live than where I lived. I just loved where I lived so much, it was so much fun, we had the whole marsh to play in. The other kids didn't have what we had as far as I was concerned. We could go around the back at the Eastern Felt to pick up rejected hats, to make cowboy hats out of them, and we could take used bottles from the dye and have fun smashing them. We would go up to Victoria Park, with big trees and waterfalls. It was a nice part of Truro and I liked it, but we had the Government Farm close to where we lived. That's what we called the Agricultural College. I spent my entire childhood, every summer, on that farm, and we hayed with those guys and we rode the hay wagons. We knew all the workers, we knew all the horses, we were able to drive the horses. No one had it better than we did, we were like the chosen community, right on the outskirts of town. You could walk to town in a minute and get all of those advantages, anything they had in town we had. We had town water, and in the 50s we got TV and we had the telephone. We had all the advantages of town plus we had all the advantages of rural living, without all the disadvantages of rural living. Ideal.

The neighbourhood was very close-knit, and it was truly integrated in racial terms. There were a few white families. You would be closer to a white kid from the Marsh than you would be to a Black kid from the Hill. The Leamonts were white, my grandfather's great friend. So were the Mingos and Lucases, and the Shipley family, who lived back in what we called the Lane. We all identified with the community, the Marsh. The rest of the families were Black, but even a couple of them had some white mixture. We had some real characters. Mrs. Morton was something of a clairvoyant. She could see things you couldn't see. She knew what had happened and what was going to happen. She loved to tell ghost stories and we'd all gather around. She was a real presence in our community. Mrs. Morton was part of the Clyke family, Black. Mr. Morton was very fair skinned, but I don't know his complete genealogy. In any case you didn't think anything of that. He was a retired stage coach driver. Jim Clyke worked in the shipping department for T.S. Patillo, a wholesaler. He was one of the few people who worked at a store, not serving customers but in the warehouse. He was able to get all kinds of goods cheap. Mr. Aubrey Borden across the street was Robert Stanfield's chauffeur, which gave him probably the most prestige, in terms of occupation, for our entire community. Next door to us were the Whalens. Mrs. Whalen was very fair and Mr. Whalen was dark. The mother was Catholic and the father was Protestant. The Whalens were the only Catholics in the neighbourhood, and the only Black Catholics I ever knew of as a child. We called them the "half-breeds." No doubt this was a pejorative term, but everybody used it and I didn't think of it as bad. Interestingly, nobody referred to the Mortons as half-breeds, but they were just as mixed. The Simmons Clyke family had 20 or so children. The father worked for the railroad. So we had Borden, Clyke, Collins, Green, Jones, Paris, Halfkenny, Ince, Morton, Tynes, Wood, a dozen or so Black households on Ford and Cross Streets. Only about half the men had steady jobs. The rest worked in construction when there was something available, or did odd jobs. We were all basically poor. All of the women were domestic workers, the mothers and the grown-up daughters. One of my very best friends growing up was Dougie Collins, and another was Ronnie Mingo. One Black and one white. Ronnie and I used to trap muskrats in the marsh. We'd skin them and sell the pelts. We knew every rat hole for miles. Race didn't matter. All that mattered was that you were from the community.

All the families were large. We had a small family with only 10 of us. Some had over 20 children. When you have that many children, there is no way in the world a parent can look after that many kids, so the parenting is left to the older children. The older kids were always responsible for the younger ones and the younger kids always had to listen to the older kids. If an older kid told you that you couldn't do something, you couldn't say, "You can't tell me this" or "You don't have any authority over me." Everyone knew that that existed, that all of the children in the neighbourhood were raised exactly like brothers and sisters. At a certain age, you were responsible for so many younger and you had to listen to those that were older. Even for instance when we went picking blueberries. You were able to start picking blueberries at a very young age, like five or six years old. You could go to the blueberry fields but in order to get there you had to hitchhike. I could get up in the morning and say I was blueberrying with one of the older kids in the neighbourhood. I would be allowed to go with them, hitchhike out to the blueberry fields to pick blueberries. Now they would be totally responsible for me and I would have to do whatever they told me to do. If the younger kids got into trouble and there were older kids there, the older kids got into trouble for letting it happen. We'd always said you have as many mothers as there are women on the street. Any mother had the right to discipline you. So if you were caught doing something, as I was many times, you got two punishments: one from the mother who caught you and who then told your parents, and then you got it again at home.

In the winter big hunks of ice would come down the Salmon River and they would jam. The ice cakes, as we called them, would back the river up and then it would flood over its banks. It would come past our house and right up the street. Then it would freeze because it's not deep water, and then we could skate. Literally, we could put our skates on in the house, go out on the porch, step on ice and then skate for miles and miles. We used to make ice boats. We'd take the blades off four skates and we'd pound them on a piece of plywood or boards to make a floor. Then we would get an old sheet or an old coat and use that as a sail and the wind would blow and it would take you for miles out on the marsh. If you wanted to go skating in the evening it meant that somebody had to get tires. So the word would go out, tonight we are going to have a skating party. The older guys would go get the rubber tires so we could have a bonfire at night. That's how we made bonfires in the winter. When the young kids got cold, as inevitably happened, the older kids would have to take the younger kids home. You get your toes cold and feet cold and everything and when that starts happening you start crying. They have to make sure you get home, they take you on piggy-back or whatever. We had no organized sport at our school at all. I played on a hockey team, but that was not part of the school activities. Generally speaking we had to make up our own games. We had boxing gloves in our house so we had matches in our back yard, not organized in any way but lots of fun.

The big entertainment in the summer was baseball, open to all ages. We had a big field, and on any one team you'd have kids as young as six years old and grandmothers. So not serious ball, but we treated it seriously. There were so many people that you'd have your pitcher, your catcher, your first baseman, second baseman and third baseman, and then you could have a whole bunch of people out in the field. As long as it was the same number, it didn't matter too much. And there were always a lot of spectators. It was a real community sport. I remember one time that my mother was playing, and she was a big woman. She hit the ball, and she started running. Harold Morton, who was a big man, a big boy, he had his hands out to catch and my mother was running and she ran right through him and right over him. After that they called her the Acadian Coachline. The whole community would turn out for these games and we had them all the time.

And we swam together a lot as a community. My Uncle Vic had a truck, and he would come around and try to scrounge up enough money in nickels and dimes to get gas. Everybody piled on the back of this old flatbed truck and he would drive to the swimming hole, Murray's Dell, which was ten miles away. Everybody would go because nobody had cars, and this was the only way we could get there. Closer to our community was the Salmon River, a place you could walk to, so the teenagers would go down there to swim and the younger kids would of course follow. This is the place where you had the highest tides in the world. When the tide comes up, the river is nice and high, and it is really good swimming. Quite dangerous, mind you. I learned to swim under water but I couldn't swim on top of the water. So the boys would throw me in and I'd have to swim in under water. And all summer long there would be picnics. Different places would have picnics and these picnics were well organized, well attended and planned for months. The church picnic was a big one. They rented buses to carry everybody to the picnic ground. It was a major event. The Eastern Hat and Felt Company, where my father worked, had a picnic. All these big industrial places had their own picnics, Stanfield's for example. These picnics in those days were really important parts of community cohesiveness.

One summer activity I learned to regret began when a bunch of us went out onto the marsh on Gordon Shipley's horse. There was Gordon, Bookie Wood, Wayne Erving and me. I'm the only Black kid, but we are all from the Marsh. We went riding out on the marsh and we found a tractor sitting there. A ball game was going on, so everybody had their attention on that instead of on us. We decide we are going to get this tractor going, which we do, and then we decide we're going to run down some fertilizer bags that are stacked up. We run them down but there is a ditch in behind which we didn't see, so the tractor dropped down in the ditch and broke the front wheels off. Well, we get back on the horse and we beat it back to the community. It just so happens that the farmer who owns the field has his spy glasses and he is sitting there and watching the whole thing, and he calls the police. The police are giving everybody a hard time. They went to talk to my parents and have my parents straighten it out, which is what they do. Now they talked to my mother and they say I was involved, but I lied and I say, "No Mom it wasn't me." My mom says, "Okay, are you sure?" "Look Mom no, I wasn't there." So my mother goes and checks with people in the community. They had all seen us at the ball game, and they didn't realize we had taken off and were away. And everybody said to her, "Yeah, he was around the ball game, he was out there, right, he was one of the kids playing there." This went on for ages, so finally my mother says "Well I'm not letting the police, I'm not letting Purdy," he was the farmer, "I'm not going to let them railroad you. Purdy can say you did it but we are going to get a lawyer." Well as soon as she says that, that means money and even at 10 years old I knew we can't afford a lawyer. We don't spend extra money in our family. It is okay for me to lie and go on, but the instant my mother said she had to get lawyer, then I had to tell the truth. So I had to say, "Mom look, I was there." My mother said, "He will pay for what he did. I won't pay for it, but he will pay for it." I picked blueberries for two years, and every cent I made I had to give to my mother and she saved it and she gave it to Purdy to pay for the damage that I did to that tractor.

We had a good relationship with the Mi'kmaq community. We used to call it Hollywood in those days, that was the name of the reserve. Now it is Millbrook. My father had a good friend, Art Cope, who was a Mi'kmaq. He used to come to our house all the time. People from the reserve would make baskets, axe handles, pickaxe handles, a lot of stuff that was made out of ash. And they would come around selling it, house to house. They were very much involved in that kind of commerce. There was never, to my knowledge, a time when I actually saw an Aboriginal person drunk in my community. I saw them many times selling things or interacting with our own people. And there were always ball games, between what at that time was the Indians and ourselves, who were then known as Coloured. We would go to Millbrook and play ball; they would come in with a team and play ball. I do believe there was a point where the Catholic Church put an end to the ball games because the guys would play ball on Sundays, and they were drinking, and the Catholic Church said they couldn't play ball with us anymore.

The church was the centre of our social existence. Apart from the few Anglicans on the Hill and Mrs. Whalen and her kids, all the Black people in Truro went to the Zion Baptist Church. It basically brought us all into one faith community. The church was an inspiration to me, and even as I moved away from it as I grew up, it remained very central to my life. It was the people in the church who were always there: the minister was always there, the people who were active in the church were active in the community, it was always the same people. The organist Mrs. Clyke lived across the street from us; Jack Tynes and Aub Borden, the deacons, lived across the street. The church and my community are almost one and the same; you can't separate your upbringing from the church. It is just there. I always admired the ministers, and in fact as a young fellow I wanted to be a minister myself. I always thought that would be really cool. There was a sense that the minister would speak up for you and for all the people. I really felt they were good. They were always kind to me. They had everybody's respect; everybody looked up to them.

I think the ministers I admired most were Reverend Albert Thompson and Reverend Harold Cornish. I was much younger when Rev. Thompson was there, so I didn't interact with him directly. He was a fire and brimstone preacher. Everyone called his wife "Aunt Annie." You could go to Aunt Annie and she would always have something special for you to eat, and she would spend time with you. At one point my sister Elaine had some issues in the family and went to live with Aunt Annie for a month or two, so in that way she was just an extension of our family. Rev. Thompson was replaced by Rev. Cornish, who had more direct influence on me. He was progressive as a minister, perhaps a little too progressive for Truro. He talked about discrimination, right there in church, and he internationalized the Black condition in the sense that he talked about African civilizations and reminded us that we are African people. He raised the race consciousness in his congregation. He wasn't a radical by any means, but he was aware of being Black and he wasn't afraid of saying so. Although my personal consciousness of race came later, he certainly awakened an interest in me.

I used to love Sunday services. Sometimes I'd fall asleep, but mostly I didn't because the singing was so great. We always started with singing, all these spirituals: you just sat and sang. Somebody would say, "Let's sing this," and we'd sing this number. If it's going good, the service might start as late as 11:30 or 11:45, when it was supposed to start at 11. Our services were more conservative than in a Baptist fundamentalist church. No clapping or stomping or jumping up and down, mostly just the communal "Amen." The one thing I didn't like at all was "testimony." You are sitting there in church, enjoying the service, and now we are going to have testimonies. Everybody gets up, one by one. "This is when I found the Lord," "I praise God that this happened to me," "Praise God, I was down and out and the Lord came to me and saved me." Then I'd be sweating. It is down to the wire and you are sitting there and people turn around and they look at you. They turn right around and look at you, "What are you going to say?" You have 40 or 50 people and they are looking at you and the sweat is popping out of your forehead. I managed to ride it out. I never gave testimony in Zion Church. I've gone back there in later years as a speaker, but I never spoke up in Sunday service.

I did speak up more in Sunday School. That was the hour before church, and attendance was mandatory until you were about 12 years old. We also had

Mission Band every Wednesday afternoon, that was mandatory too. My older sister was in charge. We learned Scriptures, we did activities like arts and crafts. It was in Mission Band that we talked about Africa. We had a little box for our African mission, so you tried to get your box filled with pennies to send to our selected missionary. My whole family was very involved. My father was not a deacon. I don't know why, but he was a well respected member of the church. My mother was very active in the church, always. Everybody in the family was baptized, but I wouldn't do it. I think maybe Alvin avoided baptism too. My mother didn't force it on me. They believed this was something you wanted to do, a decision you made on your own, and I never wanted to do it. To me there was always something wrong if you have a God who is going to threaten to burn you in hell, or punish you in ways that I wouldn't do to my worst enemy. I couldn't buy into that, it didn't make sense to me. I would say that I am spiritual, but not religious. But I never stopped going to church as long as I lived in Truro. People made remarks, but they just had to accept the fact that I was not going to be baptized. I continued to read the Bible. In Sunday School I used to win prizes for learning the Scriptures. I especially loved the Old Testament, and I think the story of Noah and the Ark was my favourite. The idea of saving the life of the fishes and birds and animals so they don't become extinct, that was significant for me. And I continued to go to the Baptist Young Peoples' on Sunday night. All the Black kids went to church and then we'd go to Reid's Snack Bar afterwards. The Hill, the Island, the Marsh, everyone went to Reid's on Sunday night, and you saw everybody and had a great time.

The other important institution in our lives growing up on the Marsh was the Willow Street School. My experience at Willow Street was really good. I loved that school. My friend Bookie, who went to the same school, says he hated it. The teachers treated him in a disparaging way because he was from the Marsh and he was poor. My experience was different. I had a lot of fun, and the teachers, I felt, were really nice to me. I always got good marks and a lot of little stars in my workbooks. My older sisters Elaine and Marie were very good scholars, and perhaps it was because of this that the teachers had high expectations for me. I was a Jones. When I'm coming through the school system I have a certain protection. Kids from other families could have a completely different experience.

I had special treatment, I was privileged, and I think this shaped not only my life at school but my life in general. I am not saying I didn't get into trouble occasionally, but the teachers expected me to do well in school and I was going to behave like they expected me to behave. When I did something bad, it was out of the norm, and they would say, "You should know better. You're not supposed to do that," whereas for another kid on my street, the expectation might be that he was going to screw up and no matter what he did or the least little thing wrong and they were all over him. They knew he was going to be "bad." It is interesting to reflect on the segregation that existed in that school. We had a separate bathroom for Blacks, but since I never tried to go to the other bathroom I wasn't told that I couldn't. I just did as I was told as a child. I didn't have any confrontations over the bathroom. I would never dream of confronting a teacher at that time in my life. This was not an issue for me. I'd have to say that I didn't even notice. My memories of Willow Street are all positive.

I was one of the top, if not the very top, student to graduate from Willow Street School. But then I went uptown to go to grade 7, and I failed that year. I now came face to face with all the things I was protected from. The teachers at Willow Street had two Black communities feeding into that school, the Island and the Marsh, and they also had the Stanfields in the same school. Those teachers had to learn how to handle that, and they did, they kept a lid on things, they were good teachers. But when we left Willow Street School and that really protected environment, things changed. Now we go into a school known as Central Junior High. All of a sudden you've got kids from the Hill, so there are three Black communities, and Aboriginal students from Millbrook, trying to fit into a white environment, and the teachers couldn't handle it. I wasn't known as a Jones anymore. The Black kids became a problem. Our voice level was 17 decibels higher than the white kids, so the teachers just wanted to put us in the back of the room and tell us to sit there and shut up. The reason I flunked grade 7 was that I decided I did not like this school, I am not going to be here. I didn't have anything that I wanted to do. It wasn't like saying I wanted to be a lawyer or doctor and you are blocking me. I didn't have any real goals or aspirations, I was just going to school because my mother said you are going to get an education. So when all of this started to happen, I just decided not to go. I skipped classes, and I forged my mother's signature every chance I got. I would even sign my own report cards. I did two years in grade 7, and then I did two years in grade 8, for the same reason. By the time I got to grade 9 I was 16, and I could leave school. There was nothing that was important to me in junior high. It was the worst possible time of my life. I didn't like the teachers, I didn't like their attitudes, I didn't like what was happening in the school. As far as I was concerned it was a kind of genocide, I felt like I was being eliminated. Because of my low marks I wasn't allowed to play sports. I didn't participate in anything in the school. I didn't turn to delinquency or any sort of deviance, I just opted out of everything, for four years.

When I say I opted out, of course, I mean out of *school*. I still had a life, of sorts, and I was learning some of the same lessons out of school about what it was like to be a Black adolescent in the 1950s. There were a few things that happened to me during that time. One, it was my first experience with overt racism, or the first time I was conscious of it. I had gone up to grade 7 with all my friends, a mixed group, from Willow Street School. We went across to the pool room, which was the next street over from the junior high, and all the kids would think it was a big deal: you were in grade 7, now you are going to go over to Jack Spencer's pool room and have a game of pool. So I went over with the other kids and was watching, standing there. It cost one cent a minute to play, or 60 cents an hour. I didn't want to jump in playing because I only had a quarter and the loser had to pay. I had never played pool before; in fact, I had never been in a pool room. So I watched, and then I decided okay I'll play because I had seen how they did it. I said to one of my friends who was with me, "I'll play now." It was going to be my turn and the owner of the pool room says to me, "You can't play." I had been there watching for half an hour or an hour, it was no big deal, tee heeing with the guys and carrying on, just comfortable as all get out, and then when I take the stick down from the rack and he says, "You can't play." So I said to him, "Yeah, I know but I think that I can." And he said, "No you can't play," and I said, "Well I've been watching. I'm not going to do anything wrong and I know I can't play but it's okay. I see how you do it and everything and I'll be okay, don't worry about it." I didn't know what the hell the guy was saying to me. I was ignorant as all get out. By then the guy is getting a little pissed off and he is bigger than me and he's got the guys that work there and hang out in the pool room all behind him, and he looks at me and says, "Look, you people cannot play pool here." And that's when I realized what he was talking about. So, here I am, I swell up like a bloody peacock and I'm going to challenge him but he's bigger than I am and he's got these other guys there, so I'm scared of him and I don't know how to handle it. It had never happened to me before. I didn't know whether to try to fight and take a beating or what to do. I just said, "Well fuck it I don't want to play anyhow." And then I left. He's saying, "Well you don't need to leave if you don't want to." That was their attitude, you are allowed to stand around and converse but you are not allowed to play. Now, what sense does that make! I was just 13 and the guy has dehumanized me, he just cut the balls right off of me, standing there in front of my friends. Nobody says anything. It's a new thing for all of us. That was my first direct experience with racism and I'm 13 already. You would have thought that I had faced it before. I had people call me "nigger" or whatever before, but they didn't have any power. As kids you get into a fight in the school yard, but they don't have power over you. But here was someone who has power over me, he's got physical power, he's got the power of the state because he owns the place. He's got all this power and he's exercising this power over me. I was helpless. There's nothing I could do to protect myself except get out of that situation. How can you destroy a child more than a kid going to a new school with his friends and do that to him. I'll never forget that until the day I die.

It was also the same year that I got a job setting pins in a bowling alley. Robbie Clyke was basically the head guy at the bowling alley. He looked after the pin boys. In those days they didn't have automatic machines. Now, here in this alley it is "candle pins," so you sit between the two lanes on a little stool while the guys were bowling. What they tried to do, a lot of them, they would bowl as hard as they could to try to make the pins fly to see if they could hit the pin boy. You are sitting there, and you are dodging these candle pins that are flying all over the place. If you get two of them bowling at the same time and they are both throwing hard, especially if they lob the ball, the pins go every-where. It's a really dangerous job, but that's what we were doing for our pocket money. Black people were not allowed to bowl, but the owner had a deal: the pin boys could bowl from 4 to 6, because the league started at 7 so you were allowed to bowl before then for free. Also you could bowl Saturday morning for free. But Black kids who were not pin boys never got to bowl at all. You could go and watch in the bowling alley, but don't touch the balls, don't try to bowl. You could stand around and watch and sometimes the Black kids would go and keep score for the guys who were bowling. This is the strange nature of Canadian racism. There are these little pockets of openings that are making people feel better who are exercising power, exercising discrimination. They say, "Okay, we will let you have this much, and these others will have nothing. But as long as we can say we let so and so have this much, we are not bad people and don't you accuse us of this or that."

There were about 16 barber shops in Truro, but only one which would serve Black people. In the movie theatre, we had to sit upstairs. But it's all a ques-tion of when it happens and what it means to me. Everybody had a favourite barber, so what's the big deal? When I went to the theatre I wanted to sit in the balcony, so the fact that Blacks had to sit there meant nothing to me. It didn't present a problem for me, whereas for someone else who may have wanted to sit downstairs it would be a problem. One day Bookie Wood was going up to the balcony with a bunch of other kids from the Marsh and the usher tried to stop him because he was white. "You're not allowed up there." So Bookie says, "But I want to sit with my brothers," pointing to the Black kids, and the usher had to let him go up. In the Truro cemetery they have a whole separate section for all the Black people. It's not an integrated graveyard, and the way they justify it is they gave the land to Zion Baptist Church. That's where all my relatives are buried, and when that was fully occupied they made another section for Blacks. Now, if you said that you are not allowed to be buried in the Truro graveyard you'd be a liar. Of course they would allow Black people to be buried in the graveyard, but only where they were buried all together. They don't integrate the plots. It's the same when you are not allowed to bowl but you're allowed to be there. They won't let you play pool but you're allowed to be there. You are allowed to be buried but you can't be buried just anywhere. It may be the Nova Scotian way of keeping you in your place, of being totally a hundred percent racist but in a way that doesn't look racist. They can feel good about it. When I was growing up there was not one Black person, not one, who had a job in any commercial establishment in the town of Truro. You couldn't go into any store and see a Black checkout person, not one. Any of the jobs we got was carrying out people's garbage, raking their leaves, scrubbing their floors. We were all, the entire Black community, relegated to the menial tasks that had to be done in that town. Mississippi North.

It's interesting what happens with adolescence. When I was a preteen, none of the Black girls found me at all attractive. I had a crush on a couple of them but I didn't get anywhere with them. Mostly the girls that I started to hang out with were white girls. We never actually had dates, we just talked on the phone or we met after school. But they were all from Willow Street School, and we were really tight and we stayed that way for years and years, in fact even as adults. There is a certain bond or closeness with those same girls. What happened was, when they were becoming old enough that their parents were thinking these girls might be getting serious about boys, the parents stepped in to stop this inter-racial mixing. One of the girls, who was sort of like my girlfriend, as much as I had girlfriends in those days, was having a party. I was going to go to the party and it was a great expectation. We all travelled around together, and I would go to the party and never thought anything of it. Then she had to tell me that her parents said I wasn't allowed to go. I was about 14. That was my first confrontation with the sexual anxieties of white families and that sort of thing. What happened, which was really interesting, was that the whole group that I travelled with thought that was really wrong. Everyone was sort of upset about this and so I was home and they were on the phone and they were all taking turns talking to me on the phone to give me a running description of what was going on at the party. It's bizarre! So I was sitting at home on the step talking on the phone, and one would talk for a while and then someone else would come and they would talk for a while. I felt good that my friends could understand that it was wrong, and they still wanted to include me because they were my friends and they had to deal with this girl's parents. But it just really made me aware that in that town that's who I was. I was Black, they were white. This was a white girl from across town who had gone to Willow Street School and we had been friends since we were in grade 4 or 5. Her parents were concerned with race, strictly race. I was a Black male and they didn't want me at their house, at their party. It's really strange. I don't know what it says about the difference in generations but with the kids I went to school with, there seemed to be a real break from the racist attitudes of their parents, and this was good.

Although I stayed friends with these young people, including the girls, there could never be any suggestion of getting physically close. For that, we had to stay within the group of Black teenagers. We used to have what we called house parties. When we went to a house party it was just the Black teenagers, and that was it. We had a fantastic time. The whole town, all three Black communities, came together when we had a party. Most of us would be connected to the church, and by the time we were in junior high we were at the same school, so we all knew each other. So there were restrictions, and I was becoming more and more aware of them, and aware that those restrictions were particularly aimed at me because I was Black. There were places I couldn't go, things I couldn't do, people I couldn't socialize with, jobs I couldn't get. By the time I left Central Junior High, at age 16, I just knew I had to get out of Truro. I had no absolute goals, other than somehow I knew I had to get out of that town. I didn't want to get into trouble, I didn't want to go to jail, and I didn't want to spend my life taking out somebody else's garbage.

Chapter Two

ON THE ROAD
AND IN THE STREETS

By the time I was a teenager, the safe, comfortable Truro of my childhood imagination had been destroyed. I still loved Truro. But I knew I had to get out. I was feeling suffocated and growing increasingly frustrated. There didn't seem to be any employment opportunities in Truro. I had no education, I had no training, I had nothing to offer. I knew that if I were to hang around Truro, the only solution would be to accept the most menial jobs or be involved in some sort of criminal activity. And I certainly wasn't prepared for that.

Some of the men in our community joined the railway. I had this idea in terms of the railway of being a servant. I wasn't going to shine somebody's shoes and make beds. The idea of being a servant was far from what I wanted to do. I was also aware that there was no room for advancement. It is not like these guys were starting off as porters and then getting jobs as conductors, engineers or all of that. They were basically locked into being porters. Only the very occasional person became a conductor. Besides the railway there were a couple ways of getting out of poverty in Nova Scotia at that time. You could join the army, where you get three squares a day: "three hots and a cot" is what they'd say. The other way was to go to Elliot Lake or Sudbury, or to Toronto and work in factories, but you had to get away.

I had that family background of going into the military, so that seemed to be my best choice. I kind of moved sideways into the armed forces. I would have been in grade 7 when I joined sea cadets, and I really liked it. The uniform was really cool, and I found it all very exciting. I was looking at a picture recently, and saw that Jimmy King, that is a fellow that my Uncle Vic raised, he joined, and I think Francis Collins was a sea cadet. But there weren't that many Black kids in sea cadets. It was in sea cadets that I got out of Truro for the first time, except for visits to my grandparents in Springhill. They took us down to Halifax, where we had a whole day tour of an aircraft carrier, ate lunch in the cafeteria, talked with a number of the men aboard. We saw the guns and got behind them and were able to see what a sailor sees when he is looking through a gun. We got to go up to the tower and see where all the radar is.

My taste of military life led me into the reserve army when I was 14. You had to be 16, but I lied about my age. That was even more exciting than cadets. The summer I joined, I went off to Camp Aldershot, where I got to see the Black Watch. The Black Watch in the Black community, they were the soldiers of all soldiers. They were the toughest guys, they saw combat and they happened to be at Camp Aldershot the year I went. There were a lot of Black guys in the Black Watch; in fact the guys who joined before '55 mostly went into the Watch. From my community, Earl Leamont, he was white but he lived across the street from us, he joined the Black Watch. Snookie Tynes from my community, he went into the Black Watch. Those are the guys who joined the army to get away. And then there were other Black guys that I met, a number from Halifax. One of the Downey brothers joined the Black Watch.

But at Camp Aldershot, the Black troops didn't have an easy way to go. They were still experiencing a lot of racism, in the service and in the town, in bars and restaurants. And again, true to most of my experiences to that point, I wasn't affected by it because I was too young. I wasn't old enough to go to bars. I wasn't really able to go to the dances, though I snuck in one night. So I spent the summer doing what the other reserve soldiers did, march and drill and shoot. The time at Aldershot was likely six weeks, which took up most of my summer. I remember how good it was to get your paycheque just before Christmas. You got so much for how many nights you went, and they paid you in cash too. I got along very well in the reserve. I've read the reports from what my officers used to say about me —that I was very intelligent and a good soldier and good potential but very immature for my age. See, they thought I was older, but I was 14, not 16. But they didn't say nasty things.

After about two years in the reserve I spoke to my superiors in Truro, and they said they would give me good recommendations to get into the regular service. But, at 16, I was too young. The Canadian government had a new program based on the idea that if they could get some of the young bright students to go into the army they could make them into the non-commissioned officers. They were looking at expanding the army, but they needed NCOs to take over the troops. They already had the military college in Kingston and they had Royal Roads, which were officer training schools, but they didn't have any training schools for the non-commissioned officers. So they set up the apprentice program, where they were taking them at 16 and 17, when they knew they could mould them. They could do all the psychological testing and IQ testing and everything. This meant they could skim and get the cream of the crop. My mother wasn't in favour of it so I had to forge her signature. She didn't know until after the fact that I had joined the service. But there was another problem: I only had grade 8. I came down to Halifax and wrote all the tests and passed the tests but they said I couldn't get in unless I had grade 9. That was in April and I hadn't been to school since the previous summer. I had passed grade 8, but I just hadn't gone to grade 9. So I had to come back and I had to go to school and get the books and everything. I only had two months to do all the work. They gave me a whole stack of books, and I was able to go into the library, and I read all of the books. I was a self-taught grade 9. I passed the exams. Then I get accepted, and I'm able to leave in September of '58. By the time I get on the train I am 17.

I was sent to Chilliwack, BC. I joined up at Windsor Park, and because you are a soldier apprentice and a future NCO, you are sort of special, so we had a choice. They say "What outfit do you want?" and I say "What outfit is furthest away from Nova Scotia?" They said Royal Canadian Engineers in Chilliwack, and I said "That is the outfit I want to go in."

When I was going there on a train, I was still Burnley. Burnley Jones was all anybody ever called me. I was on the train and I was scared, my first time away from home, no other Black kids on the train. And it was a troop train, so they were picking up these soldiers all the way across and dropping them off, a couple of cars attached to a regular train. My bravado was "don't knock the rock." Bill Hailey and the Comets were popular with "Rock Around the Clock." Some of the soldiers said, "you think you're rocky, do you?" I said "yeah." And that is where the nickname came, on that train trip. It was 6 days and 5 nights. I went on as Burnley and I got off as Rocky.

That was pretty exciting because it is at that point that I am able to shape my persona, whichever way I want. It is all new people, nobody knows me, I can basically be whoever I want to be. I decide I'm going to be this hard-nosed rock. Like Rocky Marciano. I was scared, right, but I wasn't going to let anybody mess with me. And that was the message I sent out right from the word go. You mess with me and you are really going to get hurt. And of course most of these guys had never met Black people before in their life, so I had a real advantage. You know they had this image that Black people could fight, that Black people were tough. I promoted that. I was taking a hard line, "don't fuck with me." By the time I got to Camp Chilliwack, nobody knew my name was Burnley.

The soldier apprentices were organized by age, so each intake all of the recruits are the same age. I was seventh intake, which meant I was the seventh year the program was in existence. Every intake was 144 guys, and you were identified by the intake you were in. They'd know your age, they'd know who else might be in there. So the sixth intake were now the seniors in camp, and they ran everything, the same way as a college with the hazing, the bullying and everything. I was determined that these guys weren't going to do anything to humiliate me. We were getting needles, and the older guys would come hit you on the arm and it hurt. That was part of your initiation. So I took the position, "You might be sixth intake, but you hit me in the fuckin' arm, you've got a problem." So the only guys who would dare to hit me on the arm was the really big hard guys in the sixth intake. Because of my stance and because I had already been through sea cadets and the reserve army, I was already like a senior, so I got away with acting like a senior in a lot of things I did. And I got along well with a lot of the seniors.

I was the only Black guy in the seventh intake, and there were none in the sixth. There was a Black man who was a cook in the camp, and there was a Black man, who was regular service, but he was a sergeant. I tried to make friends with him, but he was above everybody and that didn't work. The other Black guy lived outside the camp and he was married to a Black woman and they had children. I spent a fair bit of time at their place, and they were real nice to me. They were originally from Alberta, from Amber Valley. I never saw another Black face.

In Chilliwack I really got into boxing. I was never defeated in camp. I was 149 pounds. We went over to fight in Esquimalt, for a tournament with the Navy apprentices. What we didn't know was an apprentice in the Navy was anybody they had taking a trade, whereas an apprentice in the army was anybody between 16 and 17. I will never forget the guy that I was fighting on that day. This was a big fight, a championship fight. This guy came out and he had no neck. He was 149 pounds same as me, but he was only 4 foot 8. He was built like a tank. He was about 25 or 26 years old. I was in tip top shape, and faster than him. I jabbed his nose and his face kept getting redder and redder. I could see the blood coming into his face, and I'm jabbing him, bop bop bop. We had to do five two-minute rounds and for the first 3 rounds I made mincemeat of this guy, I tore his ass up. He came out in the fourth round and he was puffy and everything, and then he goes wshhh, and he hit me in the stomach. And I'm still banging him and he hits me in the stomach on the other side, and again. He didn't even try to hit me in the head because he could hardly reach it. The guy tore me up. I remember going down and the ceiling going around and me saying I'm not going to throw up because there are these girls sitting there I've been trying to hustle. I lost that fight but it was a good fight.

We had to go to school as apprentices. You not only did your military duties and work but you also had to do school work. And I was interested in drafting, so I was doing my school work pretty good and after you were there for so long you were allowed your first pass. There was an Indian reserve close by, and under the standing orders of the camp you weren't allowed to go into this Indian reserve. I questioned my CO, "Why aren't we allowed to go into the Indian reserve?" He said, "The women have VD and we don't want VD passed around the camp." But I found that really offensive particularly because I was looking to be around some brown-skinned people. Everybody was white, every single person, and I wasn't. I did have some difficulties related to race but very little. By then I'm integrated into the company and I've formed some strong bonds and friendships with the guys. Race within the service wasn't a big issue for me, but it was an issue for me that they would take this position with regard to the Natives. And in questioning it, I think I raised some hackles. I wasn't wise enough and experienced enough to know how to deal with it except to deal with it head on.

There was a restaurant outside of the camp grounds called the SNAFU (Situation Normal All Fucked Up). We would go to the SNAFU restaurant and the Aboriginal people would also go. So I met some of these people and they were just like all the people I'd met at home, and they kind of looked like me and I wanted to make friends with them. But I wasn't allowed, they told me, to go onto the reserve. So for whatever reason it seemed that after I had raised that as an issue, I seemed to get into trouble. I'm not sure whether that gave rise to an attitude in me that was that defiant, or whether that gave rise to an attitude in my superiors that I was a potential trouble-maker.

Because we were apprentices we had to be signed out; we couldn't just go out and stay overnight. There had to be a local family that would take responsibility and accept you to go to their house on the weekends. There was a local family called the Moggs, who I've kept in touch with to this day. They sort of adopted me, as they did some other guys. They were good, good people, so they'd sign me out and I would go to their place. They had two daughters, who would come to the dances in camp. Shirley at the time was only 13, and her sister Val was the same age as me. So I met them at the dances at camp and from there got to meet their parents. The Moggs were incredible. I don't think they had any prior experience with people of colour. I nicknamed the father Feathers and the nickname stuck The girls were like sisters to me and I've always corresponded with them. They also had an adopted son named Rod, Rod Jermaine, who later became a lawyer and formed a partnership with my good friend John Baigent. He went on to become a very well known jurist. So the connections, the smallness of Canada is unbelievable, when you think of this family that brought me in. Just an incredible, loving family, who opened their house to me and I'm forever grateful.

For the first time ever I was popular with the girls, not just as "golly you are a good friend" like when I was growing up. Then I was always popular as the friend who was going to help the girl meet the other guy. They weren't interested in me, they were "listen look, can you hook me up?" When I went to Chilliwack it was a whole different life. While I was in camp I met this girl Ruth, with an Armenian last name. Her brother Nat was in the sixth intake. He was a well-respected soldier. He was big and strong and could march and drill and do all the other stuff that great soldiers should do. We were quite good friends. The family lived in Galt, Ontario. Nat had written home I guess a number of times, told his folks that he had met this friend while he was there. And so when she came out to visit Nat for his graduation, we met and fell madly in love. It was just the most torrid love affair that you could ever think of. She was the same age as me. I thought she was extremely beautiful. I don't know if she really was or not. Black hair, sharp nose, olive complexion. Well mannered. She was just absolutely the most attractive woman I'd ever seen in my life. Certainly she stole my heart. We had about three weeks together. Nothing sexual, mind you.

One weekend a bunch of us go into Vancouver to get our tattoos. There is a very famous tattoo artist, Doc Holiday. I'm looking at all these tattoos and I'm still very connected to my mother. And I wanted a tattoo for my mother, but I know my mother is against tattoos. I was going out with a girl named Rose and I was going out with another one named Chris. At the time the guys were getting these tattoos "death before dishonour." I'm not putting that on my arm! But I've got to get a tattoo, it is a rite of passage. But anyhow, I finally got a rose. I figured that solves all my problems. To the girl Rose I could say, "I got it for you." I figured that would make her happy. I figured I could put Chris in the thing, then I could say, "look Chris I put your name in here." I knew I would break up with her eventually and then I could add a T. I didn't dare to put "Mom" in it, but I thought if I put "Chris" in it and then "Christ," my mom wouldn't be so mad. But I broke up with Chris before I got her name in there and I never got involved with a woman that I thought "this is going to last forever" enough to tattoo her name in there. So I still have the rose on my arm with a place for a name that has never been filled in. It is hard to see now.

I spent most of my time, when I wasn't training, with a group of girls and a group of guys at the camp. We were a pretty tight bunch. The camp was on a river, which has some of the most exciting salmon and steelhead fishing in the world, and I often went fishing. I wasn't too serious about my academic work, and they kept reminding me that if I didn't pass academically they wouldn't keep me. I didn't keep at that too much. I kept getting into trouble. They said you had to be in camp by 11 o'clock and I was always late, and then I'd get charged, and I'd get CB time, "confined to barracks." This meant you had to do everything else that everybody had to do, you had to be on the parade square, you had to do everything, and then when everybody else was finished for the day, you had extra duties. You might be in the mess hall peeling potatoes, plus your kit got inspected all the time. Plus, you weren't allowed out anywhere. Oh I hated it. Then you had to do fire picket, which meant when everybody else is sleeping you are doing the rounds checking to make sure there are no fires or break-ins. I had a lot of fire picket duty. I didn't take orders all that well. A lot of the things I didn't agree with I questioned, which I never should have done. But I loved the army. I really loved the experience, but I didn't like that everybody who came by could tell you what to do. I had a real problem with authority; I couldn't abide by the rules. Not being able to go to the Indian reserve, that to me was a stupid rule.

I think the big thing that happened is that my sister was getting married and I asked for leave to go to her wedding. And they were going to give it to me, but then they asked how many sisters do you have and I said seven. They said well, if you leave every time you have a sister who is getting married you'd never be here and we can't do that. They said no. I decided I was going anyway. Me and this other guy, Sam, we made plans to go AWOL. The guys tried to talk me out of it. They said nobody has ever successfully gone AWOL from this camp, you are sitting here in the Fraser Valley, and there is nowhere to go. There is a border to cross if you go that way. I made up phony ID and everything. These false documents got us across the border, dressed in our Canadian uniforms. It was a very interesting trip when I went AWOL. We got into Seattle and I went to a theatre, and I wanted to buy a ticket. The woman spit at me through the hole in the glass window and said, "No niggers are getting in here." So we leave there and we go to a bar and we are going to have a drink. I'm 17, I'm in uniform, and I know I can walk into any bar and Sam is a fairly big guy. And the bartender says "We don't serve niggers," just like that. This is very aggressive, this guy is very aggressive. I sort of bristle and draw myself up to my full height, and I'm going to try and be a bit intimidating and he just reached under the bar and pulled out a sawed-off shotgun and set it there and looked at me. That was the end of my dissent. I said, "Yeah well okay, we are out of here."

It was such a blatant confrontation. All my life I had all of these subtle things that happened. And in one day I had those two things happen to me that showed me, "This is exactly where you stand." And people have power over you. I was powerless, I couldn't do anything. On that same trip, there is an example of the opposite. We are hitchhiking through Washington State. It was cold, there was snow. We get picked up by an old guy in a half-ton pickup and the truck was held together with bailing wire. It was hardly making it going down the road. The guy asks us where we are from, where we are going? Of course we are sort of half lying. He knows we are Canadians. I think we might have told him we are heading to Boston. "You don't seem to be doing pretty well," he says. He was pulling off into a flat area, and I was looking down this road and I couldn't see the end of it. There was nothing. I couldn't see anything in front of us and there was certainly nothing behind us. And he was pulling off this road, this old white farmer. He reached in his pocket and pulled out a $5 bill and he said, "Here this will help you along your way." I couldn't believe this guy would do this. I said, "I want to get your name, and I would really like to send you this back." And I got his name and I wrote it down and I lost it and I always wanted to send him back. He gave us $5. I know that $5 was a fair bit of money to him. Old beat-up truck and he took off down the road.

Well, we go along further and we are freezing cold. Sam kept wanting to stop. I said, "You can't stop man, you gotta keep moving, you'll freeze to death on this highway." He was crying because I was grabbing him and I said, "No we are not stopping." Then we see this pen with buffalo in it, and we see this pile of manure in the snow. I had seen in the movies about the heat that would come from a manure pile. I said to Sam, "You may not like this, but this is what we are going to do. We are going to pull back this manure and get in it." He argued and I said, "This is going to save your life." In the morning we pull out of that, and I know we must have been rank. And along comes a state trooper, and he says "You are not allowed to hitchhike here." We said, "We have no choice, we are in the middle of nowhere," and he says "I'm going to have to take you in." So we get in his car. The trooper says, "Whoo, cough, what the hell? You stink to high hell." I explained to him that it was so cold and we had to do something and this is what we did, so he said, "Well I'll tell you what we are going to do, we are deporting you." So he radios ahead that he has got these two Canadians and they are being deported. And he drove us to the border of his state and at the border there was another cop and he turned us over to him. They drove us all the way to Fort William, Thunder Bay, Ontario. The cops in the states passed us from one to another and gave us a ride all the way across. They did this despite the smell. In fact, I think that the smell was the reason they did it. I think they would have taken us to jail otherwise and then they would have found out all of our documents are forged. At the Canadian border they told us, "This is it, get out here, you are deported, don't come back."

We got cleaned up and then we hitchhiked down to Toronto. It was a terrible trip. The final ride we got was a guy hauling lettuce and produce. It was winter and in the back of this van it was freezing cold. But he took us down to Toronto, where all the trucks come in, the food terminal. I had never been to Toronto. We went looking for my sister Elaine. I knew where she worked, and so I called her at work and we were going to go there and she gave me an address. I remember walking down Yonge Street looking up at these great big tall buildings. We went to her place at 126 Spadina. That is where all the Nova Scotians lived, so there was a bunch of people there.

Now I don't know if she phoned or I think Mom phoned. Either my mom or sister called the army and told them where I was. She didn't want me to get in trouble. They picked me up the day before she was to get married. Military Police picked me up and couldn't believe that I had made it all the way to Toronto without getting caught. So I made a deal with them: if they let me stay for her wedding, I would get on the train myself and get back. So I said, "If you let me go to her wedding, I will go back." And so anyhow they let me stay. I don't know what happened to Sam. We broke up after we got to Toronto. He had people in Kingston or something like that. And when the wedding was over, I caught the train back to Chilliwack. I got 14 days digger time.

When you have a serious discipline issue you have a hearing with your commanding officer. So he told me what a lousy soldier I was and I couldn't take orders and didn't do exactly what I was told. There was no place in this man's army for me. When I grew up maybe I should try again. I was Sapper Apprentice Jones! I was heartbroken then because I was leaving all these new friends I met. They had these parties for me and everything. There I was. I didn't quite see it as a failure but I did see it as a disappointment. I'd been in the Royal Engineers for 14 months. I cried when they kicked me out.

I left B.C. and went first to Nova Scotia, and of course my mother wanted me to stay home. I didn't know at the time but she was pregnant with Roger. I said, "No, I'm going to Ontario. I'm on my way to Toronto." So off I went to Toronto and stayed with my sister Elaine. Toronto was diversity. Toronto was Nova Scotia planted there. Most of the Nova Scotians who went to Toronto lived west of University Avenue and east of High Park and south of Bloor Street at that time. That's where the Black people lived. That's where you knew people. You see you know somebody and you go down and there's a sign in the window room for rent. It was quite communal. You had the Jewish district there, which is where a lot of people shopped. The Chinese district at the time was way down at Elizabeth Street, Bay and Dundas. It was only a very small area. The Black people basically were the majority of the people in Grossman's Tavern, the Hub Tavern, the 300 Tavern and sometimes the Holiday at the corner of Bathurst and King. The Hub was on Spadina between Dundas and College. That whole area was where mostly everybody hung out. Periodically we'd go down to Yonge Street to some of the other places. But mostly it was all in that area. And then there was Rudy's Restaurant, which was an all-night restaurant.

For me Toronto was different at different stages, different times. When I first went I was trying to be a successful rounder. Toronto was Spadina. That was where all the action was happening. To me Toronto was different individuals and it was divided between the Nova Scotians, primarily men, and American men and the women who were on the streets. The American men were the top street corner hustlers, the guys who came over from Detroit and Buffalo. When I'm hanging out on the corners, my world is made up of these guys from Nova Scotia who were hanging in the clubs, who were gambling and hustling, and the American guys who were gambling and hustling, and the women that surround all of that. It's all integrated but there's always an underlying tension between the Nova Scotian guys the American guys and the Ontario guys. The Ontario guys were a minority. Some of them are really tough but the Nova Scotians are the majority. And there's no white males to speak of involved in the street. After I started working, it became the guys from Nova Scotia and the work people who are your friends. The people I worked with in Toronto were predominately white. At first the people that I socialized with were all Black. Because I was working with white people, the group I socialized with became integrated. The women were integrated the whole time.

I really wanted the fast life. The Nova Scotians that were there included a lot of gangsters and pimps and robbers. A lot of the guys that I met really travelled in the fast lane and made lots of money. Now coming from Nova Scotia I had no money, and I would see these guys and these women just ready to give me money. Some of these gals would just give me money and say buy me a drink. Don't worry about it. Here take this. You buy. So you'd go to a bar and all of a sudden this woman had given you a 100 bucks to buy drinks. That's not hard to take. I didn't want to get into all the robbery and that sort of stuff. I never wanted to do that. But I didn't mind playing out. I played a lot of poker and we played cards all night. I was really into that, being in the fast lane and being with these guys. When I first landed in Toronto I found my old friend Midgie living in the same place as Elaine, at 126 Spadina. He grew up in Truro across the street from our house. We called him Midgie or Midge or Mitch. He was quite a ball player, so he went off to Newfoundland to play professional baseball. Then from Newfoundland he went to Toronto. We took an apartment together, sharing with lots of hookers. Some of them had kids. My sister Marie came, with her religious fervour, and she put them all out. And the kids are crying and the women are going on. Oh it was just like the tower of Babel. It was none of her damn business. But she's gonna put all of these hookers out.

So I met this hooker. And she asked me to stay with her. Wouldn't cost me anything. I said, sounds good to me. And I'm hustling trying to make a living. And she said, "but you have to go to school. I'll pay for everything but you will go to school." She would have been around 27. She was white with a dark complexion. She was bound and determined to get me off the street. She only had a big room that she rented, in the west end. She took her customers to hotels. This woman here, she was real. All the guys were trying to get her because she was an independent, making serious money. So I registered at Ryerson for a course to be a mechanic to fix airplane engines. I didn't know much but I had to go along with the program.

I stayed with her and I was going back to school. But I couldn't keep the hours. I couldn't go to school, stay up, be around with her. I just couldn't do it. She ended up moving on; I just wasn't what she needed. But what she did do for me was she made me realize that I had to get off the corner. And I didn't really have the aptitude to become a mechanic anyhow. I thought it would be good because you'd make good money fixing airplanes. But it really was a good time of my life. She talked to me at great length about what life was like on the streets, and why I shouldn't be on the street. People look at hookers like they're bad people. But in my experience they would go to great lengths to stop a young person from getting involved with that life if they could. It worked for me. I was lucky. Connie Carrington was the one who eventually did get me off the street. But it was only because I'd gone through people like her who softened me up. Because I was determined that I was going to be a gangster when I started. I just didn't want to steal and go to jail.

My brother and my sisters were all involved with St. Christopher House. I used to go there as often as I could because they had some pretty gals. That was the place where the nice young gals went. It was a drop-in centre, working mostly with young people, trying to get them off the street. There wasn't so much drugs as there is now, but a lot of runaways and delinquents who needed a place to stay or a meal. Connie Carrington was the guy who ran St. Christopher House. He was a registered social worker. Connie would see me coming in all the time and talking to all the gals and that. He sort of took a personal interest in me. He knew my sister Elaine. He knew my family. He felt that I should get off the street. With his experience he'd know what the end was for me if I really got deeply integrated into that whole lifestyle.

So he talked to me and said, "So listen. You've got to re-assess what you're doing. You've got to figure out where your life is going to go. And you've got to get a job. A decent job." And I said, "Connie look, you get me a job where there's lots of women, where I can dress the way I want, I'll take it. Otherwise don't bother. I mean look at the life I've got: I'm hustling a dollar, I'm doing OK, I always have a place to stay." Now Connie was smart, and he was really committed to his job. He went off and talked to the manager of the Unemployment Insurance, the uic. That was at 174 Spadina at Queen. Connie told him about this young fellow that he wanted to try to get straightened out. The manager was also involved with St. Christopher and he could keep his hand on me. So he said, "Okay, I'll hire him."

Anyhow Connie gets in touch with me, and I go over, and he says, "I've got a job for you." And I say "Yeah right." He says, "I got a job. And there's all kinds of fine women at this job. You can dress up. You'll be dressed up all the time." I said, "Where is this job at?" He said, "The Unemployment Insurance office." I said, "You're joking. They're not going to hire me down there." I only had grade 9 education, you know. He said, "You go see Bill, he's expecting you. Just tell him that you're the guy I'm sending over." I said, "I'm not doing anybody's janitorial work or sweeping the floor or shining shoes. That's not what I'm cut out for." So I go and meet the manager. He talks to me and says, "Well I'll offer you a job. The pay isn't good but you have a chance that you can go some place with it." And I said, "What kind of job?" He said, "We have a problem. We need some help and both Connie and I think you can help deal with it. We have people on unemployment insurance. And when it runs out, they have to come and talk to one of our officers. But usually when that happens they are very angry and aggressive, so our officers can't deal with that. So what I'm proposing is to have them come to talk to somebody first and then get referred to an officer. You could be the person for them to come and talk to. And you can help them fill out the form. And calm them down before they have to see the officers." I said, "How much?" He said, "$1 an hour. Yep $37.50 a week is what you'd be making." I said, "Damn, man! I can make that in one night! In no time. $37.50 a week? You got to be joking." He says, "Well that's what the job pays. A casual job. You might prove yourself. You know you might be able to go somewhere. But that's what we pay. Casual job $1 an hour. $37.50 a week, and we expect you to be here on time and there is no overtime."

I went back to Connie and said, "Connie, what are you trying to do? Set me up? $37.50 a week?" He says, "Yeah that's what the job pays, but you told me that you would take any job I got you as long as there were all kinds of beautiful woman and you got to dress up and you could come and go. That's what this job is. This job is being created just for you. And you know, work your way in and maybe you can make some money after. You talk about you want to do something. Well here's a way you can go straight." So I took the job. And it was right across the street from Hub Billiards, a poolroom that we used to hang out at.

So I get all dressed up, man. Dressed to the nines. I go into work at the right time. I go over to the pool room. They say, "What you doing?" I say, "I got this job over here." And they say, "What? What you do over there? Sleep?" "No man! I got my own desk." Now as it turned out most of the guys from the poolroom and the streets were the guys who were coming in. They were the ones where their pogey was running out. And they had to come to my desk. Now all of a sudden I have authority. Originally, the way they treated these guys, they were looking down on them. But as I got to know my way around and knew the workers better, I'd go over and I'd say, so and so's got this sort of a problem and here's what we can do here. I had started studying unemployment insurance. Now all of a sudden the guys are getting good service. I'm keeping them coming through me. And at night I'm still playing poker. I'm still out there hustling 'cause I can't survive on that $37.50 a week.

The job at the unemployment office was a term position and after a year, the money ran out and they couldn't get funding. Then I got a job driving a dump truck. It was interesting because I didn't know how to drive one. They wanted me to spray out gravel. The guy asked me, "Do you know how to do it?" and I said "Yep I know how to do it." Because I had seen the dump trucks going and back up and the gravel coming out of them. So they loaded me up with gravel, and I had this yard I had to spread, and he said, "I want a 3-inch spread" and I said okay. And I figure what you do is you drive at the right speed and that is how much gravel comes out. So I got in, pulled the thing that lets the gravel come out and put the thing in gear, and the whole damn load just dumped. He said, "I thought you knew what you were doing," and I said, "Well I thought I did too." He gave me a shovel and said, "Here now you spread, 3 inches." Didn't fire me though. I worked all day spreading gravel, sore hands, but I learned how to ask questions and I learned what my mistake was. I didn't have the chain hooked on the tailgate right. I learned to do that and I sprayed gravel and I learned how to drive a truck with water in it, because it sloshes back and forth. So then I wanted to move to the tractor trailers. Lou Skinner was the guy who taught us how to hook them up. I was going down to a job interview. Lou told me, "Back up as hard as you can and the thing will hook up itself." I went down to CPR and I had a test to drive the tractor trailer and the guy was loading in the back and they told me to go hook on that load. I floored it. Knocked the load all down, on top of the guy, hit my head on the window of the truck. It was a disaster. But they gave me a job. I could have killed him, killed me, killed everybody.

It was during this time in Toronto that I had to go to the dentist as I was in pain with a toothache. I don't know if it was Elaine or someone said Dr. Best was just down the street. So I went to his office, and the receptionist was white. I asked her if the doctor was available, and she said, "What is the problem?" And I said, "I've got this tooth and I'll have to get it out, it is killing me. It is bad." At that time, I wouldn't have been thinking of filling anything. So she took me into the room waiting for the doctor to come and see, because I was an emergency walk-in. Put the thing on me, and you know the little bib and that. She said, "The doctor will be in to see you shortly, he is with another patient." So I'm sitting there, I know that I'm afraid of the dentist anyhow, because we didn't go see the dentist very much when I was growing up and I knew it was going to hurt. He comes in and says, "I'm Dr. Best." And he is Black! I think to myself, "Hold it, I've never seen a Black dentist before." He said, "Well let me look, and we'll see what the problem is." I said to him, "Yeah you take a look and let me know as I'll have to make a decision as to what I'm going to do." I knew right away I was not letting this man do anything to me. He was not putting a needle close to me, period. If he is saying it had to come out, I'd say, well, I'll be back. No matter what it is, I'll be back. Because this is the first time I've ever seen a Black dentist. I didn't have faith that a Black man knew how to be a dentist. I'd never seen it, I'd never heard of it. Now I'm not sure if he said it had to come out or if he said he could freeze it and fix it, but I do know what my response was. It was "Thank you very much for the examination, I will be back." I couldn't get out of that chair fast enough and get down the street. That is what my life in Nova Scotia had done to me. And that to me is where I was at at that point. In that sense the "he" is "me." I'm looking at him and seeing myself. I am seeing myself and saying, "You are inherently inferior because of your skin colour, and your skin colour is me, then I am inherently inferior." This is what that analysis says to me. And in order to overcome that, unknowingly (it certainly wasn't by any design), the process of overcoming that perception began my self-education.

When I first came to Toronto, I used to hang around 126 Spadina quite a bit. It was a rooming house, where a bunch of people from Nova Scotia lived, and from Truro in particular. Midgie Ince lived there, Jimmy King, Robbie Clyke, Marion Clyke, Joan King from Glace Bay, Tilly King her sister. And there was a white boy, Jack Lapage, who became a good friend. He had been in the Guelph reformatory, but he wasn't a gangster by any stretch of the imagination. He was about the same age as I was, sharp dressing, fast talking. We ran a poker game together at 126. Jack and I were sharing a room there and he had brought home this woman. She stayed for about two days, while I was either staying in another room with a friend or with my sisters or whatever. But in any event, after she left I was back to my regular room, where we actually shared a bed. One night we were running our poker game and talking about what to do with our future. Neither of us had a regular job at the time. We would work at the car wash, you know you go there every day, and if they were busy, you got your job and you washed cars and you got paid at the end of the day, cash. All of us who came from Nova Scotia, at one time or another, likely worked at the car wash.

So this evening we were talking about going away, maybe out west, when suddenly he said, "Look the police are outside. What's going on?" "Well obviously we are going to get raided." We were certainly glorifying how seriously the police saw this two-bit penny-ante poker game. We were quite convinced that we were under surveillance and they were going to take everybody at 126 to jail who was involved in this poker game. We decided rather than let that happen, why not take off and go to Vancouver or wherever. So it was at night and we figured what we will do is go down and jump a freight train. Down we go to the freight yards and we talk to some of the guys and we figure out what trains are going to go west, we get this train and we jump on it. We ride the train, it rides all night and was kind of fun. In the morning the train goes to Hurst and then it heads south in Ontario to a town called Oba. And breaks up, so there we are we are stuck in this town.

We had no money and it was a railway town, no roads in, no roads out, just the railway. So we hung out there for a day and I thought well maybe we can hustle money playing pool, and we go to the pool room and you couldn't possibly hustle money playing pool because there are these old guys there who play pool all day, and the tables had so many rolls in them that you hit the ball and it would roll back into a certain pocket. These guys knew the tables. We bummed a bit but eventually the OPP came and picked us up, told us we were under arrest and the next day we had to catch the next freight train out of town. So they threw us in jail and I called home, as I always did when I got in trouble. I called my mother for money. Mom said, "I'm sorry we have no money." So I said I want to talk to Uncle Vic because he would always bail me out. The story came back, "Uncle Vic said he won't give you any money, you have to get out of this on your own." This was the time that my parents and my family decided they were drawing a line in the sand, and I was going to become a man. At the wrong time for me of course because I really was stuck. So in the morning the cops took us out of jail and said, "Catch the next freight train out of here!" The train takes off right there from a dead stop in Oba and gets up speed, but we had to find a door open on one of the cars that was going by. So gee whiz the train is going and it is getting a little faster and faster and we haven't found an open door. Eventually there is a door open and I run along side and jump in, and Jack is running along side the train and he goes to jump in and I could just see him diving under the wheels, I knew he couldn't make it. I don't know how I did it but I reached out and grabbed him with one hand and lifted him right into the train. There we were, the two of us. Then we started to cry. It was actually quite cold in this thing so we got some pieces of cardboard and there was a little bit of straw and we are using that to keep us warm. And the train takes us right back to Hurst, practically where we started!

We still had no money, so we are trying to figure out how we can get money. It is not a big town. We go down to the tavern and we hang around there, and try to see if there is somebody we can hustle or beg some money from or something. There are some men in there and they are arm wrestling for beer. At the time, neither Jack nor I drank beer, but it was 10 or 15 cents for a glass of beer and we figured if we could win one of them we could get 10 or 15 cents, and we didn't need to buy beer. So we hung around and watched. This guy, who was obviously the guy to beat, he said to me, "Come on young fellow, you look big and strong, I'll arm wrestle you." I figured I can't beat this guy at arm wrestling. "Come on, come on." I said "No, no, no, no, oh no." He kept saying, "Come on." "Well we got no money," I said. "Don't worry about it," he says. "If you beat me, I'll buy you a beer." So I sit down and sure enough the guy let me beat him. He had arms like a tree trunk; there is no way I could beat him. He was going to buy me a beer and I said, "No we'll take the 15 cents." I guess he felt sorry for us. We talked a bit and he ended up saying, "Come on home with me, my wife will give you something to eat." As it turned out he was the engineer on the train that ran from there to Winnipeg. But his crew only went half way. So he took us home, and they fed us. He said "Tomorrow morning, when I take my train, I can't take you down to the station and put you on it but when I go around the turn right up here, I'll slow right down literally to walk and crawl and you can get on the second compart-ment right behind me." His wife gave us a lunch and we went up to where he told us and he slowed the train down and we got on the second compartment. Now this is luxury, we could see all over, this is the greatest trip. When we got to half way between Hurst and Winnipeg, he told the next engineer that we were on the second compartment and that they should take us to Winnipeg. But while we are on this train we are starting to scratch. We are scratching and we start digging and we find out we have got crabs. Jack had had this woman back in our bed and she had crabs and now we had crabs like nobody has ever had crabs in their life. It was the worst dose of crabs you could possibly have. Jeez you could pick them off. I swear they were in our eyebrows there were that many. Oh it was awful.

Now if you can imagine, it had been about five or six days since we'd last had a bath. We likely put crabs everywhere we were. We weren't really aware until we got on this train where it was warm and we were sitting around and not doing things, just being there. All of a sudden these things start roaming around, they are eating up a storm.

So we get to Winnipeg and we've got to jump off the train before it gets right in there. When you are hoboing you get the word from all of the hobos where the CNR police are rough, and Winnipeg was known to have some mean mean police. So we had to get off before we got into the CNR yards, just as the train was slowing down. We got to a drugstore and we bought this stuff they call Blue Butter, for crabs. Then we hitchhiked from Winnipeg to Portage Le Prairie, where Jack had a brother, Todd. We got to Todd's house and he was quite pleased to see us. I could sense he wasn't too happy about Jack arriving with this Black guy in this small town, but he never said anything.

He had two kids and of course they have to find a place for us to stay. So Jack goes in to take a bath, and Todd says "Jesus what is that smell?" You could smell it all through the house, this sort of putrid smell. And he says to Jack, "What the hell is that smell, what is going on?" Jack says, "I got piles and I have to put this on my piles, it's a special ointment that they got for my piles, they are really bad, they are hurting, oh man." So Jack comes out and now it is my turn to have a bath, and I have to put this stuff on too, this Blue Butter. Todd says, "What the demon God is going on?" He can smell this stuff going through his house again. So I said, "I put Jack's ointment on, I didn't want to catch his piles." "You can't catch piles, you are so stupid. You are stinking the house up." I said, "Oh I apologize, I'm sorry." So he never knew that we had crabs.

Todd was in the airforce at Portage La Prairie, and he went back and told everybody on the base about this stupid Black man who comes to his house and thinks he can catch piles from his buddy. And I had to take it, right. And I go by and the guys would yell at me, "Did you catch any piles?" In the meantime, we are the ones who are having a laugh because we got away with getting cleaned up.

Something happened that summer that sticks out in my mind. The very first or second day we were in town, we were going down to a pool room. We liked to play pool. Jack was a real good pool player and I wasn't too bad and we used to hustle pool a little bit and try to make a dollar. And we happened to be going into the pool room where the Native guys play. So we're going there and the RCMP pulled us over. They said, "You are new in town." We said, "Yeah, we are staying with Todd Donnelly, he is in the air force." They said, "You guys shouldn't be around here, this is where the Indians all hang out and you

could get into a lot of trouble. We'd advise you not to hang out in this area."
We said, "We are just going to play pool." "Yeah well you shouldn't do that.
We advise you if you are going to be in Portage la Prairie, you should be up at
the other section." Literally they were running us out of the area. I already had
learned from being in the army in Chilliwack that racism was directed towards
the Aboriginal population more than it was directed to the Black population.
They didn't quite see me as one of them but they certainly didn't see me as low
as they saw the Aboriginals. It was unbelievable. It opened my eyes to racism
and how it played out.

Soon after that I met the Ogilvies. There was a woman, in her 40s I guess.
She had a very pretty daughter around my age and a bunch of other kids. She
was raising these children by herself, very poor. They hardly had food half the
time. After I got a job driving cement truck and gravel truck I left Todd's and
boarded with these people. They were really nice. I had a lot of fun with the
kids. The board money meant a lot to them. I stayed in Portage for the summer and I saved as much as I could of my paycheque every week. At the end
of the summer I was going back to Toronto, and my landlady's son Charlie
wanted to come with me. I agreed that he could come as long as he didn't
mind hitchhiking. The money I had saved up, except for what I thought I
needed for the trip, which wasn't much, I gave to Mrs. Ogilvie. I said, "Now
when we get there, I'll get in touch with you and you can just send me my
money." When we arrived in Toronto, I phoned to get my money. And I never
could get her, and after a while it was pretty obvious that she wasn't going to
send the money. I was really thinking, there went my summer. And then you
know after awhile I began to think maybe she needed that money and that she
didn't intend to steal it. She may have taken a little bit to use because the kids
needed something or something happened and then maybe she took a little
bit more and then she couldn't pay it back and eventually there was nothing
she could do. But she certainly was not the kind of person who was going to
steal my money. So I was able to get over my anger and just chalk it up. It was
meant to be, I guess. I don't know why in the first place I would have left the
money; I was used to carrying money. I carried money all the time. I do also
believe that for some reason I was meant to leave my money.

When I first came back to Toronto, I wanted the money, I wanted the
clothes, I wanted to get back on the scene. Her son was with me, and I was
supporting him because he had no money. I took him to 126 so that all my
friends are now helping to feed him. Not only do I lose my money but I end
up with him as a liability and I can't tell him that he has to get out on the

street. He doesn't know anything about this. He's just a kid from Portage la Prairie.

Back in Toronto I began socializing more with some of the West Indians. I had never been exposed to West Indian food. My first real exposure was at a "do" at Palace Pier at a boxing match. They had ox tails and pig feet and all kinds of exciting things, you know. And they had curried goat and peas and rice. It's the first time that I ever had rice as a vegetable. And I said, "Man these people are so backwards. They're eating their dessert on their plate with the goats. They're eating goats." I had always had rice as rice pudding. It was quite an experience. And then they had a place called the WIF Club (West Indian Federation), and Harry Gairey was the head of it. It was a good social place, and he would engage me in discussion about unions, about the role for Black people in the world, all of these things. I also went to events at the UNIA Hall on College Street (Universal Negro Improvement Association) and the TNVA (Toronto Negro Veterans' Association). Mr. Gairey was a very unassuming, small man, an older man with an apron on, and talking philosophy. He was one of those persons who I think helped me to understand the need to develop a Black consciousness. He was always talking about the future of Black people. My recollection is his idea that we must be proud. African people must be proud people and we had to be educated and we had to be organized. I think he was first and foremost a union man. The sleeping car porters were always first in his mind, but included in that was the idea of organization. So he translated the idea of organized labour to organized communities and organized people; it was all part of his continuum. And that is what he was imparting all the time that we had to organize, we had to be educated, we had to be committed, we had to do it ourselves, we had to look inward. He may have been the first Black person who instilled in me this idea that we had to be organized ourselves to find a solution to our problems. Lenny Johnson also, he took time to explain things, and Stan Grizzle from time to time. Because you've got to understand, coming from Nova Scotia I didn't know any of this stuff. I had never met people who talked about this sort of thing, this is a whole new world. This thing is just exploding in my head.

These people were really powerful to me. Those were the kinds of thinkers that I was so fortunate to be influenced by. It is strange now that I think about it, but we weren't talking about the civil rights movement in the States. These guys were talking more about Africa, and our need to organize and things like that. They were really focused. They would have functions, dances, parades, you know all kinds of things way before the sit-in on University Avenue, and

Toronto, 1963, Big City Rocky.

yet none of those people were involved in that sit-in. Not one of those organizations was involved and yet they were political organizations, they were cultural and political. Their politics were Canada and the Diaspora, rather than American, especially immigration policy and fair practices legislation. But I'm wondering right now why those organizations or even the individual leaders of those organizations did not participate in the demonstration that occurred on University Avenue and the immediate movement that sprang up. They may have made a political decision that they didn't want to be involved with white people doing their protests. Pure and simple. "That is nice that they are doing it but we don't see that as being our primary role here or we don't need to get involved." This is a real revelation to me, believe it or not. This recollection is making me think about it.

While all this is going on I got a job driving for a family company named

Margese, which made mannequins. I delivered mannequins. I used to have fun with them though. I would put them in my truck and have the legs sticking up, so all you could see was the legs. People would be driving up and doing doubletakes. Or I'd stand up a mannequin and just have something on and her bare breasts showing. Oh yeah, I used to have a lot of fun with them, it was a great place to work, an excellent place. It was an Italian firm, and they were teaching me Italian. I was working with Margese when I met Joan. They came to our wedding. It was the first time I knew of a wedding where they gave you money.

I remember when I first met Joan. She was a very athletic type, slim, strong, really strong. Just absolutely beautiful for me, just gorgeous. She wore taffeta dresses, oh yeah she had a nice taffeta dress she used to wear. Joan was filled with incredible energy. She was going all the time. She was a real fun-loving, effervescent person. She took no guff from anybody. She also had a sharp tongue. On the way through to Joan, I'm just playing. I'm just a young guy out there having fun. But Joan, she has substance. She was a secretary, and in those days, that was really something for a Black girl. She worked for Singer Sewing Machines, the secretary to one of the bosses there. It was a really good job. She had grown up in Oakville, which was a small town, so everyone knew her. She had played sports in the town. Her father was a figure in the town too. So she was very comfortable in Oakville. She wasn't familiar at all with Toronto. There were a few times I had her come in by bus, but it was pretty foreign to her. We became so close so fast, it was incredible. Joan really fed my interest in politics and Black consciousness. I think she got that from her father. Her father was very political, very aware of Black issues and foreign issues. He was a real nationalist, a union man too. He was originally from Montreal, a many-generations Canadian. He certainly was progressive. I think Joan took that from her father, because she had lived a pretty sheltered life. She went to Oakville Collegiate; she was likely the only Black student in all of her classes, likely in her school. She was still living with her parents until we got married.

In all of Oakville there were about four Black families at that time, and as luck would have it my sister Marie married into one of those families, named Francis. Through that connection Marie and Joan became very close friends, and it was Marie who introduced us. I'm not sure what Joan saw in me. I suppose there was a certain excitement in who I was, out there playing the game. She was going to tame me. Our lives had been very different up to then. Funny thing, my sister Marie tells the story that when Joan says to her, "I'm getting married," Marie says "Who to?" This is after I've been going over there for months. When Joan told her, Marie said, "You wouldn't, are you crazy?" Marie thought she was absolutely nuts to be involved with me.

I used to go to their house on Burnette Avenue in Oakville, just off the Lake Shore. We would jive in their rec room. It grew from there between us. And I would get into interesting discussions with her father, Eugene Bonner. He was in the Olympics in 1924 and had been a railway porter. He was just a superb man, well loved in his community and deservedly so. Her mother, Elsie Bonner, was from Fort Erie. They had two children, Joan and Donna.

It was Joan who got me reading. This was not something I had done a lot of up to that point. Really reading, and thinking, and figuring out my positions on important matters. It wasn't quite the same as with Mr. Gairey and the older men. They were more like gurus; they inspired and instructed. But Joan challenged me and made me articulate what was in my head. A lot of it was race-based, in terms of this is what was happening with Black people. Mostly our focus was the United States and Canada, but Joan also had an interest in global affairs. We read W.E.B. DuBois, Frantz Fanon, C.L.R. James, Ralph Ellison, James Baldwin. We read about Marcus Garvey. I remember we read *Black Like Me* and *The Autobiography of Malcolm X* later on when it came out. Every one became a seminar with Joan.

I always relate my excitement to the fact that when I was in Nova Scotia no one talked about politics. It just wasn't on the public agenda, maybe not even polite. Just about the time I met Joan, in the early sixties, this was beginning to change. We didn't have any formal connections with anything. It is surprising today to think that two people on their own could study and learn the way that we did. We just collected. We didn't have a mentor. Our friends that we had at that time were not into anything political, let alone Black politics. My friend Midgie certainly wasn't, Joan's best friend Marilyn wasn't. She was a white girl from Oakville. There were discussions about issues affecting the Black community at St. Christopher House, and I continued to drop in there, though not as much as I used to. Basically it was just the two of us. The thing that this literature did for me, I think, was articulating what I already knew and believed but had never heard said: that it is okay to be Black, racism exists, you've got to struggle. Dare to struggle, dare to win, all of those things that were always in the back of my mind that had never come to the front, that is when they started to take shape, during that early period of spending time with Joan in Toronto.

Chapter Three

TRANSITION

Joan and I got married in October 1961, and I had just turned 20 that August. We had a very exciting wedding. Midge was my best man. The wedding is at 3 o'clock on a Saturday afternoon, and Midge and I are supposed to meet at 9 o'clock that morning. He doesn't show up, and he's the one who has a car. So I go looking for him. Of course I know he'll be at Brock's Pool Hall, and sure enough he's there shooting pool. I say, "Midge, we got a hell of a lot of stuff to do today. We've gotta pick up the tuxedos and all this stuff we gotta do." He says, "I ain't doing it." I said, "What?" He says, "No, you are not ready to get married and I'm not going to go through with it." I said, "A fine time to tell me. I'm getting married at 3 o'clock, man. We got all of this stuff to do." He says, "No I'm not doing it, you are not ready, you are going to ruin this girl's life. You are not ready to get married so I'm not going to participate in it." He says, "You can have my car and do whatever you want but I'm not doing nothing, I'm not doing a thing."

I had to borrow his car, go pick up everything, do everything myself the day I'm getting married. I'm out running around doing all this stuff. Now we are in Toronto and Joan lives in Oakville, and now it's about 2:30 when we are getting ready to start out, and Midge shows up. He says, "Okay, if you want me to still go I'll go, but you know I disagree that you should do this." So now we are on the highway heading for Oakville. Midge is driving, and of course we are doing 120 miles an hour because we are late. My brother Alvin's wife Carol is in the back seat screaming, "You are going to kill us all."

Joan is at her father's house and she's crying and going on because we haven't arrived. And she isn't leaving to go to the church before we get there.

So everything is held up. We get to the church and we have to drop everybody off. The rings are down at Joan's parents' place. Midge is still my best man, so he goes down to Joan's place and gets the ring. Now the guys had no socks; I'm doing all this and I forgot to get socks for my best man and ushers. Georgie Whalen from Truro, from the family next door on Ford Street that we used to call "half-breed," was one of my ushers; my brother Alvin was too. And Joan is a beautiful bride, wearing a long white dress and veil. Very traditional, really a very nice, nice, nice wedding. Her best friend Marilyn is a bridesmaid and my sister Marie was the matron of honour. Oh, it was quite a thing, and then we had a party after.

It was a very mixed wedding because I had a lot of Italian friends from my work, and they have a certain tradition that was foreign to us, giving money, and a lot of dancing together as families and the men getting up and dancing by themselves. That was mixed in with the West Indians, who Joan knew growing up in Oakville. And then there were all the Nova Scotians from my side. So it was very cosmopolitan and quite exciting. It was a real good party. For me it just pulled in my whole history, like growing up on the Marsh. The Marsh was so much a part of our wedding. There was no one in my party that was new. They were all people I had known my entire life, basically.

Midge was there with a woman from Nova Scotia. Joan's girlfriend Marilyn, who is white, was a sharp-looking woman. During the wedding ceremony Midge gets infatuated with Marilyn and vice versa. But his original date is there, so Midge and Marilyn disappear. Well the argument was on, you can imagine. For our honeymoon we were staying overnight at the Lord Simcoe in Toronto, and then we were going to Niagara Falls. It was going to be quite the time for me and Joan. Nice beautiful hotel. But Midge and Marilyn decide to come on the honeymoon with us. My house with Joan was always filled with people, so it started right from there. Joan is having a good time too, because Marilyn is her best friend. If you are going to have a party, let's have a party. So they come to Toronto with us, we party at the Lord Simcoe, and then we take off and go away to Niagara Falls. It was a wedding to remember.

After the wedding it was back to work. I was driving dump truck at this time, and I was feeling very sick. It was like someone was pulling my skin, it was hurting like crazy. I had just been working for two days raking asphalt, then I broke out. I had these little white bumps all over me. Joan says, "We have to go to the doctor, you've contracted some sort of disease. I don't know what it is." Then Joan's friend Marilyn came in that same night and I'm getting washed to go into see the doctor. Marilyn says, "What's wrong," and I said,

"I don't know I've got some sort of a disease or something, I have these little white bumps all over." She bursts out laughing and I got annoyed. I said, "So what is so funny?" She grabbed hold of a piece and pulled it, she said, "You have a sunburn you fool." I didn't know what it was and Joan didn't know what it was. I said, "Well I had no idea Black people could get a sunburn. I didn't have a sunburn in my life." But I was out in the sun for two days solid and like anyone else I just got dried out and burned. Never had sunburn in my life, never saw another Black kid with one. I guess in Ontario it is hotter.

My daughter Tracey was born in June 1962, so I needed to find a better job. I went to a school over on Jones Avenue and learned computer programming. I know this sounds funny, since all my friends know what a techno-idiot I would become later on. But I am a fast learner. My computer qualification got me a job at the Ontario Treasury Department, in the data processing unit. Treasury was in a big white building right at the end of University Avenue, the West side. It was brand new; everything was brand new. Our machines were new, the courses we were taking were new. No one knew anything about all of this and here we were making it happen. We were writing the programs. It was extremely exciting. We had one supervisor who was a veteran from World War II. He had lost one arm in the war. The rest of us were all under 30. Everyone was young and it was real cutting edge stuff then.

We had to work 37 and a half hours a week, but we had a certain amount of control over when we worked, because we had different jobs that had to get done and amongst us we would try to organize when we were using certain machines. The mainframe had to be used for certain jobs and they only had so many of these. Supposing you were doing a run for Mothers' Allowance cheques. You might decide to come and do your run from 6 o'clock at night to 6 o'clock in the morning and do all your work. One of the runs I had to do was corporation taxes, and I would do it at night. This meant I would have all day off to go to the beaches, or go to the race track. I loved it because of the freedom. It was a great job. If you can imagine going into work at 6 o'clock, in just shorts and shirt, and you work all night. There is nobody else around.

The government was very supportive of our particular department, and we were able to go out and take courses. I took a course in offset printing so I could run a printing press. I took all of the courses as they came up on wiring these machines and troubleshooting. When a new more complicated computer was installed I was more of an operator than a programmer. They brought in these young intellectual types, and we were forever discussing how you work with these machines.

Joan, Tracey and I were living down on Cowan Avenue, in a three-storey building. Ours was the middle flat. We had a nice little courtyard in the back. We had a lot of fun there. There are stories to remember. We were saving pennies and nickels and a guy comes and steals the jar. Joan caught him, and she beat him down the street with a broom. The guy is running and she kept running after him beating him. She beat him, oh yeah. One night our house got raided by the police. There was a Gibson's Birdland guitar in the middle of the floor and a whole bunch of clothes and all of this is stolen stuff, and the cops come and they don't even know. They were after a friend of mine, a burglar, and they paid no attention to the stolen goods right under their noses. The stories of Cowan Avenue. You've got to remember we were really young. I hadn't sown all of my wild oats by any stretch of the imagination. I remember another funny time, across the street they had an apartment building with a swimming pool. Dougie Collins, my good friend from Ford Street, and Louis Green who was also from Ford Street, came and lived with us for a while. Everybody came and lived with us for a while, that's the way Ford Street was, you didn't know who would show up. It is in the summer, and we decided to go over and have a swim at this apartment building. You had to climb the fence to get into the pool. Well Louis was a deaf mute. We climb over the fence and jump in the pool and we are having a great time. I know sign language because of him. I grew up speaking sign language to him and his sister, and I've kept it for the rest of my life. So we are in the pool, we are swimming and having a good time. Lights are coming on, people are yelling out because they can hear us, and Louis is going "Woo woo." He couldn't hear any of this. So the cops are coming and we climb out of the pool and start running and Louis is still in there. He doesn't know we are gone. The cops came, but Louis got out the other side of the fence and had to run around and come home. We used to do that all the time at night, go swimming in the pools around.

My life didn't change too much, even after Tracey was born. I still played pool regularly with the same guys, played poker regularly with the same guys. Sometimes at my house, sometimes at theirs. Joan was a wonderful influence, in just giving me ideas. "This is something you might look at," she'd say. She was totally supportive. By then she had a couple of friends who were also interested in politics: Ruby, from the West Indies, and Joan's cousin Vince from Fort Erie. There were other people around, and the circle was getting a little wider, in terms of who you could discuss things with. I didn't know much, but I was reading and talking. My education just kept going on.

When I was at Treasury I used to take the streetcar to University Avenue and then I'd walk up from King Street to work. One day in March 1965 I'm walking up, and I see all of these people. There is a demonstration in front of the American Consulate. And then at noon hour that same day I walked back down the street and they were still there. I stopped and said, "What is all this about?" "Oh we are here demonstrating because the FBI won't use their powers of arrest in Alabama, because of the Black people trying to get the vote. " I said, "Huh?" And they are all white! Anyhow I had to go back to work. The people at my work and the old supervisor are telling me about these communists that are down there, very negative. Okay, I'll keep my own counsel on this. So I go home that night and I said to Joan, "Joan there's all of these white people down on University Avenue doing this demonstration, about what they are doing to Black people down in Alabama," and I said, "I think that Black people got to speak up for themselves." And she said, "Well I agree." My position was, it's not that they shouldn't demonstrate. It is that we as Black people should be there, there should be Black people there at this demonstration and articulating if it is a concern for Black people. So we said we had better go down there. Tracey was still a baby, in a stroller. So we go down University Avenue with Tracey. I'm walking around and Joan is walking around with this stroller. I'm asking questions to these people, these students who are there, because I don't know much about it. And the press comes.

There are no other Black people. You can imagine the visual image: Three Black people including a baby walking around at this demonstration. Somebody puts a microphone in front of my face and they say, "So what do you think about all of this?" Oh of course I parrot what somebody had just told me. I say, "Well you know, I think it is absolutely wrong that the FBI don't use their powers of arrest and we are here to put pressure on the American government and make this a live issue that something has to be done and Black people have the right to vote" and so on and blah blah blah… Well that's what these people had just said and that's what I understood, so that's what I said. And, since I wasn't really familiar with the Alabama scene, I said, "And you know we've got a very similar situation today in Nova Scotia, Alabama North." Well the next day I got a big spread in the paper. I think that is the day the *Toronto Star* calls me "Canada's Own Stokely Carmichael." By this point I am a bit politicized, not truly politicized but I am certainly aware of the different issues that are happening and I'm aware of the confrontations that are happening in the States and a lot of that. But I'm not intimately familiar with all of these details. I am reading the paper and reading books. But the Montgomery March, which is occurring then, and the sit-in at the Consulate, that's what focuses my attention, really focuses it on the civil rights movement. And the press pushed me to a certain prominence that carried no resemblance whatsoever to my history or my knowledge.

I stayed overnight at the demonstration, and the next day I went into work. And I got into a big argument with my boss about being down there and in essence he told me I wasn't allowed to go, that they were communist agitators and this and that. I worked in a very sensitive job in Treasury, and I had to watch what I did and who I associated with and everything else. So that night I went home and then went back to the demonstration again. I went to stay, prepared to stay again another night. By then I'm getting a chance to really debate the issues with those people who are there. I'm a pretty quick study, I'm listening to this one, listening to that one, arguing, and being able to take my own life experiences in Nova Scotia to educate these people in return.

The demonstration was held in conjunction with a lot of discussions. I was like a sponge. Suddenly, I had a chance to soak up all of this information and stuff that I had read, stuff I knew, stuff on the radio. It is just coming and I'm just taking it all in and then being able to argue and say, "No I don't think you are right." In a way I had a built-in advantage. I'm Black, and I can say, "I'm the authority on this. I'm Black. What do *you* know?" I went to all of the meetings on St. George Street. I went to everything. I just couldn't get back to work, there was just so much going on, and there was so much to learn and it was so exciting and Joan was supportive. She was right into it, every chance she got. She was still at Singer at the time, which meant she was travelling from Toronto to Oakville. At any rate, it was like something that was just waiting for me, I just loved it, the discussions, the everything. I think one of the things that is important was the creation of this new persona, right there on University Avenue. It was so instant.

The demonstration had been organized by Friends of SNCC (Student Nonviolent Coordinating Committee). Diane Burrows was one of the major forces. In the summer of '64 she had gone off to Mississippi as one of the summer students. But there were a whole lot of others. Some of the ones I think of are Art Pape, Clayton Ruby, Lenore Proctor, Henry Tarvainen. There were a lot of students, some returned CUSO volunteers, intellectual leftists who were all interested in the same issue. I met them at the demonstration, at different times. All of this new left group in Toronto were involved in that demonstration as were the old left of the peace movement types who were still around and kicking. So it was a collection of the entire left of the Toronto scene, and eventually even included the left-leaning labour types. Because I was Black and I was prepared to talk, I rose to prominence very very quickly, in fact overnight. Then we had these sessions at the university, daily study groups, nightly study groups, workshops continually going on, on nonviolence, on how to react nonviolently when police came, how to protect your vitals and neck. There were several important spinoffs from this demonstration and the people involved, including the George Brown Camps, Rochdale College, *This Magazine* and all the SUPA (Student Union for Peace Action) projects. Those things are all a direct result of the activity that occurred in March 1965.

When the demonstration was over, a decision was made that we would go to the States to take this right to the White House. I was a member of the delegation. Clayton Ruby was able to get his uncle's car, and I rode with him along with Lynn Burrows, Naomi Wall, Henry Tarvainen and Matt Cohen. There were other cars too. This car was an Oldsmobile and you could set the speedometer so it buzzed when it got to whatever speed you wanted. We were very conscious of the speed limits and always set the speedometer. We were taking turns driving and somewhere in the State of New York, when I was driving, the police pulled us over and told us that we were speeding. And we argued, "No we couldn't have been speeding because we had the speedometer set." You know how far that got us. The option we were faced with was me going to jail for the weekend and seeing a judge on Monday or Tuesday, and the others going on. Or paying this guy cash, close to $100. We all chipped in and paid off the police and we continued on to Washington. This was in April 1965.

We had made arrangements in Washington to hook up with Students for a Democratic Society people. So the SDS group in Washington with the SNCC group there were our hosts. They were setting up different meetings for us. It was very interesting, as I of course had never been involved in anything like that before. When we first got there we were supposed to have a meeting with the president's top advisor on civil rights. This was a big meeting, with a really high-placed bureaucrat. I recall that I wore my grey silk mohair suit, and I had sort of a cream-coloured overcoat. We had to park a couple blocks away from where we were going to the meeting, and we had to walk along Pennsylvania Avenue. As we are walking down, a huge demonstration is going on. And these were all Black people who had come up from Mississippi, Alabama, Georgia; they were all from the Black belt. It was starting to half rain, half snow, and there I was walking past these people who had pieces of cardboard or paper over them and they are shivering, they are freezing cold, and I have on a top coat and my other coat underneath it. And there is a conflict in my soul, as to whether I should give my coat to somebody to keep warm or should I keep my coat on so I would be presentable when I got to this meeting, which was so important. We were going to be discussing Selma and the civil rights movement with these bureaucrats, and maybe even the president for all we know. And how embarrassed I was that these people would think that I was part of the government, because I am walking past them all dressed up and they are looking at me and I could see that they think that I am part of the enemy. And I want to stop and say to every single one of them, "No, no, no, I'm on your side." It was not very pleasant; it was in fact quite painful. They had been there for weeks already, and they were going to stay until they saw the president himself. They were absolutely committed to the cause. I took strength from that.

We got into the building and were ushered into a large office with a huge desk, maybe 10 feet wide by 4 feet, where we were to see this top advisor. First of all we had to wait for at least a half an hour, maybe 40 minutes, before we got in there, and then when we got in there, there were 14 of us but only 13 chairs. I know in retrospect of course that this was deliberate, for it kept us in total confusion. We didn't know who should be the one standing, or if all of us should stand because there weren't enough chairs. You know they just took our power away, right off the bat. So the top advisor fellow comes in, this Black man, and I'm saying, "Wow, cool, this is the boss hog." He comes in and he goes behind this desk, young nice-looking fellow. He says, "You don't need to stand," 'cause we are all standing. "Sit down." Now we all can't sit down. He has got control. They have us set up. They are pros, and we are like lambs to the slaughter. We are sort of disorganized and some of us sit and some stand.

We are pretty rehearsed in terms of what we wanted to say. We had come all the way from Toronto for this thing. We had a couple questions we were going to ask him but he goes into a spiel, giving the government line. It's so tight and we don't have a chance. It is the first time I had seen a Black man who has got a position like this. This guy is way up there, and he was as reactionary as the administration itself; it was just so heartbreaking. He talked circles around us. There is no question, looking back; we weren't any match for him, none of us. He had the statistics, the information, the rationalization, he had everything.

After this we were having a meeting at a local church. And this was the first time I realized what Washington was really like because the church was not on Pennsylvania Avenue, but three or four streets over, and all of a sudden I'm in this Black ghetto. "This is Washington?" I had no idea that Washington is a ghetto. And there were all of these Black people at this church to meet with us.

They were some of the people in the demonstration we had seen outside. And that is the first time I met Fannie Lou Hamer. I met another woman who had a damaged leg, and she pulled her dress right up and she showed me where the police horse had just gouged her leg, it was all torn up. Every time we went out around this demonstration they had these horses and the horses pranced. And their feet go up and all over the place, really dangerous, and they had gotten her for sure. I talked to them and they talked about how important it was to continue doing what we were doing. They said that it was absolutely essential that this story get out in other parts of the world. They really impressed upon us that we had to keep this story alive and in the news. Because they didn't get the same kind of press; they could do almost anything and it didn't get reported. We are there for three days, four days, staying at that church. The group there was all Black; I think our 13 whites were the only ones there except when we met white students from SDS or SNCC. Our only purpose was to meet people. It is a very good chance for networking and to learn from the people in the South, what they are going through. That is the whole thing that happens on that trip, because we certainly are not successful in any way getting the American government to do anything.

There were other organized trips to the States after that, visiting SNCC and SDS people and so on. I was making a lot of connections with Black activists, who were just beginning in the States to move from the integrationist philosophy into the Black nationalist philosophy. I was still very much an integrationist myself. I certainly believed that multiculturalism as it was being articulated was workable, that we could have coalitions. I believed that there was room for everyone in the civil rights movement as long as the leadership resided with the people we were targeting. I went to a number of conferences, but the next big influence on me was a conference in Buffalo organized by SNCC. The reason I mention it is because Jim Forman was there and I remember having a discussion with him. But there were other people there, like the Detroit Revolutionary Movement, the Republic of Africa, CORE (Congress of Racial Equality), SCLC (Southern Christian Leadership Conference), all of the Black groups that were active at the time. Our purpose was to get support for SNCC in Canada, because we had Friends of SNCC but we wanted an actual SNCC project. By that time I was quite prominent in the Canadian media. I did a lot of speaking across Canada, usually to student groups, and I was raising a lot of money that was going into the Southern movement. The Americans knew that I was a Canadian contact and someone who could help raise money for the movement.

So I met Jim Forman, and I wanted to convince him that we should be able to have a real chapter of SNCC in Canada, and that I wanted to organize in Nova Scotia. Jim Forman was so impressive to me. I thought he could walk through a wall, he had that kind of charisma and that kind of physical strength. He was one of the most powerful speakers. And he said to me, "I cannot justify diverting money from the movement in the South to send it to Canada." He said, "There is no comparison to the struggle that people are having in the Black belt, trying to vote, being beat up, being killed and murdered, and you talking about trying to integrate some place in Canada, there is no comparison," he says. "I would not support that, I cannot support it." I argued that Nova Scotia was no different, that when he talked about genocide, we were facing a kind of genocide, a cultural genocide, that was occurring even faster in Canada and particularly in Nova Scotia than it was in the States. In the States they had the numbers and they could protect the community, whereas our communities were being bought up, our communities were being taken over, disintegrating, being destroyed. And the argument that it was worse in the Southern States couldn't hold water: they couldn't vote, but they could stay Black; we could vote but we couldn't stay Black. If things kept going the way they were, we would see the destruction of an entire people. Our history gets buried, and reshaped, and becomes the history of the oppressor and we can't do anything about it because we don't have any resources. And this became quite a debate between me and a number of people involved in SNCC and CORE, and I lost. I couldn't get any support, they just turned it down: "Absolutely not, we are not buying it. If you really want to be an asset to the struggle you will do what you are doing, you will raise money and you will speak and you know, you can come down here whenever you are needed and whenever there is a problem in Canada, that is where we will send you and that is where you will go. And that is your role and that is the most effective role that you can have."

I am developing my consciousness based on my discussions with these very same people, reading these very same materials that they are reading, and it is all American and African-oriented. The literature, everything that is coming out is basically talking about America and Africa: the winds of change have blown over Africa, and the debate of whether Blacks can separate, all of these issues in terms of nationalism are American or African-oriented. There is nothing written or being said about the Canadian experience, not even, at this time in history, about the underground railroad or the fact that Black people live in Canada, nothing. We are a non-entity; we don't exist as far as the contemporary literature is concerned or the debates that are occurring. The

Black Canadian community, African Canadians, don't exist. I come into this as an African Canadian who can provide a service and the service I can provide is to send money, basically. And to spread the gospel of what is happening to them and that is my only role as far as they are concerned. I'm prepared to do that and I think it is very important, but by the same token I have now learned the contradictions that exist in Canada. My personal growth has allowed me to analyze Canada and say there are things wrong here. I look at Nova Scotia where I grew up, look at what is happening there, look at what is happening to my community, and it must be addressed.

So I'm left with a choice. Do I continue to do just what they want me to do, or is there the possibility that I can be proactive and intervene in the Canadian context? If I am going to intervene in the Canadian context I cannot do it on my own. This is where Friends of SNCC and SUPA come in, because there is a group in Canada that is interested in community development. They are interested in confronting the Canadian government. The history of those groups is the history of the peace movement: the Quakers, the Voice of Women (VOW), the Combined Universities Campaign for Nuclear Disarmament (CUCND). So it is a different evolution than the civil rights movement in the States, because they didn't come out of the peace movement. On the one hand all of the Black groups in the States are saying, "No we aren't supporting you because you ain't got no problems up there compared to what we got." On the other hand, in Canada we have these white leftists, who are saying, "Wow, is that ever exciting, what do you need, how can we help? What can we do to move this struggle forward?" It becomes for me a conscious decision to align myself with the new left in Canada, represented by SUPA, which grew out of the CUCND. It was a reformulation of the peace movement into community action, the idea that for real peace to be achieved you can't just ban the bomb but you have to build a society that creates justice for all. And this means attacking poverty and inequality, developing community participation, not just marching with signs and banners. These were the people I was meeting on University Avenue, and it was clear that they would support the philosophy that I was developing in terms of the problems in Canada.

SUPA sponsored me to go to Nova Scotia to see about setting up a project there. We were trying to base our project on what was being used in the United States, mostly in Appalachia and the Southern States. You went first to a rural community, and you were able to organize small groups because they knew each other. Their political consciousness and organizing skills would grow. And you have movement between the rural areas and the cities, and so people could carry the skills they learned in the rural area to advance the struggle in the urban area. They have already picked up the beliefs and strategies, and they can then implement them also in the urban area. This was the theory. So that was basically our plan, and we believed that Africville and the Prestons were the target area. When I first came down, it was with Gary Pearlman, a white SUPA volunteer. Joan and Tracey were still in Toronto. In fact, Joan and I were separated at that time. I was always on the road, speaking and raising money literally across the country, or sometimes hanging out with my buddies. I was never home, and Joan got tired of that I guess.

The first place I went was to Truro, of course, to see my family. I was under the influence of the American rhetoric and the American civil rights movement. Included in that was this concept that you should never call anyone "boy," and that was an insult and you could go to battle over that. I remember coming into my yard on Ford Street and my father was there with one of his best friends, Ed Crowell. He was white. He lived at the top of our street, and they had grown up together and spent their entire lives since they were boys together. They were very happy to see me of course and welcoming. They were doing some chores or fooling around in the yard. And so Ed, who I had known all my life and who I knew really cared about me, was giving me, per usual, an order to do something, and he said, "Okay boy, do this." And I could literally feel the hairs stiffen on my neck. Here is this white man calling me "boy." But I could see the absolute love and pride in his face, he was so happy to see me home. Here is a kid he had known all of my life, he loved me, and he called me "boy." And to him that was a natural word because my father called me boy and my father called Ed boy and Ed called my father boy, and in Nova Scotia, this was a word that was used commonly amongst men and indeed it may be an endearment, if I can go so far. So there I was with all of this political baggage or background that I had brought from being involved in the civil rights movement into Nova Scotia. And for the first time, I think, in my life, I had to realize that words mean absolutely nothing. Anybody can use any word to describe you; it is what they mean, it is what is behind it, it is the feel of it, because the word boy can be an insult but it can also be an endearment. And I had to deal with that and it was a lesson that I've carried forever.

From Truro we went into Halifax, where we stayed with one of my cousins. We first got involved with the people at King's College, who had connections with our friends back in Toronto. That is where I got hooked up with Bill Curry and Wayne Hankey, among others. They were Christian activists who were involved in the Student Christian Movement. They were the first people

I connected with, to try to get our project established using the university networks. Then I went out to stay with my cousin Noel Johnson, who lived in East Preston. I wanted to see if we could organize in Preston. He was one of the leading members of the community out there, and by staying with him I thought I had an automatic door-opener. Meanwhile I was joined by Denny Grant, a West Indian. He was from Antigua, and came to Canada as a student at a bible college out West. He came to Toronto and looked us up as he had heard about us from the newspaper publicity. Denny came out to Preston with me and we were both staying with Noel.

Now just at that time there was a group of white people in the Preston area who got up a petition to divide the Black voters, in effect to gerrymander the voting district for the municipal elections. There was an emergency meeting called to see what the response of the Black people should be, and my cousin Noel was chairing that meeting. Denny and I felt that we could organize the community around that issue. So we go to this meeting. Noel is in the chair and the meeting is packed. People are adamant one way or another in terms of their positions. The meeting is just filled with electricity, a lot of tension, a lot of debate because there are two sides. One side wants it and one side doesn't, so it is back and forth. I have decided it shouldn't happen. I think that it is wrong because they are going to lose. The way the lines were drawn then, they had enough votes to elect a councillor, and they had their own councillor. If the boundary lines get changed, they wouldn't get enough votes to get their own councillor, because the way the lines were being proposed would split their vote. So I was against it, or I thought I should be against it. My cousin didn't want me to get involved. He felt we were from outside, it wasn't our issue, wasn't our business, and we shouldn't be trying to influence the community. Well I was pretty hot headed and I wanted to talk, and Denny wanted to talk, but Noel wouldn't recognize us from the chair. I was saying I wanted to talk, and Noel said basically, "Sit down and shut up." Carl Evans stands up and says, "Let him speak, he has every right to speak, he is at the meeting, let him speak." Carl can't say two sentences without saying 50, very passionate, very eloquent and very strong. So Carl gives this long speech about we are all Black people and it is an issue that concerns Black people and therefore we should be able to have a say. And that we weren't really outsiders because we are Blacks and from Nova Scotia. In fact it was a very good analysis that Carl had. So Noel has no choice but to let us speak.

My whole rhetoric was tied to the fact that we are in this not as individuals but as part of a collective, that we have been treated this way because we are an African people, because we are Black. So I couldn't stand up in a meeting and talk about the redefinition of boundaries without saying the reason this is happening to us is because we are Black. Some of the people there are saying, "No, they're not treating us this way because we're Black." They were hiding from the racist actions that were directed towards them. They didn't want to hear it. Denny also spoke. He was very eloquent, a great speaker, very passionate. A typical West Indian, fast-paced talking. He spoke like Cassius Clay that night. He just could use the metaphors. The community didn't buy it. They didn't want any part of it. And part of our difficulty when we first arrived and in organizing came from the fact that we had beards, and people weren't ready for anybody with a beard. Furthermore, our hair was long, an obvious Afro. That was the sign of radicals. We dressed differently. I wore dashikis and a leather jacket. We weren't sophisticated enough to know we should have at least looked like the people. We were wearing the uniform of the Black left and they weren't ready for that. We were talking in terms of we are African, we are Black. At that point people were still Negro or Coloured. Even our terminology was out of pace with the people. We were out of step. People were very polite, let us have our say, and then said, "We disagree."

Our experience in East Preston said to us that there was no way we could break into that community without gaining trust. It meant moving into the community and staying there for a couple of years, getting the trust and developing from that. We were looking to do something in a hurry. We decided it would be easier to organize in the city where people were coming and going and the community was more flexible in terms of talking to people, because you weren't necessarily inside or outside. That was how the decision was made to locate our project in Halifax, and to focus on the younger people there. At the end of August 1965 I wrote to our SUPA people in Toronto and informed them of this decision.

In early September 1965, there was a SUPA national meeting in St. Calixte, near Quebec City, and I attended that meeting. The idea was to organize all the SUPA community projects and get them started on a firm footing. I put the case to them of my proposed project in Nova Scotia, and it was accepted. The plan was that a team of us would go down, all of them white except myself: Lynn Burrows, Jim Kinzell and Dory Preston. Added to this was another girl, a French Canadian who joined up with us while we were in St. Calixte. She is full of love and understanding, and she just steals all of our hearts, so we let her come aboard even though she was not part of the original group. The plan was that we would go back to Toronto for some training in community development and nonviolent tactics before heading off for Halifax. I had some serious concerns about taking a white group into Nova Scotia without any training. A fundraising committee was set up to help with our expenses, but we were all expected to get part-time jobs to share in supporting ourselves and any other costs of the project. Harvey Shepherd was doing the fundraising, along with Clay Ruby and Diane Burrows. The Burrows sisters managed to get some community funding in their hometown of Belleville which went toward Lynn's expenses, which was a great help.

A prof at the University of Toronto named Dr. Jack Seeley set up our training program. He later went to the Institute for Behavioral Studies at Santa Barbara, California. I was the one who approached him. "Dr. Seeley," I say to him, "we want to do this project in Nova Scotia, and everybody going with me is white. They need to have some kind of training and some sensitivity, to be able to go into the Black community to organize and there is going to be a lot of pressure." He was an expert in psychology and community development. So he and another professor at the University of Toronto said they would give us training. At the sessions there was Lynn Burrows, Gary Pearlman, Jim Kinzell, myself and the girl from St Calixte. So in our first session, Dr. Seeley says, "Look, when you go into this kind of project, you don't realize you are going into isolation. You are going in doing the kind of work where the people that you are going to work with will not understand you. So you are way ahead in thinking than the people you are going to be with. You think they should understand and support you, but they may be against you and it is going to be hard for you to understand at all times when you are out in front and right, and when you are out in front and wrong. Because no matter what it is you do the people won't always understand. It is going to be your job to try to educate the people so that they do understand and they can make the right decisions, and they will make decisions you don't agree with. But you have to go through this continually and always be reassessing." He also explained to us that to do this you had to accept the fact that the people, even though they seemed to be turning against you, you continue to love those people, that is what it is all about. You do it because, as Stokely Carmichael said, "We must have an undying love for our people." Jack Seeley said it sort of in a different way but it was the same concept: you must have that undying love that you cannot turn against the people even if they turn against you, because they are going to turn against you. But you have to just work through that. And he says, "I will give you some skills to be able to deal with that kind of conflict. It may break you. It breaks people all over."

So he is putting us through these sessions, where we are confronting each other, role-playing. It is really really intense. In this one session, the girl from St. Calixte is doing a confrontation, I think with Lynn, and Jack Seeley is drawing them out, and all of a sudden, it was just like a movie where you can see blinders come out of a person's head. Here was this girl who we believed was the most loving person, who talked to us about how she loved people and wanted to work with people and communities, and really wanted to help. And you could literally see her face start to change into contortions and Jack kept talking to her and talking to her and drawing her out, and she is saying, "I hate you people, I hate all of you." She is saying, "You think I'm this way and I have to be this way in order to survive but I'm really not like this. I hate people and I hate what they have done to me all of these years. They think because I am beautiful that men can do this to me and they think this and that." It was just the most amazing transformation. We are sitting there, the rest of us, and we are watching this girl who we were just so taken with, and Dr. Seeley is just talking to her and she is absolutely vicious. If we had taken her to Nova Scotia, she would have killed herself or someone else. I heard later that she ended up being hospitalized and spent a couple of years in an institution. She had a mental disorder, and Dr. Seeley spotted it. Anyhow we went through these sessions and at the end of it he said, basically, "Okay you are ready and you can go. But there will come a time when you are going to face that wall. If it ever comes and you cannot deal with it, call me, I am here. I'm always available for you. I'm ready to help."

Dr. Seeley was trying to give us tools to be able to deal with what he considered to be a hostile environment. But I don't think that anyone from outside who didn't know the African Nova Scotian community would ever be able to understand the depth of the conservatism and how embedded it really is, and how strong the community would actually be able to be once it made some kind of decision. If the community says, "No, we don't want it," that would be it. I think when Dr. Seeley was training us, he did give us good coping strategies. It could be that we as individuals had to then fall back on some kind of inner strategies that we may have had. Maybe we didn't have the experience or the depth to be able to just deal with it. That's not to say that we couldn't handle what it was we were doing, because I think we did handle it. But there were many, many times, when it was impossible for me to understand the reaction for something that seemed so self-evident. Like, for instance, when you had a school teacher act in a discriminatory fashion toward a child, and you have the parent or the community condoning the teacher's behaviour. I mean how can you allow somebody to hurt or discriminate against your own child? There was no way for me to understand the community response, or the individual's response, to that kind of action. So there were many occasions when I believed that the community should stand up and fight and/or take a strong position, and the community didn't do it. And I couldn't understand why not, because you've got everything to gain and nothing to lose. But the conservatism, the history of the community, was such that there was a resistance to change.

So there I am. It's 1965. I guess I had always had a rebellious streak, from resisting to be baptized as a teenager, to my short career in the army, and my life on the edges in Toronto. Conforming was never a characteristic of mine. Now I had a chance to turn that tendency into something positive.

Chapter Four

COMING HOME

The SUPA council that met in St. Calixte christened us the Scotia Nonviolent Action Project, or SNAP. I never warmed to that acronym. It reminded me too much of breakfast cereal. We just called it the Nova Scotia Project, or the Project. We weren't quite sure what we were going to do, just work with the youth. We'd figure out what to do as we went along, using community development tactics we'd picked up in Toronto.

I was staying with my cousin in Halifax, when Joan decided she'd give me another chance to make our marriage work. She had our whole house packed up in Toronto, and Jim Kinzell put it into a bus. Jim arrived with all of our worldly goods packed into a school bus. I think Joan and Tracey came by plane or train. And my mother was very clear: "You have responsibilities, and you look after them." So I find a one-bedroom apartment on Barrington Street over the 999 Jazz Club. And we had rats, I mean serious rats. I saw nights when I had a .22 pellet gun and I would sit up and waiting for the rat, and wait and wait just like when I was sitting with my father. Sooner or later Mr. Rat would put his head out of the hole, and he was toast. Tracey was a baby and so we couldn't have rats running around and they were pretty smart. They were hard to catch; they knew all about traps, they would go right around them. These were wharf rats, old Halifax wharf rats, and I even think they were immune to warfarin. I think warfarin just went and gave them more muscles.

Not long after we moved in there a social worker we knew named Janet approached us and said, "Look, they are taking children from Halifax, Black kids, and they're shipping them away, shipping them down to the States, because there's a shortage of babies and they're shipping them other places,

71

and we need to do something about it." And we were quite concerned, I mean politically this was consistent with what was happening with the disintegration of the Black community. It was just one more way to annihilate us, to take our kids. So Joan and I decided that we would take as many children as we possibly could. We weren't going to allow them to take these kids away. So within a couple of years we went from one child to five children. Once Social Services realized that we would take children, of course then every time something happened, they would say, "Well will you take this child?" Not all were permanent placements, you know, we would take children that were abandoned and have them for two weeks or two months, and some children we took for their entire life.

That was very much part of a political system that we adopted and we tried to take that position into the Black community. I approached every Black person that I could and I said, "Look, they're taking Black kids and they're shipping them out of the province and you can help by taking a child either to adopt or as a foster child and we've got to keep our children here, and we've got to look after our own children." And 99.9% of the Black people in Halifax who were in a position to be able to take a child wouldn't do it. They had every excuse imaginable: we don't have space, we travel too much, my wife isn't feeling good, my husband isn't feeling good, whatever, excuse after excuse after excuse. People just would not step up and say, "Yes, we will take these children."

And at this point there was also a debate that we were involved in over institutions. We had the Nova Scotia Home for Colored Children, where they were placing children. That was one option, but they could only take so many. The other option was for white families to adopt Black kids, and that was hotly debated too. The issue was whether a Black child was better off with a white family that loved them or being in foster care and shipped away to families that didn't love them. We had taken the position that the children were better off with a white family than no family. That wasn't popular, but in our community it was necessary because so many of the kids didn't have homes.

We ultimately raised five children, some of whom were adopted, some were natural and some were foster, and I don't know how many others were part-time. But it certainly did create some problems. For instance, as we got more children, we needed a bigger vehicle, as we got more children, we needed a bigger place to live, and as we got more children, we needed more money for more food. It changed a lot of things financially. Plus we had the sort of house where people from all over the world were dropping in continually and Joan fed everybody. So although people did arrive with food and a lot of times people left $2 or whatever on the counter, it certainly created a lot of difficulties. The other difficulty was that Joan and I couldn't take off as CUSO volunteers because we couldn't take the kids. None of the overseas projects would accept children then. I had a lot of friends who were going on CUSO and they would say, "Why don't you come, you can do this and do that," especially in the African countries. But it just became impossible, we couldn't do it. The advantage of course is there's a lot more love to go around, there's a lot more kids, there's a lot more excitement. It was a lot of fun with all of those kids.

Halifax at that point for me is a bit scary because we live down on Barrington Street, right at the water. Across the street is a big apartment building, and there's a couple of small houses around and other than that there's nothing down there; it just gets dark. All the action in Halifax is up at Gerrish and Gottingen, and it's further down Barrington Street where Scotia Square is now. And that's the circumference of the area that we're concerned with: it's along Barrington Street to Duke Street, up Duke Street, along Market Street (that's before the Metro Centre), over to Prince, and back along Brunswick. And then when you're going north, basically Agricola Street is the end of the community that we're more interested in. So all that whole area is where all the action is in terms of the Black community. You see, Halifax was a totally divided city by custom, so that Black people didn't go to Spring Garden Road; they stayed in the North End and they didn't go to the bars downtown, they just stayed in the north and that's where people were. And things could be quite confrontational between the sailors and the North Enders, mostly Black, but you have to understand that the North End was never entirely Black; it was always integrated. So when you talk about the North End of Halifax, there were white kids that were as much involved in all the things that were going on, all the parties, everything, as there were Black kids. It was totally integrated, poor, working-class, and even if their parents were prejudiced they were still going out with you because the parents wouldn't know. And there was a lot of inter-racial dating and mixing. Dances were all integrated, houses were integrated. You could have a Black family in one half of a duplex, and a white family in the other half. The schools were integrated. The only thing that wasn't integrated was the church.

Besides finding my way as a community organizer I had to have a job, because SUPA funding was really only enough to get us started. It never covered all the costs let alone feeding my growing family. I had picked up computer skills working for the Treasury Department in Ontario, so I went down to the

Technical University of Nova Scotia looking for work. There was a professor named Stan Heaps, a prestigious scholar who was doing work on acoustics underwater and as such he had graduate students and undergraduate classes. He interviewed me and agreed to hire me as one of his assistants working in the computer lab. I was to help the students with their classes and teach them how to use this computer, which was called the LPG30. Well first of all, I had never seen this computer before; secondly, they were doing work, calculus, which I had never ever done. So I would go in and see what their assignments were, and I'd go that night and study and try to figure out what they were doing and so that the next day I'd be able to help them with any of their problems. Well, it took them perhaps one or two of my classes to figure out that I didn't have a clue. The students decided that they wouldn't blow the whistle and we would just continue with these classes. I would pose a question and we would discuss it in the class, and the whole class would get involved in what the solution was and somehow or other collectively they could solve any problem that was presented. It is amazing when I look back at it; I lasted in that job maybe six months or so. Had a good rapport with the students, good rapport with the staff, played on their hockey team, and had a good reference from the professor when I decided to quit. I figured I'd better quit before he realized I didn't know anything.

We wanted to organize the youth, and we felt that we should have both educational and recreational programs. Recreational meant dances and music, along with sports. Space opened up on the floor above the Jazz Club, and we saw that as an opportunity to open a club. That was the first Club Kwacha named after the word for "freedom" in a Zambian language. We had quite a crew of people working in Kwacha and in the community through Kwacha as a headquarters. There was myself and Joan, as the Project leaders, and Lynn Burrows was also really an integral part of the leadership. Then there was Jim Kinzell, of course, and Gary Pearlman, Carl Holmes, Carol Oliver, Dennis Symonds, Tony Carter, George Hartwell. Ronnie Whalen, who had lived next door to us in Truro, came to Halifax to work on the Project, and he was quite talented and a real asset. Some of the people from the King's College student government became very involved. I remember Bill Curry, John Cleveland, Wayne Hankey, Doug Clark. Dennis Symonds and Carol Oliver were Black, but mostly we had white people working with us. Some of us are receiving a bit of financial help from SUPA; some of us are strictly volunteers, giving part-time assistance. Then the federal government decided to set up a domestic Peace Corps, which they called the Company of

Young Canadians. The idea was that they would go into poorer communities to work and organize. It was natural for the government to go to the leadership of SUPA as they were getting the CYC going; Doug Ward, Art Pape, in fact the whole leadership was consulted. The CYC wanted to send some of their volunteers to work with us on the Nova Scotia Project, and they offered to pay some of the people who were already with us. Joan, for example, agreed to become a CYC worker and get paid for doing what she had been doing all along. I was also asked but I refused; I didn't trust the government, and I wanted to be free to take an independent political position. But it sure was good to have this new money rolling in. I believe at least four of us became paid CYC workers in the Project, and there was never any open interference in our activities.

Suddenly we lost our club space. The landlord ordered us evicted, with only two days' notice. He said it was because of police complaints. We didn't do anything in that club to deserve being evicted. First of all the only one that could complain would be the Jazz Club downstairs, and they were making noises of their own, and on the third floor that's where I lived. The were only three apartments on the whole third floor, and none of us would have complained and there was no one else around us. But we got put out and we didn't know what to do. This was the end of March 1966.

We scouted around and found that the old Armouries, which is right where the swimming pool is now, at the corner of Gottingen and Cogswell, wasn't being used. And no wonder. The furnace didn't work, no water, no flooring, it was just a shambles. It was owned by the city, so we appealed to the municipal politicians, and through their intervention we were offered this spot. No one expected that we'd be able to do anything with that place, but we mobilized a bunch of volunteers to put it in working order. There was a plumber working at Dalhousie who arranged to fix all the plumbing for us. Through the union he recruited a bunch of other plumbers and tradespeople who worked for the city or the university. They actually put in a floor for us, a cement floor. Some people from Preston, some cement workers, came along too. You wouldn't believe the workers that came to this building. We had no money, not a nickel. Between the unions, Dalhousie, the community, everybody, these guys all came in and rebuilt the entire building free. I don't know where the materials came from, and they even coloured the floor, they had red colouring in it. It was just amazing how the community came together and built us this spot. If I recall the city charged us rent but I don't think that was any amount. So that was the second Kwacha and again it was very successful. We took possession on June 6, 1966. We were there for about a year, and then we moved to Gottingen Street. This would be Kwacha Three, and the final one. We were in that place when the National Film Board came and made the film *Encounter at Kwacha House* in 1967. It closed in January 1968.

Obviously this was a very integrated endeavour. The kids we were working with were both Black and white. The workers were mostly white. And so were a lot of my friends in Halifax. Many of them had been CUSO volunteers and were now back at university. Ken McKay, Stan Barrett, Colleen Ashworth, Jill Morton, John and Diane Baigent, they were all returned CUSOs. It may be that they had experienced some of the same isolation, in different countries, and had to face some of the same things that I'd had to face coming to Nova Scotia, and so they had a certain, perhaps, sensitivity to some of the things that I was going through. They certainly all understood what it was like to be a minority in Africa or India or wherever they were.

This circle of friends and co-workers was entirely consistent with my personal and political philosophy at the time. I had adopted a philosophy of cultural integration. I believed it was possible for Black people to participate in mainstream society and economic and educational endeavours. I believed it was possible for Black people to do that and generally speaking the society would respond. I was fairly close to the old philosophy that others had, that there were a few bad apples responsible for our problems. I was just beginning to see that there was a societal problem, a structural problem, though I still believed that within that structure Black people could find equality. I also believed, when we were first starting, that it was possible for white people to provide some kind of leadership and to participate with us in confronting the racism and inequality that were so pervasive in our society.

This same philosophy was reflected in the group of supporters we gathered around us. We called it the Friends of the Nova Scotia Project, and that in itself was very exciting. It was an integrated group, with some very influential people. Believe it or not, the deal was that they would raise money to supplement whatever we got from SUPA or our own employment earnings. But the Friends had no say over what we did, none. They had no say over program, they had no say over content, they had no say over anything; their only role was to raise money, and to act as resource people when we wanted, and to back our play. You can imagine the faith it took, in those days, to do that. Now, here I was as wild as wild could be out there, and these people were going to support me to do it. It was just incredible that it could be pulled off. We were at the mercy of the community. We were real idealists; if we were real organizers the community would find a way to look after us, which they did, by the way. It worked.

The Rev. Don Trivet, a white Protestant minister, was chair of the board. How we found him I have no idea. Victor Oland, one of the wealthiest men in the province, was on our board. I recall talking to him and telling him that basically what we really wanted to do was change the structure of society. He was quite intrigued by it. He said "What?" Lloyd Shaw was on the board, one of our biggest supporters. So were Allan O'Brien, who later became mayor, and his wife Nancy, Rabbi Freeman, the Anglican bishop W.W. Davis, Richard Owens, Frank Kilmore, the Kaplans, who were at the university. A lot of our support came from the old peace groups, the Quakers, the Baha'is. Fran and Don McLean were Baha'is and very helpful to our Project. We had Dr. Ian Maxwell, who was a pathologist at the Infirmary.

Dr. Maxwell was perhaps the biggest influence on the Project, other than us. Ian Maxwell was my greatest mentor. I don't know how, he showed up one day, riding his bicycle, wearing his overalls and his old plaid shirt, and began to help us do things. If anything needed to be fixed, we called the Doc. We didn't even know at the time that he was truly a doctor, we just called him Doc. And everything that we needed fixed he'd either fix it or find resources to have it fixed. We wanted to make kayaks, so he learned to make kayaks and taught us to make kayaks; he helped us to physically build the club. He was there for all of our discussions and certainly didn't understand exactly what we were about because we had many arguments. He was a committed pacifist. He and his wife Ann had four children and he'd bring his kids around. Absolutely the best thing that happened to our forum was to get involved with him because he helped us to stay grounded. You can see him and how he operated in *Encounter at Kwacha House*. A lot of times when I'd be really angry, and a lot of times when we thought all this wasn't going to work and we can't do this or we can't do that, Doc Maxwell would be the voice of reason. "Yeah, it can work, let's try this," or "I know someone who might be able to do this, let's give them a call." He was just an incredibly kind, committed, energetic worker, who did more than anyone else of all the people that we met for the Project.

Another pillar for us was Muriel Duckworth from the Voice of Women, and her husband. Muriel agreed to support us and open doors, but didn't understand at all what we were doing. We were talking about things that she didn't experience and she would say, "I don't have any experience in this, but if you say it's something good then I accept that and I'll support you blindly." She too had incredible faith.

All these people were white. From the Black community we had Gus Wedderburn and Buddy Daye. They were there, but they weren't truly supporters. They were prepared to be on the board but most of the things we were about they opposed. They both were suspicious of what we were doing. Reverend Coleman on the other hand was always very supportive of us. Charles Coleman was the minister at Cornwallis Street Baptist Church, and he opened doors for us and gave us the legitimacy of the major church in the Black community. His young people's group literally became the founding members of Club Kwacha. That was because his teaching and his stance were basically the same as ours, but his were religious. The Baptist young people were the core of the Project and the most active participants in the programming we did in Halifax. Rev. Coleman was a preacher who believed that Christians had a duty to be involved in their community, and as such the young people in his congregation had to live out this duty by being involved in our Project. I talked with him a lot and he gave us many ideas. He was a very dynamic, forceful person.

Joan Brown was always helpful, always ready. But above all from the Black community we had Mrs. Pearleen Oliver, the wife of the Rev. Dr. W.P. Oliver. She would run interference between me and W.P., who never really approved of me. Pearleen was always supportive of the Project and of me personally. She understood, she could see what I could see, she could see what I was saying. I've heard her say publicly, "I know what he means. I know what he is talking about. I grew up in New Glasgow and so I understand him." When I think of people I look up to and respect a lot as individuals, one would be Pearleen Oliver and the other would be Muriel Duckworth. I think I have the strongest admiration for those two people as almost anybody I have ever met. In their own way they just plodded along and tried to make a difference, and have been consistent in their commitment to the community. To my knowledge they have never compromised their position in any way that would endanger their real goals or endanger their community. Both of them were women in a time when women should have kept their mouths shut. Those are two of my greatest heroes, and two of the people most responsible for the success of the Nova Scotia Project.

Obviously we had a very strong team of workers and supporters. Every single day we have organized discussion groups on organized topics, which we call freedom schools. And the Black kids are very excited; for the first time ever they're beginning to learn about their African connections and they're learning about the American civil rights movement and there are a lot of people who are in and out of Halifax that these kids get to meet that they wouldn't normally have met, different visitors that come through and so the political consciousness is rapidly changing.

I was still travelling quite a bit on behalf of SNCC. I'm off to Boston or Winnipeg or Vancouver. I would go away and I would hear about something, and I would come back and talk to them, and we'd discuss it, and all of a sudden they know about it. And then we'd get a book. We were reading everything, and the people you thought would never be reading would be reading. This is what the kids wanted. We also had tutors, volunteer university students from King's, Dal and the Mount, who would come in and help the kids with their homework. We had basketball and hockey teams for the boys, and basketball for the girls. Girls didn't play hockey in those days, but we had a typing course for girls. There were arts and crafts, instructional films every Wednesday night with discussion following, a general meeting every Sunday afternoon, a coffee house every Sunday evening. Something was always happening.

Part of what we were attempting to do was to get the people to take control of their own community, and we also wanted the young people to take control of their own activities. If they had things they wanted to do there was no reason they couldn't do it if they organized. That's what participatory democracy is about and that was the SUPA philosophy; people must participate to make democratic decisions and have that kind of control. We did things that teenagers do. The only difference between us and other teenagers of the day, I suppose, was that the young people actually controlled their own activities as opposed to having the activities put on for them. They had to plan them, they had to implement them, they had to fund them. They had to do it all, and this was developing certain skills. The idea would be that they had to write their own reports. They may not want to write in school, but they had to write their own reports, account for their own money, raise it, budget it, all of these things. We would ask them what they wanted, and once they decided our goal was to try to help them get it. Now among the Project workers we discussed the theory of leadership, whether we would lead by example or whether we would lead by basically pushing, and it was our philosophy that we would lead by pushing. In their various activities we would have one of the young people be the head of it and then we would act in a supportive role and push them along. It was an attempt to decentralize the leadership of the entire Project and to a certain extent I think it worked.

We conducted a survey in the community, the Kwacha kids themselves did it, along with our Project workers, to see what the most urgent issues were as

far as the families were concerned. The two issues that emerged were housing and recreation. So we launched our community action with two major
projects. We wanted to organize the parents, and the best way we felt was to
involve them through their interest in their children's recreation, and through
their interest as tenants. First we organized what we called the Tot Lot, which
was a community playground. And in organizing that community playground
we were saying, our children need a place to play that is safe and not a lot of
broken glass, and where they have equipment. People responded to that and
so we had a lot of help clearing the lot, getting the equipment and supervising
the children. That acted as a springboard to then have people talk about what
is the role of city hall when it comes to providing service to our community. So
the small things that we organized, did eventually allow us to talk about larger
things and mobilize the community on different issues.

It was Lynn Burrows who went around and talked to all of the mothers
about developing the Tot Lot. She was able to convince them that we needed
a safe place for the children to play and that they needed to participate. We
had the mothers take turns supervising the lot so there was sort of a revolving
schedule of mothers who weren't working, or if they were working they could
come after work. It was a very complex schedule to set up and it required an
incredible commitment on the part of the parents. Lynn was able to set up a
schedule to get the people out and she was there almost 24/7 making it work,
and Kathy, the other volunteer who was also white, she worked full-time on
the Tot Lot.

It was vacant lots that were on Creighton Street, filled with garbage and
broken down cars and whatever, and we went to the guys who had trucks and
people we knew in the community and we had clean-ups. We got the men to
actually clean up the lots for us, we just took them over. I'm not sure if they
were owned by the city or the developers, but we just took them over. It was
incredible the excitement that was generated around something so simple as
making a playground. Doc Maxwell had a lot of ideas about what we could
do, what kind of things we could make with tires or just pounding planks
together, that sort of stuff. Some of the men were helpful to dig holes to put
in a tank to make a teeter-totter or a tilt-a-whirl. The whole community got
behind that project and people didn't destroy it. That was the thing, no one
destroyed the Tot Lot. There were no broken bottles. You could see empty beer
bottles or broken bottles anywhere along Creighton Street in the alleyways,
but in that Tot Lot every day we carried out an inspection, that was part of the
drill, every day before the kids went on. There were never any broken bottles

or beer bottles in the Tot Lot. No discarded condoms or needles or anything like that. It was really respected by the community.

At the same time we were organizing a Tenants Association. Housing had been identified as an issue, and we thought that we should be on the side of the tenants, because the tenants are exploited by the landlords. At the time the municipal government was re-zoning the core of the city, and they wanted to put public housing along Creighton Street where we see it today, Creighton and Maynard. Developers were moving in. We organized, and went around and distributed leaflets, and we had meetings at the Cornwallis Street Baptist Church, talking to the tenants about the impact this development would have and that they had to be organized. Our idea was that we wanted to make sure the community survived, whereas the idea of the developers was to raze the community, tear down all the houses, build high-rises, move the people out, just like they were doing in Africville. What we didn't take into consideration was that a lot of houses were owned by people in the community; they had a house and some tenants, and they wanted the development because they could sell their house for a better price. So it was in their interest to have development, while we were organizing to stop development.

People were coming out and getting involved, and then every time I would meet an owner of a property, they were upset. For example, Lynn Burrows's landlord, Deacon Cain, wanted to sell. He just owned his one house and he could get a half decent price for it and we were going around saying, "No you can't sell." That was the kind of tension and conflict that was happening in the community and we were stirring up a lot of trouble because the development was going to go ahead no matter what. So the interests of the landlords and the interests of the tenants were not the same. The landlords were not by and large absentee landlords; they were people who lived there all their life. They were other Black people or other white people who were from the community. So here we were creating a situation where we had people who grew up together, lived side by side their whole life, one owned the building, one lived in the building as a tenant, they have different interests and we're in the middle agitating, trying in the first instance to take the side of the tenant. The landlords were saying, "Look it's none of your damn business what we do with our homes. It's our homes, we worked for it all of our life and you have no right to come in here and try to stop us from selling our house." And you can see their point.

We used to agonize, we'd have these meetings and we'd say, "What are we going to do?" In the beginning we could not find a way to show the landowner and the tenant that they had interests that were common. What we started with was the idea that we would save the houses that existed. We wanted public housing erected on vacant lots, and we didn't want these huge public housing complexes. We were able to convince the community that the concept of row housing would benefit everyone. Our position evolved. Instead of fighting the landlords, we fought the developers. We put forward that if development was to happen they should build row housing. It had to be individual units, and people should eventually be able to buy the property from the government and own it themselves. If you had a house and you wanted to sell you could do it, as long as the city was going to replace that house with a unit that was not a high-rise and would still make room for the same tenant. If someone did not want to sell their house, the city could build around it, and that's basically the way this street was developed. The whole concept was accepted by both the landlords and the tenants. As it turned out, because we organized and because we were able to bring about political pressure, the city's original plans were amended. We were able to force a compromise, and now they have a kind of housing that you see on Creighton Street, the low housing as opposed to these huge public housing complexes or even as big as Uniacke Square. But one unforeseen consequence was that the Tot Lot was lost; a low rise went up where the Tot Lot was.

When we were still in Toronto Joan and I had become involved with Alan Borovoy in doing test cases to see whether there were discriminatory practices. You'd send a Black person or couple and a white person to apply for the same job or apartment, with equal qualifications and circumstances. If the whites were accepted after the Blacks had been rejected, we knew discrimination had occurred. We attempted to do the same thing in Halifax, mostly with rental housing. Our Kwacha people participated. And we did uncover some cases, often relating to students from overseas. Another big political item that emerged during the Kwacha days was the anti-Vietnam War movement. The same people who were supporting us were the main drivers behind the anti-war campaigns, both SUPA in Toronto and elsewhere, and our Halifax allies in VOW, SCM, the Quakers and so on. Some of our Kwacha young people went to their training sessions, and we were closely connected with the peace movement at the university. We took a bunch of kids from Halifax to Grindstone Island, sponsored by the Quakers, to develop their anti-war philosophy and techniques. Muriel Duckworth was involved in that. We spoke out very strongly against the war in Vietnam, and we supported a lot of things, fundraising, marches and helping with draft dodgers who came through. There was a huge march in October 1967 through Halifax. I was in the front, arm in arm with Allan O'Brien, who was mayor by that time.

And we organized a Canadian tour for the Freedom Singers. They were a group of American SNCC workers who came together to raise money and to raise consciousness around the civil rights movement, and specifically they raised bail money for jailed activists in the South. But they were involved in everything, raising money for the general SNCC coffers, too. It was a mixed group, white and Black, coming from different parts of the States. They had quite a story to tell, and they were just great musicians and singers and raised a lot of money. They had a concert in Halifax and another in Dartmouth. I went with them on their tour, speaking, not singing. It was mostly a university tour. We went to UPEI, New Brunswick, Québec, Toronto. I continued speaking all the way across Canada right through to Vancouver, to raise money for SNCC. We also raised money ourselves as Club Kwacha, through tag days and other means. Some of the money went to SNCC but it was also used to fund some of our own local projects.

It wasn't all politics, at least ostensibly. We put on a play, called *Here to Stay*. Walter Borden, Jules Oliver, Edith Cromwell and Joan and I were in it, among others. It was about the settlement of Black Refugees in Nova Scotia after the War of 1812, and it may have been the first popularization of African Nova Scotian history. That was an interesting experience. It was the first chance for many of us to be involved in that kind of literary work, but more than that it was the portrayal of Black people in a positive way in the mainstream public venues. We did that play at Neptune Theatre, in the Little Theatre in Greenwood, and we did it in schools; it was a very successful play. We even took it to the Dominion Drama Festival in Ottawa. I remember we had to drive to rehearsals in the winter down to Bridgetown, and Walter and I used to drive together. At the time Walter is writing a lot of very sophisticated poetry; he's doing readings of his work at Kwacha that's so far ahead of where anybody else is at that time. That's quite a cultural thing we had going. We also started a singing group in the Club, called The Ovations. We had a back-up band for the singers, and they played at our dances. I'll tell you it was hot.

We held a regular coffee house in the Club, and sometimes visiting musicians would put on a free concert for the kids. One of them was Gordon Lightfoot, who came to town and gave us a performance at Kwacha. He was a big star at the time. We also held fashion shows, talent shows, all of them thought up and organized by the young people. One of our highlights was a trip to Expo 67 in Montreal during Centennial Year. We took 30 or 35 kids, and they all helped raise the funds for the train trip. We were up there for several days, staying in billets arranged by the mother of one of our Project workers. We had a fantastic time, it was so exciting. Even to this day when I see some of the kids, they talk about that trip to Expo. We had the passports and went around to the different pavilions, and that was a big thing in terms of what we were able to do culturally. They had a chance to meet a lot of the African people in their pavilions and talk to them. It was just amazing.

There were darker moments too, though everything had a bright side in the end, or at least a funny side. The police were always visiting Kwacha, especially when we were having dances in the evening. I would meet them at the door and there'd be almost a confrontation because we took the position that this is our club and you've no business coming in unless there's a complaint. You've got a search warrant, show us, but you've no business coming in. The police officers resented the fact that we had the audacity to tell the police that you can't come into our place, and it set up a lot of tension. I made it absolutely clear I would meet or attempt to meet any threat to my person with an equal amount of force. Whatever they did to me I was doing it back. And that was the philosophy that I was attempting to develop in everybody I came in contact with: don't let anybody push you around, you're nobody's servant. And when we were upstairs on Gottingen Street, the confrontations with the police became more frequent. The police really felt more threatened with the stance the kids were now taking. They knew their rights. We would talk about what your rights are and what the police can do for you and what you have to do, and what information you have to give the police, and the kids were standing up to the police. And the police were determined that they were going to come into Kwacha and lord it over the kids, and they weren't going to take it. So there was a lot more general confrontation going on all the time.

There was one situation where the kids were at a big dance at the Forum. And when they were coming back from the Forum there was some sort of confrontation, and Wayne Smith got arrested. When Wayne got arrested all of the kids said that he didn't start anything, it wasn't his fault, and they were really angry. Wayne's mother came because she was going to blame Wayne for doing something and all the kids said, "Wayne didn't do it, it's not Wayne's fault, whatever happened it's not Wayne's fault." So a near riot breaks out. The kids are going to overturn the police cars, they're rocking the police cars and they are heading down Almon Street back downtown. And at this point, it's getting bigger and bigger and bigger and more volatile, and they're bound and determined that they're burning Halifax down. They just see this is a real injustice.

I'm across town while this is getting underway. Now it's really interesting because at this point I don't know that I'm under surveillance to the extent that I was. I'm at a friend's house, there's a knock at the door, it's the police and they want to talk to me. My friend says, "Huh? How did they know you were here?" Anyhow the cops say, "We've got trouble across town, you've got to come." And they're telling me about it as we're driving in the police car. I said, "Well, wait a minute you can't drive up to the middle of a situation that you're describing with me riding in a police car. You gotta let me out before we get there, I'll walk over." So they let me out at Cunard Street and I walk through the field, and see all these police that are hiding and they've got on their riot gear and I mean there's all kinds of them. And when I get to Gerrish Street there are all of these police and the police are scared because I'd say there might have been 200 kids there, Lord knows how many, and you could see the police are literally shaking. That whole area is filled with kids and they're yelling and screaming and going on and they're picking up stones and that. And so when I arrive there's Buddy Daye trying to tell these kids to be calm, but the kids aren't listening to Buddy. And they're yelling "Black Power!" They've got all this rhetoric on the go. I said, "Well what happened?" Because I didn't even know for sure what their perception was. And they said, "Well they arrested Wayne and it was wrong, and they shouldn't have arrested him and they're always picking on us, and they're always in our area and everything." I said "Well the only thing we can do is let's go down and see the chief of police. Let's go right down to the police station and we'll see what happens here." So they said okay.

So we start down Gottingen Street. Now if you can imagine we've got all of these kids, they're carrying sticks, they're carrying stones, and somebody could've been killed. I could see that because these cops were more afraid than the kids were. So we start walking down Gottingen Street and cops are walking front and back of us and we say, "We're going right to the police station." So we march down to the police station and the kids are yelling and screaming and we want to see the chief of police. It's one o'clock in the morning. They got the chief out of bed. So the chief comes out and he says, "Well, I'll talk to you Rocky, come on, I'll have a talk to you." He comes out on the step and the kids yell and then listen to him, and so he invites me in, and I say, "No, no, you're not doing that to me. We'll talk but you'll talk to me and others." So maybe six or eight of us go in and I tell the other kids, "Now whatever you do, don't be trying to tear this place up when we're talking to the chief." So we go in and talk to the chief and he says, "I've got an awful situation. I can't let Wayne out because I'll be overruling my guy and you know I can't do that," and I say, "But you've got to do something because he shouldn't have been arrested and we're not going to stand by and let anyone be brutalized, we're not going to stand for it." So we're trying to find a compromise and so he goes, "Look, we will keep him in but we will allow you to visit and make sure he's okay." So he puts Wayne in a cell, and then for the entire night three or four people could go into the cell and talk to him and be there for the whole night like a revolving group. So we made the chief back down so that we could see that he was okay, and the chief was able to say that we arrested him and he's still in jail. So it was a win-win thing and we got through the night, but it was a tense one, man. There were never any charges laid.

We had good reason to be concerned about Wayne in the hands of the police. There were all these stories of our guys being harassed and brutalized. It was not unusual for them to pick up white girls who were with Black men and either take them home or take them in for a VD test. It was a continual issue. They had a certain Sergeant Bishop, who was as racist a cop as there ever was. He arrested me once, because I was walking with W.W. Davis's daughter Margie. We were walking up by the Armouries and Sergeant Bishop pulled around in his car, "Get in." He has his partner with him. "What for?" He says, "*Get in the car!*" So we had to get in the car and he was taking us down to the police station because I was walking with a white girl. If you can believe this guy! So I told him, "Listen, you ain't nothing but a racist old pig. You know I've seen cops like you all over the place." And he hits the brakes and he says, "I'll take you down to the station and see how tough you are," and I says, "Well, just you and me go down to the station and we'll see how tough *you* are. You've got a gun pig, give me one, we'll deal with it." He says, "When I get you down to the station we'll see what you're like." Margie Davis is there with us and he doesn't know who she is. We get to the station and she says, "I want to call my father." And they say, "You just mind your business and shut up." And she says, "I need to call my father," and she starts crying. "I heard what you said to him," she says to Sergeant Bishop, "and you're going to beat him up and I'm going to call my dad." Somebody says, "Who's your father?" or something like that, and she says, "My father is Bishop W.W. Davis." Oh yeah, big mistake now. Margie looked young and she was very small. They let us go, no surprise.

Within the context of Halifax at that time we're still at a period when there are no Black fire fighters, no Black police officers, no Black people working in major financial institutions, no Black people in the stores. Black people are strictly hewers of wood and drawers of water at this time in history. We're already into the sixties and the Black community is still excluded from mainstream economic and educational activities. It's hard for people to understand how people in the Black community were treated. We were so far out of everything that was happening, and yet if you were from away, a West Indian or African, it was accepted that you could be a professional. But if you were from here there were no professionals and it wasn't expected that Black people from Nova Scotia would be in positions of power. The police were going into the neighbourhood and ordering people around, telling them they couldn't stand there, that they were loitering, and you could be standing in front of your own house. On Creighton and Maynard Street the houses come right to the street. So in order to be standing anywhere you had to be on the sidewalk. So two cops on the beat would come by, and they'd say you've gotta move, you're loitering, and people were getting incensed about it. We said they've got no right to do this, they're like an occupying force. The role of the police is to protect the community but they're not protecting the community, they're occupying the community and they're using the tactics of an occupying force and we want them out. So in order to have them out we figured we needed a force to protect the community, because drugs were just starting to come in. So we set up our own police force. My we were arrogant! We got Wayne Smith, Papa Lou Black, Woody Toliver, Conrad Black, we got all of the toughest guys in the community and we went to Kwacha House and we bought black turtleneck sweaters and black berets, like the Panthers wore. I had a white turtleneck as leader. We made yellow crests that had the Kwacha emblem on it, of a Black man breaking the chains. It was designed by Bruce Wood, known as Bookie, who was my friend from the Marsh in Truro. The same emblem was on our Kwacha letterhead. The women in Kwacha sewed the badges on to these turtleneck sweaters and it's an image that will be burned in my mind forever. And you can imagine we've got these 19-, 20-year-olds, 21-year-olds. Wayne Smith was massive, well-built, with a tight fitting turtleneck, looking like something else.

So now we're all wearing these sweaters and we don't know what to do, so someone says, "Let's go over to the shopping centre." So we go to Halifax Shopping Centre and the idea is we're going to police the community, we're going to keep the cops out of the community. We go inside the shopping centre and go up the escalator, and there's this white woman there who sees us and starts, "Ahhhh," and runs off, and people are disappearing everywhere. I can just imagine what it must have looked like to them. Here's all these Black guys with their Kwacha sweaters on and we're just strutting. I notice that one of the guys, I won't say which one, has got a something in his pocket. I say, "What the hell is that?" and he's ripped off a ring. I say, "Man we can't steal anything." I says, "No, no, no." We used to say, "Let's just liberate this…" These guys were going to liberate the shopping centre! I says, "We are not liberating anything. We're making a point here, we're showing them we have the power here. So, you know what," I say, "Let's go to the police station and let them know our position." So, I get on the phone and I call the chief of police from the Halifax Shopping Centre and I say, "We're on our way to the police station. We're coming down and we want to meet you, and me and my boys will be there. " And I hung up. And I didn't say can we, will we, or anything, I just said we are coming down to the police station and we want to meet. So there we are driving down to the police station, and we get there and there must be 50 cops waiting. There were cops everywhere. We go in the front door and there's all these cops lined up, they must have pulled all the cops in from everywhere. We've got our crests on and we walk in and man, we are feeling powerful, right into the police station. The chief is there, and we say, "We gotta have a meeting, things aren't going too well." So the chief says, "Come on in."

We're standing tall and we go into the office, and the cops don't know what to do. We're not carrying guns, but it's pretty clear that these are some able-bodied boys ready to do some business. So anyhow we go on in and the chief says, "What's the problem?" and I say, "Listen, the problem is that your officers are aggravating the community, they are moving people along, trying to tell people they're loitering when they're standing in front of their own house. Sergeant Bishop is up there trying to throw his weight around. He has got to go, Sergeant Bishop has got to be pulled out of the community, that's the first thing, and we don't want your police in the area. You've got to pull the police out, and we'll do it ourselves." We talked and talked and he said, "We can reassign the sergeant." And he did it, he agreed.

Word went around that he pulled the police out of the community, and the community went snakey. People said, "What the hell are you guys doing taking the police away?" The community turned on us. People were upset, and here we thought we were doing something good. They said, "Look at who you've got policing us! Just take a look. You've got the wolves watching the hen house." Oh no, the community was not ready for it. So the police were not pulled out, except for Sergeant Bishop. That was the big blaze of glory for the Kwacha boys. One good thing was that during that discussion the chief promised to hire a Black police officer. I truly believe that Chief Mitchell wanted to do good things for the community. He was basically a good person, but he had problems with traditions in the police department. He had to deal with the older racist guys teaching the young guys. I do believe that Chief Mitchell was a good person, but he only had so much power.

That was all about the Halifax city police, of course, but then we had the Mounties. They also had me under surveillance at this time, and they had an informant embedded in Kwacha. I got their reports under the Access to Information policy. We in Canada have placed the RCMP in the same position as we have placed gods; they are infallible, they are the greatest thing since sliced bread. In fact the RCMP were racist, the way that they categorized Black people at that time in their files. "Subversive activity amongst Negroes in Nova Scotia," that is the heading of the file. So they are looking for subversive activity and when they don't find it they are creating the subversive activity themselves. They write about me being in the Prizefighters Club smoking drugs. It was absolutely untrue, because I took such a hard line against drugs, not because of any morality, but as a tactic. I couldn't take the chance and never did. But they wrote it up in their book. They also wrote that I was teaching "free sex" to 8-year-old kids in Kwacha, and teaching them how to make Molotov cocktails. Utterly ridiculous, and it was pure lies. It was not just a mistake. They wanted to vilify me. The only eight year olds we came in contact with would be the ones at the Tot Lot, and as such they were extremely well supervised and protected. There is no possible way they could arrive at that interpretation by mistake. The Mounties exercised a very racist position when it came to Black people in general and me in particular. And their racism is coming back to haunt them with all the cases against the RCMP. They have not always been the good guys in red serge as we have been led to believe.

It's interesting how naïve we were. We would say, listen to the phone, the phone is tapped, or whatever, but we really didn't know the extent of the surveillance, except on certain occasions when it was absolutely obvious. For instance, there was one occasion when Rosie Douglas and I were doing a speaking tour at the universities, and there was another informant that we didn't know about who was travelling with us. I'm not going to identify him now. We were doing one university a day with speeches, entertainment, a social at night to raise money, and then the next day we were heading somewhere else. I think the money was intended for the Huey Newton defence. We had speeches in Halifax and then we went to Acadia, and to Mount Allison, and to the University of Prince Edward Island, and all of this time the same Mounties followed us the whole way. We were taking the ferry to PEI, and we wanted to have a game of whist. So these two RCMP guys were just sitting a couple of tables away and obviously trying to listen to our conversation, and we needed a fourth. So I went over to their table, and I say, "Fellas, we need a fourth, and you've got to watch what we're doing, or listen to what we're saying, or whatever it is you've got to do, so why don't you just join us? We're not going to talk any business, but we need a fourth, and if you can play bridge or whist please join us." So one of them did, came over and sat down, and joined us, and we pretended that he wasn't RCMP and he pretended that we weren't under surveillance. We made the trip across, talked small talk and whatever, and it was very pleasant.

Several years later, I believe it would have been in 1974, I had a secretary in the Transition Year Program at Dalhousie, Sandra MacKenzie. She had applied for a job in the foreign service, a sensitive job, and they were doing a check on her. I'm in my office at Dal and this RCMP guy comes and he wants to ask me some questions for a background check on Sandra. I said okay, and as I'm doing this, I'm looking at the guy and he seems so familiar, and finally it dawns on me that he is the same guy, this shadow when Rosie and I were going on this tour. So I mentioned to him, "Listen I've met you before," and he says, "Yeah." "You're the guy that was on the ferry with us when we were going to PEI, you were our shadow, you were assigned to do surveillance on us." And he says, "Yeah, yup, well, you know," and I says, "Now, how could you possibly see us in that light a few years ago, and I'm the same guy, I haven't changed, and now today you're asking me if Sandra MacKenzie would be a good candidate to be allowed to travel all over the world on behalf of the government. That's a contradiction. What's wrong with this picture?" He laughed and he said, "I'm just doing my job. They told me to come out here and do this. This is what I'm doing." I found this absolutely amazing, and rather disconcerting, because I didn't know if I'd become so conservative that the government would be asking me who would be safe to go overseas, or was the government just so out of touch with reality that the left hand didn't know what the right hand was doing.

In those same confidential papers that I got through Freedom of Information, I found a report that was surprising as to how far the surveillance went. I was speaking at the University of Lethbridge and to travel there I had to change planes twice, once in Winnipeg and once in Calgary, and from Calgary I went to Lethbridge. When I was in Winnipeg I had a layover for a couple of hours. It was late at night and there was nothing in the airport, so I just hung around. In the RCMP surveillance report it was interesting to read the extent of the detail. They wrote that I moved around and that I stopped to talk to this particular person, and the writer said he didn't think that there was anything sinister in the conversation but that maybe I was just passing time with somebody I'd met in the airport. That's how indepth the surveillance was. When we were in Lethbridge they knew where I was staying, where I was speaking, who was there, what time I was leaving, so incredibly detailed and complete. I think the RCMP truly believed that there was the possibility of armed insurrection in Canada, and that threat was coming from the Black community. And as I was learning, there were others, right in my own community, who perceived me as a threat.

Chapter Five

FROM REBEL TO REVOLUTIONARY

While we were still in Toronto and preparing to come to Nova Scotia, I started to keep a scrapbook of newspaper stories about our Project. The very first clipping in my scrapbook has an interview with W.P. Oliver. He had heard, through the press, about our intentions, and he described us as "outside agitators." "We don't need them," he said, and "the community doesn't want them." This appears just as we are on our way, and it sets it up so that people think we're going to be violent and get them killed. People have in the back of their minds this idea that we are going to come into their communities and we're going to agitate, and the end result will be violence towards them. We have to overcome this, which is very, very difficult. There were so many reports in the newspaper about riots in the States and places burning. We came to Halifax talking some of the same kind of rhetoric, wearing the same kind of clothes, as radicals in the States. The notion was that I was preaching hatred against whites, and there would be a backlash against the Black community. People were afraid for their children. They didn't know what was going to happen.

The traditional leadership in the Black community at that time had a "blame the victim" mentality, and that's how they perceived the community. Gus Wedderburn is quoted in the *Toronto Star* saying, "Nova Scotia Negroes are apathetic; they have lost their fight." They are in fact saying that the masses of the people are docile and need to be led and the solutions need to be found for them. It is the attitude that the solution must be imposed from the outside. It is like the Black people have created the problem for themselves, that we are

92

in this situation because we want to be, and it is our own fault, and we don't have any aspiration to change anything. We live in the slums and substandard housing because we want to live that way.

At that time they were focusing on Africville, and they were going to clear it out because the people there needed help and couldn't handle their own problems. To me that reflected the reality of how we were viewed all over. No wonder Robin Winks, a historian in the States, could describe our history as "a depressing story." He sees a community that is being victimized but powerless, and basically the masters of their own misfortune. To me it underscores the fact that we were correct in our analysis that people had to take control and run their own ship and do what they had to do. As I reflect now, more and more I can see how correct we were. Our position was, right from the beginning, and always would be, that the solution has to come from within the community, and the community have got to define the problem, define the solutions and implement the solutions themselves.

The interesting thing is that there was not one position in the Black community that was elected. And that situation continues today to a great extent, and it's a crying shame. The government decides which institutions to fund and which ones to listen to. That is why we have no opposition to government policies. I'm talking, of course, about our "official" leadership, the ones the white community and the government listen to. But there is also an internal leadership, the ones the community listens to. At that meeting in East Preston, Carl Evans was the man who stood up and convinced the others to let us speak. Carl was not a man of letters, by any stretch of the imagination, but he had absolute respect when it came to the things he talked about that would benefit the community. When I look back I recognize that contrary to what it may seem like, in the Black community leadership is not selected based on formal education, or necessarily on the job you happen to hold. Every community has people like this. Buddy Daye had no formal education. He was a merchant seaman, and he worked in a laundry after that, but when he spoke at a meeting people listened. They may not be the ministers and they may not even be the deacons, but they wield incredible influence. That is one of the things we learned in our Project. We learned who to go to to get things done. For instance Ma Carvery, who was the matriarch of the Carvery clan, wielded immense influence. If I needed something done and wanted to ensure that word got out, I'd go over and have a discussion with Ma Carvery about what I could do or should do. If she gave her blessing, you can be guaranteed that a whole large sector of the Africville/Halifax community would go along with it.

We were coming with a philosophy of participatory democracy, of self-determination. We had to connect with the internal leadership, and we had to confront the establishment. This included some of the major Black institutions, and it certainly included the government. The prevailing attitude among that "official" leadership was that you have to cooperate with government; government will be your friend and solve your problems. There was a committee known as the Halifax Advisory Committee on Human Rights. They were trying to help the people of Africville during its destruction, and they were pushing for better human rights protections generally. Jim Kinzell and I were invited to one of their meetings in October 1965, soon after we arrived in Halifax. Fran and Don McLean were prominent in this organization, and I suppose our invitation came through them. Gus Wedderburn was there, W.P. Oliver was there. We announced our plans for the Project, which of course included confrontation, which these people rejected. If you want the government to cooperate, you can't go confronting it. You send petitions and you have meetings and you persuade the government. This was not going to be our modus vivendi. As a result our relationship became frayed with this committee, with the NSAACP (Nova Scotia Association for the Advancement of Colored People), with all or almost all of the traditional spokespeople of the Black community. Despite all this I had good personal relationships with all these people. The McLeans were on our board. W.P. was a political opponent, for sure, but we never had a bad relationship. I always had respect for him; I grew up with that. He was after all W.P. Oliver, and I was as much of an upstart as I could possibly be. We had our disagreements, but as two people we could sit and talk.

Charles Coleman happened to be an influential person in the community, and he was also the minister in arguably the most important Black church anywhere in Nova Scotia. But he was too progressive for the Cornwallis Street Baptist Church. He was ahead of his time, as far as they were concerned. He supported all the things we were doing, he was really into community participation and confrontation if necessary. But he had to deal with his deacon board, and they were very conservative. He was from Raleigh, North Carolina, with dark skin and penetrating eyes. He moved quite slowly, never seemed to be hurrying. He was very engaging and had a charismatic style, really attractive to young people. His sermons included comments on social issues, sometimes the very issues we were dealing with in the Project. He even supported our Tenants Association. And he became involved in one big issue that eventually cost him his job, or so everybody believed at the time. The white merchants on Gottingen Street allegedly had an agreement among themselves not to hire Black people. We were talking at Kwacha about organizing boycotts and sit-ins, to force the merchants to hire some of us. We were going to the merchants and warning them that they would have to change their policies. Reverend Coleman spoke up in our favour, endorsing the kind of tactics that were, in fact, being put into practice in his home state. Now apparently the merchants had an understanding with the church, or some of its leadership, that they would make financial contributions to the church in exchange for no inter-ference in their affairs, including who they hired or didn't hire. I was not a member of the church and have no firsthand knowledge, but the word was that Charles Coleman became too dangerous for the church hierarchy. He spoke out against the merchants and they cut their donations. He was costing the church money, and so they forced him out. I was very sorry to see him go. But that episode does show the kind of attitudes we were up against in certain segments of the community.

It's fair to say that the church as an institution, or its leadership at any rate, did not approve of the Nova Scotia Project. The community was very religious in general, and that promoted conservatism. But it also promoted cohesiveness. People felt comfortable with each other, they could act together. So conservatism was both an advantage and a disadvantage for our kind of activity. The thing about Nova Scotia is that people are so steeped in the his-tory of families. Family matters a great deal, and I had the great advantage of being Elmer Jones's son and Jerry Jones's grandson and Sam Jones's great grandson. I had this to fall back on wherever I went, and doors were opened for me because even white people had heard of my grandfather the war hero. If your family is respected, you will be treated in a certain way. I learned very quickly when I was organizing that I had to play on this conservatism and play on my own family ties. They would never have understood this back in Toronto. Our training didn't include this type of thing. They would never understand that Lynn Burrows boarded at Deacon Cain's house, and this gave her a certain respectability she would not have had on her own, being white and female and coming from away. It also meant that she had to go to church on Sunday, she had to be home at a certain hour or have a good reason for staying out, she had to behave in certain ways. They would never understand outside of Nova Scotia how tight the community really was, and how firmly it held to its values. I didn't have to go to church but I could not smoke dope, even though it was very common among young people in the sixties. If I was going to be an organizer in the community I had to be able to say "I don't do drugs. I don't smoke dope." People would know if I was lying, because we were always being observed by somebody or other. I just could not do it or it would have destroyed my ability to organize in the community.

I had no such leverage with the government. They didn't care who my grandfather was, I was just an interfering radical. The government is saying, "We've got to do something about these militants who are getting their toe-hold into everything in Halifax." We were involved with the tenants about housing, we were involved with education, we were involved with recreation, we were involved with the police, we were extending our sphere of influence within the community, and it's all based upon a very revolutionary philosophy: "Let the people decide. Let the people control." These things we're talking about are very threatening, at all levels of government. But they can't just come in and arrest us. To undercut our influence, in order to destroy us, the government set up organizations or funded certain people in opposition to what we were doing at Kwacha. They did it by funding groups and placing *agents provocateurs* in our own group. They did everything they could to destroy us. They set up the Neighbourhood Centre because we were gaining influence within the community. They funded it so that there could be workers provided by the government to do the kinds of things that we were saying needed to be done, and they could do them with paid government workers who wouldn't be confrontational and they wouldn't be revolutionary. It's interesting to me that the establishment was accepting the notion that the Black community was docile and incapable of doing anything on their own, yet they were afraid of the things we were saying and doing. That means they understood that there was the real potential in the community to reject the self-defeating stance that was taken by certain people among the Black leadership and to reject the "depressing" version of our history.

At first I didn't understand that the Neighbourhood Centre was in direct opposition to Kwacha House, so I cooperated with them. I attended meetings when they were trying to develop programming in the community. We had a real debate about whether or not we could have programming in isolation from politics. I was arguing that you needed to have a political component, but the government was not prepared to allow that kind of activity. That Neighbourhood Centre had to be an organization to deliver recreation and to deliver welfare and that's what its role was, argument finished. So I stopped being involved in the Neighbourhood Centre. Conflict developed between ourselves and the Neighbourhood Centre because we were seen as being much too militant and dangerous. I don't think the government's strategy worked, because the young people were never attracted to the Neighbourhood Centre, so their constituency became an older group. They began to work with people in the community who were on welfare, or maybe the working poor, and that became their constituency. They gave up trying to work with the youth and that meant that we weren't in direct competition and we didn't debate the issues directly. The issues for the young people were different for the welfare people or the working poor who were in Uniacke Square.

Early on, Buddy Daye was hired to work with the youth, and he did come up with some recreational programs for the Neighbourhood Centre. Buddy Daye was a person I had a lot of love for, and him for me. I remember the day I met Buddy. I just came down from Toronto, where I was boxing, working out in the gym all the time. I went to the gym on Creighton Street, just thinking that I would work out. This guy was in there jabbing and shadowboxing and everything. I thought I could give him some good advice. I said, "Well maybe, gee whiz, why don't you try turning your hand like this, you know?" I did not know at the time, of course, that I was giving advice to the lightweight champion! I had no idea. Buddy got a chuckle out of that. At any rate, we kind of clicked, though we were different politically. Buddy was certainly well left of centre, but not as far left as I was. I was working quite closely with Buddy on a lot of things, and boy we could get into some wicked arguments. W.P. Oliver was very much a scholar, who would argue things based on his massaging of statistics. Buddy was more arguing from a position of emotion and what the people would feel. He had a real handle on grassroots responses to different issues. One of the things that you could value about him politically is that he had an uncanny sense of where people were at. From my perspective, however, his analysis at times was not dead on.

I was part of the group who were working hard to get Buddy involved politically, and to get him to run for the NDP. I was a committed NDPer. Buddy wasn't committed, but we convinced them that he should run for election as an NDP candidate. And we got him to run in the 1967 provincial election. We used our young people to do a lot of the legwork for Buddy's campaign, putting up signs, delivering flyers and that sort of thing. We tried to develop a lot of excitement around the fact that Buddy Daye was a Black man. He was not a university-educated man, he was a working man with a family. So we represented him as a lunch pail candidate and a lunch pail party, real grassroots. We were very prominent on the campaign. Of course there were the traditional NDP intellectuals doing things, but we were dealing with the community for Buddy. At any rate, there was this issue that came up the day before the election. A guy comes to me, a reporter, and says "Did you hear what happened down in the Valley? Well there is this senator down there, Finlay MacDonald, who was saying you gotta bribe the niggers." He is saying, "You gotta bribe the niggers, but don't bribe them too soon because they won't stay bribed too long." The Tories' guy is saying this. Now Gerald Regan was the leader of the Liberals in this election. So I went to Regan and said, "Look, it looks like we're going to lose our deposit and we've got a lot of expenses that we can't handle. So if you will make a donation to Buddy's campaign, we will put this story on the Gestetner, and we will put it into every door in the community and let the people know what's going on with the Tories." Well, the money came to the campaign, a substantial amount. I know it's not big money like people talk about today, but it was enough money that would make a difference to the expenses that we had. The Gestetner we used was not the campaign Gestetner. It was all done outside of the office, and Buddy never knew about it. The story was printed and all of the young people that we had at our disposal went around to every door and put this story out of what the Tories were saying about Black people. Now, the vote shifted from the Tories, not to Buddy but to the Liberals, and it elected Gerald Regan as premier. We continued to work in the Needham constituency, to build it up for the next election in 1970.

So then the nomination meetings are happening for the next election. Someone told me that Buddy had nominated Regan at the Liberal meeting. I said that was absolutely impossible, because not only were Buddy and I involved politically and doing things for the NDP, we were also close friends. I just didn't believe it. Sure enough, it had happened. After that nomination Buddy was appointed the Sergeant at Arms for the provincial legislature. It strained our relationship for quite a while, this incident, because I felt quite betrayed by it. Even though we had political disagreements, and we weren't always on the same page, we did have the kind of relationship where we con- fided in each other.

Maybe the relationship between me and Buddy was a mirror of my rela- tionship with the general community. Buddy more than anyone represented where the grassroots people were. My conflicts with Buddy were always of an ideological nature. We had conflicts over whether or not we should take government funding. That was a big issue. Buddy believed we should and I believed we shouldn't. I believed that the government would control anything they funded. Buddy didn't think so or didn't care if that happened. I think that was a sentiment expressed by many people in the Black community. He

reflected what a lot of people believed and thought. So what if we get government money? We need money to do these programs so let's take it. We had
an ideological difference in terms of the role of police in the community. I
believed the police were an occupying force and were using their power in
the community to control the community. Buddy took the position that the
police were there to protect the community. Again, I believe his position was
reflective of where many people in the community were. We had many conflicts like that. By the same token, there's so many nights that I spent with
Buddy, where we laughed for an entire night. We would spend so many hours
just having fun and enjoying each other. And then we would argue. I would
argue with Buddy more than I would argue with anyone.

There were only so many of us that were politically active in the sixties.
Buddy was one of those who fought to get the barbers to cut Black people's
hair. He was involved in helping to create the Tenants Association. He was
more a voice of the people than anyone can imagine. Since his death, that
position has not been replaced. No one has that connection to the grassroots
of the community and the inside track with the politicians and the downtown
power-brokers. When he was Sergeant at Arms he saw the premier every day,
and he could say to the premier, "There's someone I want you to talk to or
listen to," or he could talk to cabinet ministers. He was in a position to get
certain favours done. No one else can do that now. Buddy's access crossed
party lines. When Buddy was downstairs in his office, there was always a bottle
of rum. When you went to Province House, he would say, "Okay come on
down and let's have a drink." So you can go into Buddy's office for a drink of
rum and there could be a Tory member and a Liberal cabinet minister both
in that office with Buddy to have a little drink of rum. It didn't matter. Many
a time I would just go down and stop in to see Buddy and I ended up sitting
there with someone I didn't expect to sit with. It's important to recognize that
he used his position to facilitate people, to facilitate the community, to make
things happen.

Anyway Kwacha survived its rivalry with the Neighbourhood Centre. At
one point the Company of Young Canadians was assigning volunteers to
Halifax. The Neighbourhood Centre asked for five and got only one, while we
got the four we asked for. The provincial Department of Social Services was
quite annoyed about that. Getting CYC salaries was a boost for our finances.
We were still receiving money from SUPA, as much as they could send, but they
had other projects besides ours. Most of our funding came from the Friends of
the Nova Scotia Project, and then I worked, where and when I could.

We had no direct connections with the other SUPA projects, mostly just through Toronto. There was the SUPA Newsletter, published centrally, with stories from all the various activities, and we had our own newsletter in Halifax. But apart from that our connection was pretty loose, and getting looser. Moving from Toronto to Nova Scotia was more distance than the 1400 miles. People had totally different lives. There were many people we were dealing with who had never travelled out of their town, let alone travelled out of their province. So it is very colloquial in Nova Scotia and different things mean different things. In Toronto when we were training and looking at community organizing, the people were very intellectual. The Toronto SUPA people were university types, they had education and they had book learning and they had theories. They had certain theories that were connected to ideas of peace, of the global economics, of the global politics, and when we were in Toronto, we also had those ideas. But it was very difficult to try to translate the idea of a global struggle into neighbourhoods where the immediate concern was dealing with wharf rats or with feeding your children. Even the connection between African peoples and the Diaspora, and saying we are all African people and we are connected, didn't go very far. In Nova Scotia people, including Black people, are making fun of African people and they are calling West Indians "jigger foot." There was absolutely no understanding, at that time, of the political connection between the oppression that was occurring in Africa, Latin America or the Third World generally, and the oppression that was occurring in downtown Halifax.

We were trying to organize people at a very basic level, to set up a playground for kids so they wouldn't get cut, to organize tenants so that they would be able to maintain their housing, to organize sewing groups and tutorial programs. It was all very practical. And we hoped that by doing these practical things, we would be able to engage people in discussions about the genesis of it, how it all connects. The people just weren't buying it, the people were really concerned with what was happening to them on a day to day basis. In Nova Scotia there is a history of people going to war, of people being connected to the British Empire. Sometimes I say Canadians, and particularly Black Canadians in Nova Scotia, are more British than the British when it comes to their loyalties for king and empire. The services has been a way for African-descended people to get out of the situation they were in. They were trying hard to get into the army. And we come along and say, "Wait a minute, wars are bad, you know, these people shouldn't be going to Vietnam." They didn't understand why we would be saying don't fight for your country and don't go to war. We were an absolute contradiction to what people were under-standing at that very basic level.

There was a disconnect between the intellectual or philosophical stance we were taking and the organizing and talking we were doing. It was very difficult. I think in hindsight, maybe we began to become closer for a while to adopt-ing the reasoning and position of the community, and as we became more involved and ingrained into that kind of thinking, the thinking in Toronto became more and more distant. We also began to think that they don't under-stand us and we are growing further away. But I do think that in the simplicity of the movement, as it was then developing in Nova Scotia, there was an awakening for me, even more than I had realized before. The oppression was so stark. We had things like fighting in the schools, campaigning for burial grounds, facing discrimination in accommodation and in employment, and all of that stuff that was still very much alive. So we had these people here oppressed because of race and it made it even more clear that racial oppression was very much part of the international oppression of Black people. On the one hand, I become estranged and cut off from the Toronto peacenik-left-wing philosophy that is growing out of the peace and community-organizing move-ments from central Canada, and I begin to move more towards the nationalist philosophy, because it only made sense. I could see with my own two eyes and by the experience I was living and the experience of the people who lived in the community, that they were being oppressed because of race, and there was a common oppression because of race, and the common solution also had to be racial.

My evolution away from SUPA was part of a shift in my consciousness about race relations and social justice, about power and democracy. It was a sort of conceptual revolution. Maybe this transition happened to me first, but soon it was happening to others in our Project and in the community more generally. When we started we were very much committed to concepts of racial equality based on integration. Brotherhood, love and understanding would solve the problems. We did have an analysis of capitalism as being the underlying issue, but few people in the community shared that analysis; they just knew they were poor and that others were taking advantage of them. Integration made sense, because Halifax was an integrated city, with inter-racial marriages and mixing occurring in many areas. As the Project developed we became more influenced by world events and particularly the events that were happening in the United States. As we examined Black history we found things that gave rise to a belief that we could accomplish things ourselves. Long before I was ever born our people recognized the need for African people to be organized as a body with the formation of Black churches and of the African United Baptist Association. There were other organizations in the nineteenth century like the Anglo-African Mutual Benefit Association that reflected the knowledge that Black people needed to have their own institutions, and they survived and they helped the community survive. It meant that we had to become aware of our own history and interpret that history in a positive light, and we had to look to the future and say we have the possibility of controlling events in our community. And that's a big leap, because first and foremost in the context of Nova Scotia, we had never been taught our history, and there was no place for us to go where we could draw the connection between our existence in Nova Scotia and our birth in Africa.

There was no place in Nova Scotia where we could see the power of the Black community being exercised economically, so that wherever we looked we saw Black people who were poor. We were poor farmers, we were poor persons who had wood lots, we were poor people in the city. There was no economic base that showed us anywhere in this province that we could put together money and survive as a people. It just did not exist. And sadly there was no history that we were aware of where we consciously resisted any attempt to enslave us or put us in situations where we were powerless. The active outward rebellions that you hear of in the States, we weren't taught about those in Nova Scotia. So what we had was an articulated superficial history of a people who were dependent upon white people for their survival, notwithstanding that we did create the African Baptist Association and that we did have independent communities that survived. This was not taught to us in the context that it was positive or powerful or that we had the ability to survive on our own. So when we launch this Project we're buying into the old rhetoric that if we integrate it will work; it doesn't matter where the leadership comes from, we can have white people who really believe in our struggle and they can be part of the leadership and that will all help. Well, what we learn from the States in particular, and from the African independence movements, is that Black people should be in control of their own affairs. We begin to question the leadership role of whites within the civil rights movement, specifically.

In my travels, and from the visitors we had coming into Kwacha, a bigger picture is beginning to form. We are beginning now to have different kinds of discussion than we were ever able to have before. The concept of Black Power begins to take shape and it can set down roots right in Nova Scotia. We can say it's okay for us as Black people to have power, not just political but social power and economic power. We don't have enough money to have true economic power and we don't have enough bodies to have true political power, but we can begin to assert ourselves within our own community and say that leadership must come from Black people. It's at this point that we begin to reject the notion that Black people are a minority; in fact we're part of an international group of people of colour who are the majority of people in the world. We need to be connected internationally so that what you're talking about is a global revolution and we need to be part of it. This shift in consciousness and philosophy occurs over a very short period, probably not much more than two years. We go from a completely integrationist philosophy to a cultural nationalist philosophy. We're talking Black Power. You can see hints of this in the film *Encounter at Kwacha House*. The kids are just about to tip into Black consciousness at that very time.

When you figure in race, when race is the paramount reason why people are oppressed, the capitalist analysis doesn't work. The original rhetoric was that capitalists were oppressing everyone equally, so the answer was "workers of the world unite." What we found out was that the workers that we talked about being brothers and having this common bond, those workers were racist. It was the workers on the docks in Halifax who had a vested interest in keeping Black people out of the unions and off of the docks. There were no Blacks at all in the dockworkers' union at that time. So when you talked about workers uniting, here was this dilemma: you are talking about oppression of workers, and the workers are oppressing Black people. So then you had to take your analysis further. Maybe the multinationals, the people who run the ships and the shipyards, are oppressing all of us. But when you get down to the oppression at the local level, it is the local union boss, the local union member, who is also participating in the oppression of Black people. They have taken the oppression and made it racial. In order to fight this I cannot rely on someone who is oppressing me to fight my battle for me. I can have an alliance at a given time if we both have some power and there is a reason for a particular coalition or alliance, but generally speaking I can only rely on myself and others like me. I have to move away from the whole idea of oppression being general and move into letting the people understand that our oppression is race.

In Kwacha and in my public speeches I tried to teach in terms of: "Listen, you've got to understand that you are being oppressed because of your race and you have got to stick together as members of that race or you will never overcome that oppression." That is not the same as saying you have to hate other people. I never ever believed and never spoke of a hatred against a race of people. Even though the oppression was race-based the solution could not be hate-based. Our solution had to be internal, looking inward, finding strength and love amongst ourselves to overcome the oppression.

The Black nationalist philosophy frightened Black people when we were first arguing for it. They are saying, "You are going to get us killed." The reason they were afraid is not because they rejected the concept, because they had lived the concept forever of having separate institutions. What they were afraid of was the backlash because they had seen what was happening in the States and they were afraid of the violence, and they were not a violent people. My task was to show our people that they already had a Black nationalist philosophy, they just didn't call it that. What kept our community together over the generations, over the centuries, was that Black people could and did organize themselves on their own, and they ran viable institutions on their own. At the same time there's a shift in terminology, and this was not a coincidence. When we first started using the term "Black" it made many Black people nervous. They associated it with violent Black radicals in the States. It didn't help that we were wearing dashikis and had beards and Afro hair styles either. But it became a new way of identifying ourselves. "We're Black and we're proud." All the kids were saying it eventually. If you're "Coloured," what colour? If you're "Negro," you associate your identity with slavery, for that's where this term originated. But "Black" makes the connection with other Black people, in Africa, in the Diaspora. It gives you a sense of belonging to a mass of other Black people, it suggests "power" and, of course, we used the term "Black Power" too. Those of us in the Project were acting as a catalyst. We are trying to redefine the terminology, redefine concepts, redefine who we in fact are as a people; we're trying to redefine who controls our institutions.

It could be difficult because often the people who best understood this new interpretation were white! The white people in our Project, and other whites associated with us or listening to us, were themselves being educated along with the Black kids. But it created a dilemma within the Project as well. There was a lot of internal dissent and problems during the last period that Kwacha was going. In rejecting white leadership, we were actually challenging the whites who were coming around, we were challenging their own racism, and we were taking the position that we don't want you to come and organize in the Black community and we don't want you to come and organize us. We want you to go back into the white community and organize the whites in such a way that they would be more conducive to allowing more Black people to move in and move up. I think that helped to speed up the demise of Kwacha. We had a built-in contradiction, because the Black leaders could not back away from the ideas of Black consciousness, the necessity for Black leadership and Black control. By controlling the Project I mean that we had to fund it and run it. Taking the position that white leadership was inappropriate left no room for Lynn Burrows or Jim Kinzell or the others who had been with us right from the beginning. Some of them already were or became CYC volunteers, and they moved on to other projects. The resolution of that contradiction was the demise of Kwacha House as an entity in January 1968.

In the Black community itself the pressures and the tensions were even getting greater. Our rhetoric and the things we were talking about were changing. By 1968, when Kwacha closes, we had adopted the position that we would use "whatever means necessary" to change our situation or defend our community. We were not in charge of what the means were. The necessary means were in direct proportion to the oppression that we faced. This also suggested that Black people should be armed and know how to bear arms and be prepared to use arms to protect the community. That was really frightening, to everybody except those of us who had moved to that position. But it was, I think, a widely accepted position, and there were many, many Black people around the province who were beginning to understand that they had a duty to protect their home, their family, their kids, their community. And I don't just mean young people. Older people too were beginning to say, "If these people bother me, they have a problem." I think if there had been any widespread violence perpetrated against Black people, violence would have been met with violence. For myself, I never believed that violence was the only way; I never gave up on white people. I had an unshakable belief that we could change society, and it wasn't about reform, it was about restructuring society. I was prepared to sacrifice anything to bring about that change. If I had to go poor, if I had to go without food or sleep, I was prepared to do it. I kept telling people that, and I think even when people didn't agree with me they had to respect the fact that I was sincere. I think what pulled me through was the belief that we could change things. But there was no reason why Black people in particular had to be oppressed and poor. The fight against oppression to me was something that just had to be waged. Somehow I had to explain this to people. I didn't have the answers but I knew the oppression was wrong, and you had to keep trying to find ways to overcome it.

Meanwhile I'm being thrust into a position of national prominence simply because, and I sincerely believe this, I think Canada needed its own Stokely Carmichael. At that demonstration at the American Consulate, in March of

'65, I literally get introduced to a lot of these ideas and to the movement, just by being in a particular spot. But the press from that moment on give me the kind of prominence that was way above my experience. I had to respond as if I had experience, as if I knew something, even though I didn't have an academic background. I had read a number of books but I certainly didn't have any formalized study. The press had a real love affair with the image that they themselves were creating. No matter where I went or whatever I said, it was picked up, it was reported. I was speaking at rallies all across the country, interviewed in the national press, national TV, radio, everything. I did have a very high profile.

And that profile brought out the crazies all over the country to take pot-shots at me. It was ordinary for me to get hate mail, to get hate telephone calls. There was an incident, a fight I was involved in at the Prizefighters Club. I'm not particularly proud of it, but it happened and it shows what was happening to me at the time. At that point I was not as strong as I would normally be; I was starting to get burned out. Earlier that same day I knew I had reached the wall and I called Jack Seeley in Toronto. What was happening to me was what he had talked about, what we would go through, the emotions and the frustrations. I tried his office, his house, I tried everywhere, because I thought he would understand and give me support. But it was impossible and I didn't reach him. That same night I'm going into a bar to shoot a guy. As I look back on it, I had been at the forefront of not only a local movement but of a national movement. At the national level I was expected to respond to almost everything that was happening in the Black community nationally. At the same time I was responding to everything that was happening locally. And we had no money, we were just surviving. I don't know how we survived while I played revolutionary. Joan just kept things going. Someone would send a plane ticket and I'd be off someplace, and people continually coming through. When I walked into the Prizefighters Club that night I had a shotgun in my hand. And everybody saw me walk in with it.

The guy I had the beef with was a tough cookie. I won't name him here. He had been threatening me, and everybody in the neighbourhood knew he was after me. I can't say whether I intended to shoot him, or to intimidate him, or to prove to the rest of them that I was not afraid, to uphold my own reputation as a tough guy. Suffice it to say that I was standing five feet in front of this guy with a loaded shotgun, and I wasn't thinking straight. He looks at me and he comes off of that chair like a coiled spring, like a tiger. He just explodes. He grabs the gun, the gun goes off to the side and two of the guys get shot in the legs. The pellets went through the bar. When that happens the bar empties, everybody is out. This guy and I, we sort of fight for the gun and he ends up with barrel and I end up with the stock, and he hits me across the face with the steel barrel. And I know I'm not going out, I'm not going to pass out or anything because I know if I do I'm dead. The gun ends up with me, I have a hold of him and he's looking at me and we both instinctively knew that for that moment the battle was over, the fight was over. No words said. I leave the bar and somehow the gun disappears. The cops eventually come, they find nothing. They get the word that I was involved and they come to arrest me at my house. I had gone home. I said to Joan, "Look, we've got a problem."

But she was pretty cool with it. The police come, and I put my hands in front of me. "I know you have to arrest me, I'm ready to go down." The guy says, "No, you have to put your hands behind your back." I put my hands behind my back and they handcuffed me, and as soon as they had the hand-cuffs on me that cop just drives me up against the wall. Well, I came off facing them and I said, "Listen pig, if you ever do that to me again or if you ever in any way whatsoever manhandle me, you will not see the light of day for many, many days, if ever again, just remember that." And I was serious. "I'm sorry," he says. They take me down to the station, and down there the cops are quite nice, asking me what happened. Now contrary to what I later always told my clients, I told them everything. I went in there with a loaded shotgun intend-ing to shoot somebody, and it went off by accident. At that time they told me that two people got shot. They didn't tell me how badly and I thought I had hurt or killed two innocent people. I'm feeling terrible. They take a statement. Doc Maxwell comes to see me, he checks my eyes, and John Baigent comes down, and he says, "We are going to spring you." John was a law student, and he talked to Andy MacKay who was the Dean of Law, and they get me out. And they arrange for Leonard Pace to be my lawyer. He would later become attorney general, and was the best criminal lawyer in Nova Scotia.

At first I was facing one or two charges, but later I was facing a whole bunch of charges, something like 21 years' worth. Leonard Pace made a deal, or we thought we had a deal. I would plead guilty for a two-year sentence. Doc Maxwell promised he would look after my family and my responsibilities while I was in jail. So I went there that day to trial thinking I was pleading guilty, do two years, in fact I wouldn't have to do the whole two years, and then be out. But they put all these additional charges on me. So Leonard Pace says to me, "We had a deal. They are trying to burn you; I can't guarantee you anything like we have agreed to." And he got up in court and says, "Listen we had a deal here and this isn't the deal, and I want an adjournment." And the judge says, "Yeah, you can have ten minutes Mr. Pace." I'm thinking, "I'm going down big time." He came out and told me, "Look, I can't hold this deal, we can plead guilty and I can make the argument, but I don't know." I said, "Let's plead not guilty and go for it. If I do seven years I do seven years, but I'm not rolling over and having the Crown send me upriver without a fight."

We go to trial. The Crown calls Keith Paris and Lenny Sparks, the ones who got shot by the stray pellets. They ask Lenny first. "What happened?" "I don't know." "What do you mean?" "I was drunk." "Well you must have seen something." "I didn't see a thing." "Well you got shot in the bar." "I don't know how." The Crown attorney is frustrated. "What did you see? What happened?" "I don't know, I was drunk." Another witness, "Well I know there was two people fighting but I don't know who it was." "Did you see a gun?" "Somebody might have hit a stick or something but I don't know." They had all of these people who were at the bar, everybody is coming up, "I never saw a thing."

Then they call Keith, who is my cousin. The Crown says, "Mr. Paris, what did you see?" "Rocky Jones, Burnley Jones, my cousin, he comes into the bar, and there is a fight." " So what did you see?" "Well I saw them fighting and he had a gun." "What kind of gun did he have?" "He had a shotgun." "Was it a sawed-off shotgun? Was it a full shotgun? What kind of shotgun?" He says, "It was this long and it was a 12 gauge." And the prosecutor says "How long?" and he says "This long." The prosecutor says again, "I know you are saying it is this long but for the record, how long was the gun?" Keith says, I told you it was a 12 gauge shotgun and it was 12 feet long." The prosecutor was blind. The place cracked up. So anyhow, they called the guy I was fighting with. They tried to get the story out of him, but he wouldn't tell them anything. The guy is solid as a rock. But now I'm afraid I might still have to deal with him. I'm thinking to myself, this is one tough guy. I don't know if I'd rather do the time and have it over or have to deal with him on the streets. But over the years, it turned into just one of those things in passing that happens when you are young. I've had drinks with him since and we sit around. It is a moot issue now.

Well I got two years suspended sentence and probation. The judge said, "This is the case of a progressive young man who meets with reactionary forces in the community and can't cope with it." In fact he was quite right. I was lucky, blessed. I was blessed nobody got hurt, I was blessed the guy I got in the beef with was that much of a man that he could walk away from it and not carry it on years later. I was blessed that the guys who got hurt didn't get hurt badly, blessed that they only got a couple of pellets and that didn't affect any relationship I had with them over the years. And I was blessed that someone, and I know who it was, actually had the sense to take the gun and dump it in the harbour. All of that stuff just fell in place.

This incident interrupted but it did not end the invitations I was getting to speak here and there. One of them was an invitation to appear on *Canada AM*, for a television interview. The significance of that to me was not what I said, but that *Canada AM* was acknowledging that the Black issue was of national concern. The issue of Africville was mostly confined to Nova Scotia in the media, but it was the conditions surrounding Black people all over Canada that are now being talked about. The issue had moved to the national agenda. This was in 1967, Centennial Year, when Canada is celebrating itself, and here I am breaking the bubble. I said my usual things, that Canada is a racist country and Black people are being oppressed. I was the sour note in the Centennial celebration. Shortly afterwards, and even more significantly, I was invited to comment on the Massey Lectures delivered in 1967 by Dr. Martin Luther King, Jr., entitled "Conscience for Change." The lectures, and the commentary panel, were broadcast on CBC radio. Obviously by now the CBC would know my position, they would know what I was going to talk about, yet they invited me anyway. They wanted to promote some controversy I suppose.

There were three other people on the panel, all of them white: a female professor, a male professor and a journalist, who was the chair. It's interesting that after only a couple of minutes the whole panel is talking about Blacks in Canada rather than Dr. King's lectures. He had praised Canada, for its role in the Underground Railroad and almost as a racism-free paradise. He calls it a deep personal privilege to be addressing a nation-wide Canadian audience and he goes on to say how Canada has been one of the best friends of the Black people, anywhere. And naturally I rejected that. My understanding of Canada was diametrically opposed to his. Generally speaking my response to King was that he was soft. He was teaching a philosophy that I figured could not possibly work, and his analysis was shallow. In retrospect, I am aware that his analysis was much deeper and much more sophisticated than I thought at the time. I have learned to respect him as a great thinker and a great leader. I also see now how his teachings went to the very nucleus, the kernel, of American beliefs. He challenged the exploitation of workers and he challenged the war in Vietnam, and he was getting masses of people to look at those issues. But at the time I saw only his commitment to nonviolence, forgiveness, pacifism, and that was the position I had rejected.

Most people at that particular time in history would not have opposed Martin Luther King's position. They wouldn't dare because his position was so acceptable; whites wanted that position because it spoke to nonviolence, no retribution, turn the other cheek and forgive. And in the Black community, this philosophy was in a lot of quarters accepted, because it did pay dividends, and secondly people were physically afraid of being brutalized; they had gone through the lynchings and having the police as the occupying force in all of their communities. So I think people were looking for a philosophy and a position that would give them advancement without jeopardizing their physical being, and Martin Luther King offered that. There was certain safety as compared to say Malcolm X, or Rap Brown or Bobby Seale or Stokely Carmichael. That is what Martin Luther King offered. So for me to stand up in Canada and openly oppose such an acceptable position was very unpopular. The other panellists don't buy my arguments, they don't see that Canada has treated Black people in a very inhumane way, the same as America had.

When I was on the Massey lectures panel, I considered myself the resident expert on what was happening to Black people in Canada. No matter how many degrees these people had, if they were coming from the white community, they didn't know anything compared to what I did. I could challenge any assumption they made based on experience and understanding and knowledge, and I guess that does make a difference when you are in a debate and firing back at their questions and comments. I always believed I had that advantage. That is strange when you look back at it. I was 26 years old. Just a pup. It is amazing to me now. In those days, doing whatever it was, it was just the thing to do, it was just as natural and as normal as anything else. I would think nothing of having a debate with anyone, or speaking anywhere, or being at rallies of 5,000, 10,000 people. Sometimes I think the biggest fear you have is being judged by your peers and the people you feel are important. If I had to speak in say Truro at something, I'd get really nervous, because you want to be what you should be there, but Toronto, Montreal, Massey lectures, whatever, it didn't make any difference to me then. I felt that I had a mission, and I had the confidence of youth that I could fulfil my mission. Canada would change.

To support myself and my family at this time, and to contribute to the Project as long as it lasted, I was pretty much making my money by playing poker and shooting pool. I didn't always win, but I always came out ahead in the end. But it wasn't enough, so I had to find something else. I didn't want to work for the government, and I knew nobody would hire me because of my high profile, my reputation. I decided to go into a small business, in part so that I could say to other Black people, "You can do this, it is not impossible." I looked at whatever skills I had and Joan had. Joan was a great seamstress and she could type and do the books and so on. I thought I'd be a reasonably good salesman; after all I was selling Black Power all over the country. So we decided that with this combination we could open a store. We could sell women's clothing and accessories, and some African-oriented products. We would call it the Nile Leather Shop. I went to the bank and they wouldn't lend me any money, the Royal Bank at Gottingen and Cunard. Even with Doc Maxwell signing for me, they refused us a loan. We only needed $4,000 to open our shop. Then I went down to the same bank on Spring Garden Road, and they approved our loan right away. That's the kind of prejudice that existed on Gottingen Street against people from the area.

With the $4,000 in hand we rented a place on Birmingham Street, a ground-floor one-bedroom apartment. We used what would have been the living room for our showroom, and the bedroom was for my cutting table for doing leather and a sewing machine for Joan. Our customers could use the bathroom as a place to change. I bought some leather and some equipment from the Tandy Leather Factory, and then I went off to Montreal and Toronto to buy items that we could sell. In a Toronto factory I found some old leather suede skirts that went way low below the knee. By then the mini-skirts were in, and all these skirts were out of style. I said to the guy, "I'll take them all. I'll give you $5 a piece. They are out of style and no good, but I might be able to get rid of them where I come from." He agreed, probably thought he saw a sucker coming. I think I might have had $2,000 left at this point, and I spent it all on these skirts and brought them back to Halifax. I took a knife and cut the bottom off those skirts, Joan turned up the hem, and we hung them up as mini skirts. We opened the shop in the spring of 1968. Opening Special on Mini Skirts, $34.95! So we had all these girls coming in. We put pictures up on the wall, cut from magazines with nice leather outfits. We said "If you see it and you want it, we can make it." Made to measure. Joan could make any-thing. There were so many women coming in we didn't have space for them all. I'd say, "Come back tomorrow." At the end of our first day we had sold 30 or 40 skirts. I paid $5 for them and I'm selling them for $35. The bottoms of the skirts I cut into ribbons, and I had a section of the showroom for ribbons at $5 per pair. They'd buy the skirt, they'd buy the matching ribbons. Perfect, perfect. Then in Montreal I found a warehouse where they had a discontinued line of studs. I bought a batch of them for 15 cents a piece, and sold them in our shop as earrings for $3. Then we'd have a big special, $1.99 earrings.

Women would be coming in. People were even stealing from us. I didn't care, let them steal.

We were doing quite well on Birmingham Street. The rent wasn't high. And then when Scotia Square opened I was invited to move our store over there. I said to them "Why would I move into Scotia Square? We are the only place around where you can get handmade sandals, handmade vests, hand-made skirts, handmade purses. We have a good business." I had made sandals for Gordon Lightfoot when he was in town, and lots of other musicians and folk singers. And they said, "If you come to Scotia Square, you'll have more traffic, you'll be able to do really well, and we'll put you on a percentage. You know, your rent will be 8, 9 and 10 percent, over a three-year period. Only 8% of your gross sales, then 9%, then 10%, plus heat and air conditioning and so on." So they talked me into it. We also thought that by moving into a prestigious place like Scotia Square, we would be showing Black people that they too could be involved in legitimate commerce, they could compete, they would know they belonged in a place like the Square. So we moved, in 1969. But it was a bad deal. It sounded good, 8%. I only had 150 square feet, but I was bringing in money. The thing is, they were making all the money, they were getting the profit, but I didn't know that going in.

Our shop was still on Birmingham Street when I decided to go to university. I still want to be involved in organizing and protest, and I am aware that I am a marked man. I'm just having all these confrontations with the police, confrontations in the community, I have been arrested, I have a record. But if I could be a student then I could continue to do all of this and I'd just be a student. Students do it all the time. If I'm in a demonstration, I'm at a demonstration as a student. If I'm organizing something, it is as a student. That was the main reason I went back to school, for protection against the police. I didn't have any particular goal. It wasn't part of a career plan, it was a strategic move to keep me from being under too much pressure at a certain time. I had already been thinking this way when I attended a teach-in at Dalhousie. The issue was the war in Vietnam. There was a speaker, speaking in favour of the war in Vietnam and what should be done. During the question period I went to the mic and I argued against the speaker's position on the war. I offered a fairly well-reasoned argument. Afterwards Henry Hicks, the Dalhousie president, came up to me. "That was a very, very impressive speech young man. What university did you go to?" I said, "I've never gone to university." He said, "If you ever think of going to university, I hope you would think of coming to Dal. We would love to have you here." I thought, "Right!"

He should never have said that, because I called him on it. Not too long after that I went to his office and I said, "Dr. Hicks do you remember me?" He says, "Oh yes, I do. " I said, "Do you remember our conversation?" "Well no, not exactly." "Well you told me if I ever wanted to go to university, you would love to have me at Dal, and I've decided I'd love to go to university and I want to come to Dal." He was choking. He said, "You don't have the qualifications," and I said, "No but I can come to Dalhousie as a mature student." He said, "It would be much better if you went to St. FX, I could get you into St. FX." He was saying at St. FX or Acadia you could go with a grade 11, but Dalhousie had a higher standard. I told him right there and then, "Dr. Hicks you told me that you would like me to be at Dalhousie, and this is where I want to go. My family is living in Halifax, I've got every reason to stay in Halifax and I want to go to school at Dalhousie." And he was stuck. He was an honourable man and so he said, "Well if you come over the summer and you pass a credit, then we will let you in, but you cannot be involved in any student politics. You are not coming here to be a radical, you are coming here to get a degree and learn to study." "Okay Dr. Hicks." So I took my summer course. I chose to study Spanish, because I figured you didn't get Spanish at high school and no one else had Spanish, so I'd be at the same level as everyone else going in the class. I passed it, and so they had to let me in. That same fall I was part of organizing the "Freeze the Fees" campaign. That was the year we had the biggest march ever. Oh was Hicks annoyed. We organized a big campaign. I've got pictures of me walking down Spring Garden Road with Bill Curry and Wayne Hankey, big banners, "Freeze the Fees." And Henry Hicks saw me. He was so angry.

That fall I took the most fascinating history course you can imagine. It was taught by George Shepperson, an eminent scholar who came to Dalhousie for one year as the Canada Council Visiting Professor. The course content was perfect for me: Africa and the African Diaspora. It was a graduate course, with PhD students in it. I went to Dr. Shepperson and told him about the reading I was doing and the community things I was involved in, and how I'd really really like to be in his class. Somehow he agreed, even though I was a first-year student. We had Hagos Yesus, an Ethiopian PhD student, a hard-line Marxist who had participated in a plot against Haile Selassie, Lafayette Surney, a Black SNCC worker from Louisiana, a Nigerian woman, beautiful, named Okeke Okpepe, several white Canadian grad students. And, importantly, Jim Walker was in that class, a former CUSO volunteer who I had met during the demonstration in Toronto in 1965. We saw each other for the first time since then, in Shepperson's class. Jim was starting a PhD on Black history in Nova

Scotia, on the Black Loyalists. That class was the most exciting educational experience of my life. First of all, the readings overlapped with what I was doing already, and it furthered my thinking about the international history of Africa and Africans. The discussions were so stimulating, and Shepperson would challenge everything. You couldn't get away with sloppy reading or sloppy arguments. You couldn't say anything you couldn't back up. It was just knock down, take off the gloves, when you came in the door. For me it was an intellectual awakening that was profound. I had a chance to read, to challenge and be challenged, to exchange ideas with some really bright students. I was the only Nova Scotian there, but Shepperson included Nova Scotia in our readings and discussions. We examined the racism faced by Black people throughout our history, the attempts to overcome it, the problems we faced and their historical background. My understanding of the Diaspora and even of my home province was expanded that year. There is no way I could bring out the excitement for someone who wasn't there. And I was doing this while some other very exciting things were going on.

Chapter Six

BLACK POWER

Tariq Ali wrote a book about 1968, the great year of revolution around the world. It doesn't even mention Canada. Well, we had our own 1968 in Canada. For me, the most exciting part of that revolutionary year would start with the Congress of Black Writers, which met in Montreal in October. I was invited to give two talks, one on the opening night of the conference and then another at the closing. These two jobs gave me a fairly prominent place on the agenda. The conference brought together not only Black writers but many important intellectuals and community organizers from Canada, the States, the Caribbean, Africa, England. The organizing committee in Montreal had Rosie Douglas as chair, and Clarence Bayne and Juanita Westmoreland. From around the world we had C.L.R. James, undoubtedly the most respected person at the conference, Carlos Smith, who had given the Black Power salute at the Mexico City Olympics that year, Michael X, Bobby Hill, Walter Rodney, and above all Stokely Carmichael, who was then prime minister of the Black Panther Party. Most of our reading list in the Shepperson seminar at Dalhousie were there in person. Here I am, this boy from the Marsh, with all these leading lights in the global Black community. Joan was there with her camera, and she took pictures of me with all these great people, and I took some of her with them too. These were people I had been admiring from afar. It was exhilarating, and humbling at the same time. A lifetime highlight.

There are some published accounts of the Congress of Black Writers, reporting on the speeches and deliberations. My own most valued experiences were in private conversations or small groups in the hallways or in hotel rooms. Because I was on stage for the opening, everybody there could call me by name as I moved through the hall. One speech, and I'm known by all these giants. Of course I spoke about the situation in Canada, and in Nova Scotia particularly, and this seemed to interest the people from away. The first person that I get to spend time with, for whatever reason, is Michael X. We were sitting around talking and he would roll a joint of marijuana out of newspaper, like a long funnel. My eyes were like saucers, I had never seen anything like it. He is rolling these joints and he says, "Brother man did you ever eat anybody?" I said, "Huh?" "Did you ever eat anybody?" I said "Hell no." "Oh brother man, don't know what it taste like, that human flesh, man, some good." I'm looking at this guy and saying to myself, this guy's smoking weed, he is on some sort of trip. He says, "Oh man, up in the hills man, we had lots of good food." "What you talking about?" "Brother man, we eat people, you know, we like people." He goes on to tell me about being a cannibal and what human flesh tasted like. He explained it was nice and sweet like pig. He'd say "Man, to eat people is to make yourself strong, because you get what they got and double your strength." It was hairy. He knew what he was talking about. Eventually they find all these body parts buried in his yard. In fact he was a cannibal and was later hanged in Trinidad for murder. I spent hours with this guy. He took a liking to me; maybe he wanted to chop me up! But at the same time he talked a lot about the movement in England, where he was living at the time, in London. He talked about how difficult it was to organize because Black people there identified so much with their oppressor. "Afro-Saxons." And "skinocracy" was one of the issues that they had to deal with, the light-skinned West Indians who really didn't want to be Black but helped hold other people down, and they became the real gatekeepers. He would talk this way: "You have to off the gatekeeper man, the gatekeeper must be put down." And the way he talked about it, he was serious. You were supposed to kill the gatekeepers so the masses can get a chance to rise up. What an experience it was, just talking to him.

One of the other people I met there who was so intellectual and so kind was C.L.R. James. He would sit with me and talk and explain things. He was a committed Marxist; it was all very theoretical with him. He could take a particular set of circumstances and talk in terms of how it fit into a certain theory, what that situation would mean to the masses. And he was interested in Nova Scotia and what was going on there, and how the organizing was going, whether the people were close to the point where they were ready to rebel, and whether there was any chance of armed insurrection. (Well no, not really.) I had read him some time before, and that is why it was so exciting

Montreal, 1968, Miriam Makeba, Rocky, C.L.R. James, Stokely Carmichael.

to meet him. He was a very kind and gentle guy, by far the patriarch of the conference. Everyone wanted to sit and talk to him. Whenever you saw him there were people around. What shone through with him was his gentleness and intelligence. He took time to ask you what was going on in your life and with your issues, and explain how he would see it. He was quite free with advice. He made you think. Another person I spent a lot of time with at the conference was Walter Rodney, from Guyana. There was just something about him. When you talk with him he is talking about concepts, and you are trying to follow him and he corrects you, challenges you. It was another eye-opener for me.

But the person I spent most time with in Montreal was Stokely Carmichael. I had never met him before, and here I was associated with his name all across Canada. He was so energized by what was going on. This plus his natural charismatic self made him sort of a star the whole time. The energy was fantastic. For some reason again the two of us just hit it off, there was something there. We'd get off in the corner whenever we could. He was interested in learning about Nova Scotia. He made one comment during an interview, telling the reporter that "aggressive violence is essential if the Blacks are going to change their status. In performing such violence the Blacks would do to the whites only what had been done to the Blacks many times in the past." And he was including Nova Scotia! We'd be sitting in a hotel room talking, and he was saying he was feeling so pressured. I knew the feeling. So I said, "Come on down with me and chill for a while in Halifax. Nobody will know who you are." He said, "That is a good idea but we can't tell anybody." "No we won't tell anybody, we'll make the arrangements. You'll come down, spend a week or so with me," I'm saying to him. "You are starting to get fried man." So he said okay. Now he goes to speak to Miriam Mikeba. They would change their arrangements and nobody would know. Joan and Miriam had been getting along great all through the conference, so it was okay with them. We would all quietly hang out.

Well, he makes his arrangements. Joan and I fly home and Stokely and Miriam are to follow in a day or two. It is interesting to me now how naïve we were. We thought we could keep this a secret. Back in Halifax I decided that if the Mounties are following my car, I'd better have a different car. So I borrowed a car from my friend Jim Walker. He would spend the day driving around Halifax in my red VW bug, and let the Mounties follow him. I could go the airport anonymously to pick up Stokely and Miriam. When their plane arrives, the airport is full of cops. They knew every move we were making. But we manage to slip away in Jim's car and I'm thinking, "How are we going to get into Halifax." I was speeding a bit desperately, and I'll never forget Stokely's words to me. "Slow down brother, you can't organize a revolution around a car accident. It is okay if I get shot dead; people will rebel because of it. If we just have a car accident, I'm dying in vain." That is what he told me on the way in. Anyway we come into town, to our house on Pepperell Street. There are cops parked in front of my house, press too. All of a sudden this nice little quiet getaway is now a public thing. Stokely Carmichael is in town!

We switch our cars back again, and I made arrangements to have dinner upstairs at the Arrow's Club. By then we had quite an entourage; it sure grew all of a sudden. There's the four of us, then we had the Kwacha bodyguards, our boys, then we had some people who were from South Africa who had been invited for Miriam's sake. All of a sudden this quiet thing had become quite a deal. So we went over to the Arrow's Club, and we ate upstairs away from everybody. We had a good meal, lots of fun. Then we were going to go downstairs to party, but Stokely didn't want to. I don't think people understand to this day. The issue has been portrayed as him not wanting whites around, but he was really concerned at the number of people there. The only way we could control it was to keep him and Miriam and that party separated from other people. People would say, "Can I have your autograph?" Miriam was a big star at that time, so they are crowding Miriam, crowding him. He is in a strange place, never been here before, and all these white people are starting to crowd in, so he is pretty nervous. And they want Miriam to sing. So she agrees to sing and then the party is on, there is no way we could hold it back. She brings the house down, everybody is up dancing, and the police are all surrounding the club. What a scene.

The next day we were invited to eat at the home of a South African doctor, a woman, a very swank, South End house. And these women from Africa are there, cooking this incredible food. Miriam and the hostess get into an argument. Miriam tells the woman, "You are a sell out." They are getting right down at it. Miriam is saying, "You come over here and think that you are this and you are that, and you got nothing to do with the local community and wearing your wig and putting on airs. People are living in poverty and you don't care. You are a disgrace to your people." Miriam was taking no prisoners, she wouldn't let up on the woman. The woman was actually trying to get away from her. Miriam was really upset about this woman wearing a wig. The woman said something to Miriam and Miriam reached over and snatched the wig off her head in front of the whole party. The fight was on. This doctor is hooking now, she is hooking right or left, and Miriam is trying to hook too. Stokely jumps between them, other people too, trying to break up the fight. So now the party broke up. Everybody's got to leave. We've got cars that are lined up outside, and the police are out there. I'm getting people out, trying to keep things calm and ushering people to the cars. By the time I get everything straightened away, all the cars are gone. Everybody is gone, and there is me. The cops are parked across the street, so I go across to the cops. "Listen buddy, I know you are assigned to be following me, but everybody is gone, so if you have to follow me, can you do me a favour and give me a ride over to my house. You'll know where I am and I don't have to walk." The guy says, "I'm not assigned to follow you." I said, "Even if you aren't me can you give me a lift home?" He says, "Yeah, I guess so."

When I got home Stokely said, "I came here for a little rest and relaxation, and I've had nothing but aggravation. I'm leaving." There was a report that there was something that happened, and he had to leave town. The reality was this man had gone in two days to face all of these people at the Arrow's Club, surrounded by police at every move, badgered by reporters all day, his wife gets in battle royal at some party, he hasn't had a wink of sleep, and he's saying, "Brother, I'm going home to my bed to get some rest." I said, "I'm sorry." All I could say is "I'm sorry." Welcome to Nova Scotia.

The radio, the TV, the press, they all thought Stokely was coming to start a riot. The revolution was on! People were frightened, and not just white people but Black people too. To have someone of his calibre, by far the most famous Black militant in America, and to have him come to Halifax and be staying with me, at that time maybe the best-known Black militant in Canada; you have these two putting their heads together, you know it is revolution time. The headlines had a field day. Stokely told the reporters, "We are internationalizing Black Power. We recognize all the problems that Black people of Halifax have and we wanted to begin some coordination so that we can move against racism and capitalism." Even Gus Wedderburn was alarmed. The press asked him for comment and he said, "Time is running out, let's start finding solutions to the problems of the Negro." So all this attention, though we were thoroughly annoyed at the time, actually had a payout. It got everybody thinking, even if they were scared, and they had to focus on the racism and all the things that were wrong for us in Nova Scotia. There is no doubt in my mind that Stokely's short visit was instrumental in swaying public opinion and starting to get changes made. It turned out to be revolutionary after all.

Stokely goes back, and as he had promised, other Panthers arrive. And most of them were staying at our house. After our daughter Casey joined the family we needed more room, so we moved out of our Barrington Street apartment to a rented house on Pepperell Street. Soon we were crowded again. There was George Sams, alias Wadell Smith, or I think Smith was his real name and Sams the alias, and there was T.D. Pauley, and Coco Hughes and another woman named Ethel. Altogether I think there were eight Panthers who came to Halifax, but not all at once. T.D. was the intellectual law-school type, really sharp, as were the two women, who were university types.

George Sams was the only one with a different background. He had been a gang leader and had been shot up a number of times. He had all of these bullet holes in him. He used to sleep with his thumb in his mouth. He was a very tough, tough, tough guy, obviously coming through that background, but he was very gentle with the children, he loved our kids. But any question you asked him he answered with a quotation from Chairman Mao. He had memorized the Red Book and he used it to handle questions. He had every catch phrase, like "Political power grows out of the barrel of a gun." My friend John Baigent took George Sams over to the law school, where John was a student. John was doing a seminar and Sams was going to participate. Now George Sams wasn't the sharpest knife in the drawer for sure, and when the other students started talking to him his response was, "Well you kill them." Or something like that. Sams actually wanted to stay here, he liked Nova

Scotia. He got along well with Clarence, who was then one of our boarders. They used to sit around a lot.

That house on Pepperell Street was crowded for sure. We continued taking on more children: after Casey came the three boys Augy, Patti and Shaka. So there's five kids, Joan and me, and we always had boarders who were just like part of the extended family. We needed the income to help pay the rent, for one thing, and they helped with child care and so on. My sister Wilma and Walter Borden were there all the time, and Clarence, Jackie, Bobby, Wayne, Rubin. We'd have at least four boarders at any one time, and any members of my family who happened to be coming to Halifax, and visitors, political people who were involved in the civil rights movement, and Panthers for a time. They were there when Rosie Douglas came to town. Rosie loved Halifax too. He would show up and come and stay for a few days or a week or two, it didn't matter, then he'd be on to another thing.

This particular time he got involved with the police. I've mentioned before about the police wanting people to just move along, on Maynard Street in particular and on Creighton Street, when the people were standing there doing nothing wrong. A bunch of us were in the Prizefighters Club one night and Rosie was carrying on about how the police don't have the authority to do this. When the cop tells you to move along, you ask him if he's arresting you, and on what charge. Otherwise he can't order you around. We were outside on the street a little later and sure enough, the police come along and tell Rosie to move along. Rosie said no, he was not doing anything and he wasn't loitering, that he was in fact talking, and the officer said you have to talk and walk cause you can't stand in one spot. Rosie's position was, well you know this is our neighbourhood, this is our community and I have every right to stand here and talk to someone. So they arrested him for loitering, and it was a big deal because it was consistent with our political strategy of heightening the contradictions, and then have a confrontation. Well the contradictions that were heightened in that situation were between being able to live in a community and having the freedom to stand outside your door, and the police power to tell you to move along. It just heightened that to such an extent that confrontation was inevitable. They take Rosie down to the station and he says this is not a criminal issue, it is political. And so he refused to pay bail and refused to have anyone else pay bail for him. So Rosie went to jail on this issue and it raised an awful lot of interest. Then someone anonymously paid for his $200 bail. The rumour was that the deputy police chief paid it in order to avoid all the trouble it was stirring up. Eventually it went to trial and the

Crown pulled it. The loitering situation was never tried as an issue, so that it was sort of pushed into the background as opposed to being resolved.

That was going on, and the police and others in the white community seemed to be getting more aggressive. Some Black people were convinced that we needed to be prepared to defend our communities with arms. And we knew that we weren't. Consequently there was an interest in trying to set up a training camp in Nova Scotia. We knew that we had rural areas where everybody had a gun. It wasn't anything special, everybody knew how to use a gun. And there would be areas where Black people controlled the land so we could have some kind of a training camp. Our boarder Clarence had land in Shelburne, so we were going to Shelburne to look at this land and see if there was some way that we could set up a training camp there. I had that little Volkswagen and we drove off and we spend a day in the Shelburne area, talking to people, shooting off some guns for target practice. We come back and my vehicle was parked in the yard at Pepperell Street. I still had the shotguns in the car, and there may have been rifles; they were legitimate long guns as opposed to restricted weapons of any kind. In those days you did not need to have a licence to have any kind of a long gun. George Sams wanted to go out to buy some cigarettes or something, and he was going to drive my car. When he pulled out with the car and went down the street the police pulled him over. Routine check, they say. It is my belief that he was set up, he was targeted in as much as their informant said, "Sams has got the car and you can get him." They find a .38 revolver under the seat, which was a surprise to me because I didn't know it was there. Sams says he didn't know it was there. I have no reason not to believe what he said; in fact I believe that that gun was planted. We were very careful, knowing that we could get stopped at any moment. A bunch of Black guys in a vehicle, being followed all the time by the RCMP, with this American Panther in the car: the chances of us being stopped were pretty good, so we did not have a restricted weapon in that car. There would be no reason for us to have one. It was not our intention to go target shooting with a pistol. So from the time that we came home, and the time that he took that vehicle, that gun was placed in the car; that's what must have happened. And it had to have been placed there by one of the *agents provocateurs* that was in our group. I have very strong suspicions as to who it was. So George is arrested for being in possession of an illegal weapon.

The same night that George Sams was arrested, the police came to the house and picked me up too, as the illegal gun had been found in my car. A bunch of people put together my bail money, I forget how much it was but not nearly as much as for Sams. The charge against me was dropped. Bail was set for Sams at $1,500, so naturally nobody could pay that to get him out and he was kept in jail for several days. I held a fundraiser at Dalhousie to try to raise enough money, but we only got about $150. His case came to trial just one day before Rosie's. Sams was found guilty but sentencing was delayed. As soon as the judge pronounced, they whisked him out a side door. The next thing we know he has been taken to the airport and deported back to the States, just like that. We never saw him again.

It wasn't all confrontation, and apart from George Sams, the Panthers did not talk about or advocate violence. They were really good ambassadors for the American civil rights movement, they were extremely polite, they were very informative, they took time to talk to people in the Black community. They explained what the Panther party was, and they were really interested in trying to get a breakfast program going, along the lines of what the Panthers were running in the States. They did a lot of education around the issues of love and self-love and how we had to love and respect each other as African people. They didn't talk at all about insurrection, they were really smart enough to understand that Nova Scotia was a different environment than the large northern cities in the States. They talked more about building the community so the community could have more control over institutions. They talked about the possibility of a Saturday school, and about how to organize Black people as a group, and what kinds of organizations might work. They were very low key while speaking in the community. Most people would not have known, either by dress or fiery rhetoric, who any of these people were except maybe George Sams, who could not get rid of the black leather jacket and beret. Coco and Ethel and T.D. were just like university students who were out there talking and bringing the concept of the true meaning of Black Power, which is simply power to Black people. The training they were bringing and the way they were presenting it and the attempt to make us believe, truly believe we were part of this international Black struggle, was really important. They helped us to turn the corner I think, from being a Nova Scotia project to being a project that was part of an international struggle.

My sister Janis and her husband Bryan organized meetings at Acadia, where Coco, T.D. and I spoke. There were meetings at Mount St. Vincent, and T.D. came several times to the study group Jim Walker and Jules Oliver and I had organized at the Dalhousie Student Union Building. To mixed audiences they emphasized that there was a role for the white activists, which was to go into the white community to educate other whites about racism. In fact, they were really encouraging, they were the exact opposite to what you get of the image of the Panthers, of "hate whitey." They were quite willing and ready to talk to white people but they were saying, "We don't want you to come into the ghetto and try to organize our community. We don't want you to try and take over our organizations, and to tell us what to do, but we do want you to go into the white community. Somebody has to do what we can't do. Somebody has to go into the white community and organize it and educate it." That is not to say that we didn't talk at a personal level of the need for armed rebellion, but when they were talking to the people, whether they be white or Black, they were not putting out that message at all. They were too smart for that. They were putting out the message that Black people must unite and Black people must have the kind of symbolism that people can relate to. We've got to develop symbols, we've got to have songs, we've got to have meaningful things in the community that people can respond to, to be able to say "I'm Black and I'm proud."

The Panthers were encouraging us to hold a Black Family Meeting. There were two preliminary meetings, both of them held at Cornwallis Street Baptist Church, leading up to the big meeting on November 30. The first meeting didn't attract too many people, maybe only about 20. It was a sort of tug of war between me and W.P. Oliver, and no conclusions were reached. I was supporting the idea of a Black Family Meeting, but W.P. would have none of that. It is true that every time I go up against W.P., I have to overcome all of the romance around him. He is W.P. Oliver. He is the biggest thing in the Black community and a name that I have known since I was born, a person who has almost walked on water. And I've been brought up to respect authority, to respect the leadership and all of that and now as this young man I am in a position where I've got to take this person on in different ways. Every single time you have to go up against someone of that stature, all of that history is there to make you nervous, to keep you thinking. He was formidable. When you went against W.P. you had to know what you were doing. He would eat you up.

So we had to have another meeting, and this second meeting was packed, the church hall was absolutely full of people. This is the meeting where T.D. spoke. Again the question was, "Do we have a Black Family Meeting?" We've got the room filled with people and we've got to make a decision about the idea of a Black Family Meeting. W.P. was the greatest politician I have ever met, absolutely brilliant and an orator of orators. When he spoke he was thinking of his sentence four sentences ahead as words are coming out of his mouth. His mind is just going. So we are at it again, trying to get the minds of the people and I'm trying to get them on my side, to approve of the meeting. And W.P. is saying that is a bit radical, perhaps we should think of doing it a little differently. T.D. Pauley explains to the people what we need or what we could do is have an organization that is an umbrella, everybody still has their own organization and nobody loses any control. He says we can force the government to talk to this group, because all of the groups will be represented and we'll have a central body and this central body will be united. We'll have a united front. But it will always be made up of all of these separate organizations. It is at this preliminary meeting where the concept of a united front is first introduced. People are nodding in agreement and quite clearly they are going to buy this. W.P. knows which way the meeting is going to go, so he is the first to endorse this as a concept, and he offers to chair it! The Black Family Meeting that we had been trying to get, that he has always been against, now he says we could have this meeting and all of a sudden it's his meeting. He was brilliant, one of the smartest politicians that you could ever ever deal with when it came to community politics.

So we have an agreement to hold the Black Family Meeting, which means Black people only, and the date of November 30 is chosen. Now there is not much time between this second meeting at Cornwallis Street and the Family Meeting; we've got to get organized, get the word out as widely as possible. It was soon obvious that we would have more people than would fit into the church, so we went to Allan O'Brien, the mayor, and got permission to use the North End Library. Meanwhile the press are going crazy about this radical, reverse-racist Black thing. In the Black community there is all kinds of movement and discussion because we had to deal with who is Black. Does that mean if your father is Black and your mother is white, you are Black? Does it mean if your grandfather is Black you are Black? Who is Black? And in Nova Scotia that is a difficult, difficult question. And we had a little group who was trying to organize this and make decisions because we knew on opening night we had to deal with this at the door. And it was something we couldn't resolve, because in Nova Scotia the politics of who is Black is so interesting.

By the night of the meeting our definition is self-identification: whoever self-identifies as Black we'll have to accept it. I'll never forget that night; it was one of the most difficult nights I have ever gone through. People are arriving early, people are coming to make sure they get their seats. There were women, particularly white women, who were married or living with Black men who had children with these Black men, who showed up and said, "We want to come in." And our position at the door was "You're not welcome." And they were saying, "What's wrong with me, I'm married to him, these are my children, and this is my future you're talking about," and we were saying, "No you can't come in, no, we're sorry," and it almost came to blows. "This is a Black Family Meeting and you are part of the extended family and we love you, but this is the nuclear family, this is Blacks only." And they were right at the door, and for the Black community, people were embarrassed. They knew these people, they lived with these women, they were their friends, and they would say, "You know, can't we just let them in, she's lived in the Black community all her life, she's married to so and so." They were embarrassed and upset, but we held the line. People wanted to kill us that night. You've got husbands who are mad. "This is my woman and she is the mother of my children. Who the hell do you think you are to say she can't come in?" For Black people in Halifax that was such an incredible shift in terms of position that no one was used to it, including myself, but I knew what I had to do in terms of fulfilling a leadership role and moving people to take control of their own destinies. We had to do that, but the people we were doing that to were our friends.

Nobody knows what is going to happen, and they are afraid. The Panthers are here, so are we planning a revolution and going to have to pick up a gun and go to war? W.P. is involved, so they have a certain sense that it should be safe if he is there in the chair. I'm involved, so that is another side: maybe he is going to finally get the chance to get us all killed. And the press are questioning why Black people should be allowed to have a meeting without whites. Then we get in, and there are 500 people there. You've got the political spectrum from the most arch conservatives to the anarchists. There are Black people who take the position, "Let's get a gun and bomb everybody in the world"; others are saying, "White people have been good to us and we shouldn't be like this." We had it all. No matter what was put on the agenda, no matter what we tried to talk about that night, there was some extreme position that was taken by someone, so you couldn't get through anything. What did happen, and what was really good, was that for the first time, even in that meeting with all the dissension, people realized that we as Black people could control what we did. We told the press they couldn't come in, and we were in control. Cops couldn't come in, we were in control. I think that what was accomplished that night was the sense of power that the community had for the first time ever, with all of the pressure that was on the community to do something different: the press didn't want the meeting to happen, the politicians didn't want the meeting to happen, a lot of the leadership in the community didn't want the meeting to happen. And we pulled it off and gave a sense of "This is what we can do."

T.D. got up and described the situation in Washington, D.C., where they had formed the United Front to give them more influence with the politicians and more coordination among the different Black organizations. We really couldn't get very far during that meeting except to say we needed something like they had in Washington. We got agreement at the meeting that the new organization should not take the place of any existing organization, and all existing organizations should have the right to be a part of the new organization. It was very clear and definite that this organization was to be a coalition of all of the organizations and not something in its own right. And they would be able to have representatives, and we would make decisions from there. The meeting definitely then said, if this is as far as we will go, we will agree. The decision was to name it the Black United Front of Nova Scotia (BUF).

So then the meeting elects the Interim Committee, which was charged with three tasks: to design a program that would be relevant to the needs of Black Nova Scotians; to suggest a permanent structure, an umbrella structure, for the new organization; and to explore sources of funding for its programs. The idea of government funding was discussed and rejected by the meeting, so we are looking for alternative funding opportunities. And then the Interim Committee was to carry its proposals back to another family meeting for approval. Like most meetings, everybody knew who should be on the committee and so somebody would just say, "I think Rocky should be on it." My supporters are going to make sure I'm on it, so everybody would say okay. "W.P. should be on it." Okay, and he would be the chair. So the people who ended up on that were pretty well representative of different interest groups or different factions. Buddy Daye was very active in the community at the time, and would have been seen as someone who represented Halifax city interests. Although he was connected to the church, people would have seen that he was more representative of the community. Edie Grey would be representative of a group of people in the Halifax area who are not associated with the church. She would have been seen as part of the real old guard in Halifax, the old B.A. Husbands types, the Coloured Citizens Improvement League. Keith Prevost was younger, a very good talker and part of the Prevost family and represented the business interests in the Black community. Also Keith would have had a broader base in those persons who were outside of all of the established groups. He had a more militant stance. Arnold Johnson was a returned veteran from North Preston, well respected, conservative, church-oriented. People would trust that he would tell them the truth. If he was on this committee then whatever was going on, he would certainly represent the interests of North Preston.

And Gus Wedderburn was seen as an educated person who knew what was going in the community, a Jamaican immigrant who was an established leader as president of the NSAACP. He was involved in a lot of groups, including the Human Rights Advisory Committee and engaged in the Africville situation. So he was knowledgeable. And Denny Grant, who was basically the same constituency as I was. So we had our collection of moderates like Buddy, Gus and W.P., and those considered more radical like myself, Keith and Denny.

The Family Meeting was on a Saturday night, and the very next weekend there was this human rights conference at Joe Howe School. Every year for the past four or five years the Halifax Human Rights Committee, by then called the Human Rights Federation of Nova Scotia, had held a conference around Human Rights Day in December. The 1968 one had a special theme. Gus Wedderburn was its chair, and he sent out an advance letter to invite everyone to attend. He says, "You see on your TV and the newspapers the tragic consequences of the denial of human rights to fair housing, fair employment, education and dignity in the United States." By "tragic consequences," Gus would be meaning the reaction of the Black American community to the denial of fair housing, not how poorly the people are being treated. Essentially he is scaring people, reminding them of the race riots that were going on in the States at that time. Then he also says that Premier G.I. Smith would be attending and he would have an important announcement pertaining to the appointment of a full-time human rights commissioner for the province. Obviously Gus knew what was coming down. Several weeks earlier the NSAACP organized a meeting with the premier, which I also attended along with others. Gus presented a series of demands, or rather requests, including this full-time coordinator for human rights who should be a Black person. They also argued for more economic development in Black communities, paving some roads into the more remote settlements, and that the Black contribution to the province's history should be recognized. I was asked to comment on the impact of Stokely's visit on the Black youth, and I said they were becoming more militant. This gave Gus and the premier the idea that the "threat" from the militants was becoming more serious.

The night before the conference opens I am approached by reporters from the *Chronicle Herald* and the TV. "Do you have plans to disrupt the conference?" they ask me. "Is it true that 200 Panthers will be coming to Halifax?" My response is of course 200 Panthers will not be coming, and I have no plans to disrupt the conference. My interest is in having people come together to talk about what their role is, the definition of society and the solution to problems. That has nothing to do with disruption. I was not concerned with the appointment of a Human Rights Commissioner. As far as I was concerned that would do nothing to confront the systemic problems faced by Black people, specific problems coming from racism. They must have got this idea that I was out to ruin the conference from somebody; certainly it was never my intention. Somebody was planting these ideas to exaggerate the threat and frighten the people. It was all orchestrated.

The opening night of the conference, Friday, December 6, Howard McCurdy addressed the conference. Among other things he praised the system they had in Ontario, where there was a full-time Human Rights Commissioner. Whether Howard was briefed to say this I have no idea. Then on Saturday afternoon John Cartwright from Boston University gives a really rousing talk, very progressive. At the end of his speech he raises his hand in the Black Power salute and calls out "Freedom now!" Well, the audience went wild. There must have been 700 or 800 people there and Cartwright's talk was thrilling them, especially the Blacks. We have to control our own destiny! There was a panel discussion right after, which I was on, and I endorsed what Cartwright was saying. So the audience is already getting hot when Premier Smith gets up. Basically he goes over the list that the NSAACP had given him; he must have been reading from a prepared speech, maybe prepared by Gus. The road into North Preston would be paved; more industries would be located in Black districts; blah blah. Then he makes his "important announcement": a full-time Human Rights Commissioner has been appointed, and he introduces Marvin Schiff, a 31-year-old journalist, white, from Upper Canada! No consultation with the community, no local connection. Even the NSAACP had asked for a Black commissioner, though by this time Gus may have known who had been appointed. I jumped up and started complaining about all this, and the premier looks really surprised. Obviously he expected his announcement would be welcomed by everybody. I pointed out that I knew there was at least one Black applicant for this position, and they had not even had the courtesy of a reply from the premier's office. Some people thought I was referring to myself, but I would not apply for a job like this. Anyway people started shouting and standing up and complaining about this. Hell is breaking loose in that hall, it blows up. After hearing about Black liberation from Cartwright, people were feeling snookered by this Schiff appointment. Well Schiff himself gets up and apologizes for the way his appointment was made. He says, "I'm mad as hell that it happened this way," and the conservative people in the Black community said, "He shouldn't swear." The fact that he said "hell" was the issue! I think that conference, and the appointment of Marvin Schiff, is something that polarizes the community, into people who are prepared to accept the government position and those who are committed to opposing the government position.

Exactly one week after this, on December 13, I am back in Toronto again, speaking at a rally at the Ontario Institute for Studies in Education on Bloor Street. I was exhausted, but this was a very important meeting. In Toronto then there was something we described as "tribalism," a lot of organizations that were associated with particular islands and people's origins: the Jamaican Canadian Association, the Trinidad and Tobago Association, and so on. The organizers' idea was to excite the Black people of Toronto with a rally that would address the Canadian situation, to form a collective viewpoint. They wanted to show the connection between our situation in Canada and the situation of Black people in other countries, and to keep the movement focused on the nationalist philosophy rather than integrationist. Wilson Head was one of the organizers. He was seen as the intellectual guru, really way above the rest of us when it came to analytical abilities and knowledge of progressive political movements and history. He was very highly regarded in the Black community. The other organizers were much younger. The chair was Jose Garcia, of the Afro-American Progressive Association, a Marxist, Black nationalist organization in Toronto. Although that organization was Canadian, its name reflected the interaction with the States; there was continual movement back and forth across the border with Detroit and Buffalo, with Panthers and CORE and various Black nationalist associations. Many of these people were also at the conference, in particular a group known as the Detroit Revolutionary Union Movement, DRUM, extremely militant and connected to the Panthers.

The conference was scheduled to go from Friday to Sunday, and I was to give the keynote address on Saturday. When I arrived the organizers explained that there were problems with immigration officials and the RCMP, and a lot of the American participants were being turned back at the border. So they said, "Look, will you address this issue in the opening address?" This was because I was Canadian, and I could adopt an anti-government stance. Now the auditorium was jam-packed that afternoon, and I'm up to give the opening, welcoming address. I blasted the RCMP as a bunch of white racists, targeting Black people at the borders, and we won't stand for it. We are becoming organized and we need to stick together to stop our people from being treated like this. The audience is standing up and yelling and screaming; they are almost whipped into a frenzy. I finished the speech and people are standing up, cheering as I go down from the stage. One of the preconditions for when I was travelling was that I would be provided with security. I did not feel safe moving around these conferences and being in these places. I was having death threats and phone calls at home all the time. White supremacist groups were active, and there were disorganized skinheads and nutcakes out there. On this occasion I had been assigned two bodyguards. These guys dwarfed me, absolute towers of steel. I'm walking down the aisle with these two guys toward the back door when this young, extremely beautiful white girl who is wearing the shortest of skirts calls out "Rocky," and she starts to run toward me. Well the bodyguards see this and they grab this little girl and hustle her out through the door. When I go through I find out that she used to babysit Tracey back when we lived in Toronto, for Joan and me. She came because she heard I was going to be there and we hadn't seen each other for years. All of these people are looking at me, quite suspicious. Here is this beautiful white girl coming at me with arms wide open. So I'm explaining this away, saying this girl used to babysit my daughter and so on, standing in the foyer. Just at that moment a good friend of mine, Diane Burrows from the Friends of SNCC comes up and kisses me. We hadn't seen each other for years either, ever since I moved back to Nova Scotia. She is white too, extremely pretty, tall with a dark complexion. She had come as well because she saw in the press that I would be there, and she wanted to show me her baby. So she is holding up the baby saying "Rocky you haven't seen our baby yet." Oh my God, I'm thinking, this is the end of my credibility with this crowd.

The conference went on for two more days, and it was instrumental in uniting the African-descended people living in Toronto and surrounding areas, because there was no acceptance of any kind of philosophy or rhetoric that would accent island or country of origin. Most of the people involved in the movement in Toronto would have been born somewhere else other than Canada. Likely 80% or even more had been born in the islands. Some Americans, some Africans, some people from eastern Canada, but the bulk of the people would have been first generation immigrants from the West Indies. The most positive result may be the part it played in the genesis of the National Black Coalition of Canada less than a year later. It was a fostering spirit, it got a momentum going. Jose Garcia and the people at the conference were insistent that we begin to look at the Canadian consciousness as opposed to country of origin. This doesn't mean that there weren't disagreements and arguments and lively debates at this conference, just that our focus was on adopting a Black nationalist perspective, no more tribalism. This is 1968, when everything is happening and everything is on the table. The Black community is in a state of flux. There is excitement going on, the Black Panther Party in the States is at its peak, there are the different philosophies raising the level of debate in terms of what are the solutions and where do we go. There are people advocating back to Africa, there are people advocating that there be a Black state set up in America. There are people advocating basically a separate but equal doctrine, separate schools for Black people, separate living conditions. You have people who are advocating complete and total integration and then others who are saying assimilation is the answer. And that's the debate at that time in history, maybe the most exciting time that I know of, from both reading or participating. It is the most exciting time in the history of African people in North America in terms of open debate on philosophy. And we had all of these lines of thinking there at the conference, and we know it's crystallized to an extent that the debate can continually occur and it is happening all over. We also knew it wasn't just an academic debate. For some of our people at that time in history, we are talking life and death. When you are saying, "Either society will come around or we'll burn it down," that is really confrontational. When you have confrontation occurring at that level that is deadly, that is people's lives. When you are talking about breakfast programs and the fact that Black children were basically dying because there was not enough food, that is life and death if you are poor and living in a ghetto somewhere. So all of these issues were being debated right there in that meeting, an attempt by one particular philosophical group to bring people together to implement programming based on their understanding of what was happening and where to go from here. It was amazing that that philosophical debate didn't fracture the Black community. It is a testament to the strength of the Black community and it also may be a reflection of the oppression of white society. People left determined to keep the momentum going.

While I was in Toronto W.P. approached the federal government in an attempt to get government funding for BUF. The government responded positively, and W.P. began consulting with the Secretary of State field officer in Halifax. W.P. is saying there is a real urgency, we really have to get this money. I come back to the Interim Committee in the middle of this discussion about federal funding, and some of us are saying no we don't have the right to do that. We have to go back to the community and we've got to have a structure that the community has endorsed. We have a particular mandate that has been given to us and we have to follow it. W.P. is saying no we don't have to follow it, we are going to do it this way. Basically he's saying that the people don't know what it is that is good for them. And that is why W.P. exercised his authority as chair to appoint additional members to the Interim Committee, when it becomes clear that more votes are needed to carry his agenda. I'm not saying they were unqualified, but they were not elected. There was his own son Jules Oliver, who was not a political activist in the community, though he and I and Jim Walker had recently founded an educational program at the Student Union Building, a night school for Black kids who had dropped out of regular school. I suspect that he was in his father's shadow and there wasn't a lot of room for him to manoeuvre. Not to say that he didn't have the smarts or couldn't do things in different groups, but in these big public meetings, Jules wasn't a factor. So his father appointed him, not that he had a constituency to represent. And then there was W.P.'s brother, Donnie Oliver. Donnie is a Conservative, a lawyer and later Conservative senator in Ottawa. He was not particularly involved in the community. He lived in the South End of town, on Vernon Street, and he socialized in the South End of town. So his constituency was never the Black community. Another appointee was Murray Warrington from Liverpool. He is outspoken, has his constituency of Southwest Nova, and I would say is fairly radical in his rhetoric and very conservative in his actual votes or the way he does things. Clyde Bishop, from Cherrybrook, would represent his local people but more so he was seen as a pretty level-headed guy who wasn't able to be easily controlled. Eldridge Brindley was a porter, from North Preston, very respectable and close to the church hierarchy. And there was Jesse Dillard, a rather strange appointment. He worked with the Halifax recreation department and was its director, or soon would be. Jesse was well-liked but he wasn't even involved in the Black community before W.P. put him on the Committee. So you'd have to say, by the time all these extra appointments came on, that we had an overbalance of conservatives and other people close to W.P. who would be setting up the new Black United Front. Denny and Keith and I, and sometimes with Clyde Bishop depending on the issue, would be on one side, and the rest of them would be on the other. It wasn't exactly what the Panthers had in mind when they first came up with the idea.

Then, when they had a proposal ready with the help of local federal officials, W.P. and Gus made a secret trip to Ottawa to talk to Allan MacEachen, Minister of Manpower and Immigration and Nova Scotia's representative in the Cabinet, and Gerard Pelletier, Secretary of State, along with some senior civil servants. Keith Prevost was supposed to be included, but he took the position that this was wrong so he backed out. They met in Pelletier's office in

January 1969, but apparently Pelletier himself was ill and couldn't be there. The basic pitch was that the militants were a danger and would take control of BUF, but if they had government money and a tighter structure then the moderates could keep the radicals out of it. Of course I didn't know about these details at the time, or even that Gus and W.P. had gone to Ottawa. I didn't find out until they returned to Halifax to tell us that the feds were agreeable, and that all they had to do was refine their proposal and the money would be coming.

This is why we go off and create the ACLM, Afro-Canadian Liberation Movement. We were holding these meetings in the Prizefighters Club, freedom school type discussions about how we should get the initiative back. This is when Lemuel Sealey surfaces. Lem was a medical doctor. I don't recall that he had been involved in the debate up until then, but he was friends with Keith Prevost and when we used to go over to Keith's club, the Prizefighter, on a Sunday afternoon, Lem would show up. Some of us were disillusioned with the way BUF was shaping up. We didn't have any influence within the church framework, and we recognized that we had to have some sort of secular organization, and we also recognized that we had to have an organization that was cultural/nationalist in approach that would recognize the international aspect of the movement. Lem Sealey had the intellectual background about these issues and he was articulate and committed to the struggle, and he became a natural person to chair this group. We were careful in choosing the name. We wanted the word Africa in it to show that it was international and connected to our perception that we were Africans in the Diaspora, and we also wanted the word Canadian in it, to make it clear that it was not an American movement. We used the word Liberation to portray the revolutionary nature and philosophy of the organization, and we didn't want it to be seen as an organization that would have certain fixed parameters that would be limiting. We wanted it to be seen as a movement that would be fluid and flexible and open to all of the people.

The leadership of the ACLM was basically the same leadership that was in the left of BUF and what I would call the cultural nationalists in the movement. Keith Prevost, Denny Grant, Lem Sealey, myself, some of the people who had been involved at Kwacha, Woody Tolliver, Dennis Symonds. First and foremost our role was to educate each other and to educate the community, so we had a lot of study groups, just a lot of talk. We formed the ACLM because there was a void and there was a need for a cultural/national organization to speak to the needs as we saw them. I'm not saying there wasn't a Marxist element, but a classical Marxist analysis would not account for the racial issues. You can talk about the dialectic, the role of the proletariat, and all the things that a Marxist analysis gives, but we superimposed a cultural analysis that was important for us.

We adopted the philosophy being advanced by the Black Panther Party, which says that self-defence is essential to the survival of the people and in order to defend your people you must be prepared to defend your communities, and you must be proactive in your community. Self-defence is not only the power to pick up a gun and fire a bullet; that is not the only way the community needs to be defended. The community needs to be defended against economic inroads and people buying up the land and taking over the land base that a community can develop. The community has got to be defended by the educational programs being opened up, people being allowed to get an education so they can compete. The defence has got to be to feed the community. And so in Nova Scotia that is what is being played out, exactly the same as the Panthers. Both Lem Sealey and myself had gone through a pacifist stage, both Lem and myself had adopted nonviolence as a strategy, and both Lem and myself had moved through that to develop a Black nationalist strategy and to reject the concept that nonviolence is the solution. Both of us move to the position where we were believers in a philosophy that says, if it is necessary to use violence, and if violence is perpetrated against you, then you can respond in kind.

So we issued a manifesto, published in the first issue of a tabloid newspaper we called *The ACLM*, in March 1969. We wrote: "The time has come for Black People to unite. We must come together as a race of people, and work towards solving of our problems collectively." We said our aim was to revolutionize the Black community from within, to create "a Black consciousness and identity through the awareness of our history and the revival of our culture, a liberation of the mind from the deliberately imposed conditioning by white society in order to enable a proper re-evaluation and a true definition of ourselves." We ended on a militant note, dedicating ourselves to "the elimination of all forms of racial oppression, social and economic injustices against Black People — *by whatever means necessary*. To this end we pledge our lives." The echoes of Malcolm X, of course, were quite deliberate.

As a community development technique, to get people aroused and involved, we decided to rename Citadel Hill as Maroon Hill. There was already the Maroon Bastion, with a plaque on it, recognizing the role of the Maroons in building it in the 1790s. We wanted the whole Hill, or really we wanted to put something out that would unite ordinary people in claiming their history. We had about 200 people there for an elaborate dedication ceremony, and everybody was very excited, but the name didn't stick. We also got the ACLM involved in any of the political hot-button issues of the day. We submitted a brief to the Human Rights Commission when it was undertaking a review of the Human Rights Act, arguing that they should be addressing the underlying systemic issues rather than limiting themselves to daily instances of discrimination. In a reminder of Kwacha, we called for a special police force of 12 men, jointly appointed by the city and by the community, to patrol the Black neighbourhoods. The NSAACP opposed it, of course, and the idea was crushed. The most important thing about the ACLM was that it provided a different voice for the community besides the BUF apologists and the NSAACP. We did consider ourselves to be in "opposition" to a certain faction in BUF, but we were not opposed to BUF itself. After all BUF was supposed to be an umbrella, and the ACLM could be included under that umbrella. Our existence was not a rejection of BUF at all. There should be room for everybody in BUF. The politicking would continue, and our side continued to be out-manoeuvred.

While all this was going on, I was still a history student at Dalhousie. I especially tried to keep up with my reading for the Shepperson seminar on Africa and the Diaspora, and with my written assignments, sometimes with the help of Jim Walker, a PhD student. He also helped me with some of my speeches. We'd go to the History Department house on LeMarchant Street in the evening with a bottle of rum and a few cigars and knock around some ideas that I could shape into a speech. Sometimes we did this in the kitchen at our house, with various other people participating. This way I was able to expand my ideas, and get some meat into my presentations, though I'd have to say that mostly they were spontaneous, driven by adrenalin on the spot. I believe that of the hundreds of speeches I was making at that time, only one ended up being preserved in print. It was in a transcript of a teach-in at St. Francis Xavier University in January 1969, in a publication called *The Black Man in Nova Scotia: Teach-In Report.*

The St. F.X. teach-in occurs at a time when Lincolnville is going through some changes. Lincolnville is a Black community outside of Antigonish, one of three Black communities in that immediate area; the other two are Sunnyville and Upper Big Tracadie. There are also some Black people who live in the town of Guysborough and a few in and around Canso. The Coady Institute had attempted to organize Black people in that area and set up a pottery kiln, and help them in terms of community development. The Coady tried to help them define their problems and to help the community work on them. The land where the original Black Loyalists had settled had been taken over by whites, and the Black community had shifted to the worst land possible. It was almost impossible for the Black people to make a living. It was the same kind of land as Preston, rocky, very thin soil, scrub trees, that kind of thing. All they had was working in the woods part-time, or sometimes working partially in the fisheries. They had all of the problems in that area of abject poverty, with no real chance of long-term employment. At the same time there was a landfill going in at Lincolnville. It was at a time when all of these problems were surfacing, plus there were racial flare-ups between some young people from this outlying area and the people in town. Additionally, there were problems with Black people in Antigonish proper, finding employment and accommodations in the town. So the whole area there was just percolating.

People were brought in from all over the place as speakers at the teach-in. You had people at the Coady, Africans for example, who came from countries where Black people had control of their own affairs, and they had a different perspective. W.P. was speaking, and Donnie Oliver, and Joe Drummond from New Brunswick. Henry Bourgeois, a government official, gave some interesting statistics: at that time in Guysborough County, in a total Black labour force of 3,658 people, two-thirds earned less than $2,000 a year. Donnie's position invariably was that racism was a direct result of an individual's attitude towards other people, and that you could eliminate racism by cleaning up those individuals, those bad apples. Donnie was part of the establishment so he never took the view that the society had to be restructured. Joe Drummond on the other hand was very grassroots. He saw the system as being corrupt, he believed that racism was institutionalized and that we had to attack and change institutions, and that it had to be done by Black people for Black people. W.P. explained what was going on with the Black United Front, and in answer to a question he mentioned that he had just returned from Ottawa and government funding was more or less in the bag. I believe that was the first public admission of this government arrangement, and it's possible W.P did not intend to make an announcement, maybe it just slipped out as he was answering a question.

I gave them a very provocative, racially-charged speech, and I guess I upset a lot of people, especially when I called for separate meetings for the Black people in attendance, separate from the whites, the idea that we should have mini-family meetings during the afternoon session. My suggestion was accepted, but there was a lot of disagreement from the white people there.

There were about 800 or 900 people altogether, and probably almost half of them were white. I did encourage the young Black people to become involved with BUF and make sure BUF truly served the needs of the community. As much as I thought BUF was corrupt I also realized that you had to be inside of it in order to have any influence in it or even to know what was going on. And I believed that if they carried on with all their hand-picked people then we were really in trouble. In my speech I also pressed home the systemic definition of racism. I said you could shoot all the honkies you want but it still won't cure racism; we've got to get to a new level of analysis, to identify the real roots of our problems. The people coming from Guysborough County and Antigonish were really starting to get a sense of their own power, because prior to that teach-in the Coady hierarchy were making all the decisions. Even though the Coady was talking about participatory democracy and teaching it to the students from all over the world, when it came to the local community they were very paternalistic. At this teach-in the people said we don't want you telling us what to do, we're going to have a separate meeting and we're going to discuss our own problems, and people from the Coady were very upset. In fact the people at St. F.X. thought I was inciting their local people and that I was a really bad influence. It was my suggestion to have that separate meeting, but people will only do what they feel is important to them. Out of this St. F.X. teach-in I do believe there was a decision that the community would take over the kiln and control it, instead of the control being in the hands of the people from the Coady, which was a really quite a revolutionary thing for them.

Almost immediately after the teach-in I get a call from Rosie to come to Montreal and speak to a rally at Sir George Williams University. In fact I think at first they were calling it a teach-in. There is a large literature now on this event, "the Riot at Sir George," "the Computer Centre Party," but I have a different take on some of it. The outline of the story is well-established. There is a conflict between the Black students and a professor of biology, and the rejection by the university of the legitimate concerns of the Black students. The students, Black and white, stage a sit-in in the foyer on the main floor. This is an urban university, all in one high-rise building. The leadership of the occupation was mostly Juanita Westmoreland, Rosie Douglas, Anne Cools, Leroy Butcher, Leon Jacobs. They wanted me to come to speak to the students who were there doing the sit-in. That's where I spoke, in the downstairs foyer, to a couple of hundred people. I don't know what I said to this day, but it was a fist cutter. I said things like "Either this society will come around or we'll burn it down" and "We have to storm the Bastille." And right after my speech the students went upstairs and took over the computer centre. Now that was not my intention, I had no idea. I don't want to put myself in the position for taking any praise or blame, but that's the way it went down. So the students do this, but it's not the Black students that do it, it's the white students. And now we have these meetings and there's a debate. The Black students are the leaders, and they have to decide what to do now. I don't know that I've seen this so much in the published accounts. We know it's not going to last forever, and sooner or later the cops are coming, so the debate is what should the Black students do. My position is, and some of the others agreed, that the Black leadership had to get out, that they couldn't afford to go to jail and that we didn't have a broad enough base to have these people put away. But the other side argued that the white students were young, they had no experience, they didn't know what they were doing, they were just being very emotional, and they couldn't be left to take that kind of heat without Black people staying with them. And this was quite a dilemma, especially for Rosie. I said, "Rosie, you cannot go to jail," and Rosie said, "Well if it happens what do you expect, I mean I can't leave, you just can't leave these kids out there." And I said, "These kids have got rich parents, they've got money, and you haven't got anything. You can't go to jail Rosie." So this was the argument, and then we tried to determine if it happened, who was expendable enough to let them be arrested. But that's a pretty hard discussion to have. It was an impossible, impossible situation. If the whole thing had been planned, there may have been some contingencies set up to deal with all of this, but because it was an impromptu occupation, planning after the fact became extremely difficult. And at any rate I was leaving to go back to Nova Scotia on Sunday night, and they were still involved in the sit-in.

So I'm not there when the big thing goes down, but I did talk to the people involved at the time and this is what I understand. The decision when I left, as far as I knew, was that if anything happened the Black leadership would get out. But they got soft-hearted and went up with the white students. What happens is that there's a fire in a wastepaper basket, either purposeful or acci- dental, the fire creates smoke, someone pulls the fire alarm and there is mass confusion. The fire brigade comes, and in looking for the fire they cut the wires to the mainframe computer. There was never a deliberate attempt to set the computers on fire, it was totally accidental. It's true students were throwing computer cards out the window, etcetera, but that was all spontaneous, all in the confusion and excitement of the moment. Ninety people were arrested, 40 Black and 50 white.

But the Black leadership was not supposed to be arrested and they all were, and that creates another problem because with the leadership now in jail there's no one to organize quickly to get them out. The people who can do that, the ones who have the skills and contacts, they're the ones who are in jail. It creates a complete and total confusion. Eventually you have the intervention of some of the Black professors and some of the people in the community, and they start getting people out of jail, but by that time some of the mindset in the white community has already been formalized that these students have wrecked the computer, started a fire, and it seems like it was a total intent to destroy everything in the university, anarchy, and it wasn't that at all. It's really interesting how the Black students got vilified when in fact they tried to protect those white students and help them. The press and public opinion were determined to leave the Black students in jail. It took a lot of work for a lot of people. The judges didn't want to let them out, the community, everybody blamed the Black students, that's the bottom line, which really bothered me because I knew a different story. I did a lot of speaking at the time, travelling, trying to raise bail money, but also to say to people "Hey listen, the Black students didn't cause this."

By now I'm really getting a reputation as a radical. Because of my association with Stokely and now, after Sir George especially, I'm regarded as a real threat to Canadian society. People are coming to me, interviewing me, to get the "radical perspective" on this and that. One of them was Martin O'Malley from the *Globe and Mail*. Jim Walker was in the house when O'Malley arrived, in the basement cleaning a shotgun of mine after we'd been out duck hunting. That trip was a couple of weeks before. Meanwhile I went out after geese and got a frozen foot. O'Malley comes into our house and I'm lying on the couch with this frozen foot. He's asking me all these questions about the radical movement, when Jim comes back upstairs to return my clean gun. O'Malley of course assumes he's a white revolutionary coming to my house to give me a gun. That's what he wrote. That was his perspective on my whole existence at that time. He was focusing on violence, potential violence. The story, when it appeared in the *Globe Magazine* in February 1969, had the title "Rocky the Revolutionary." I was always being called to speak on the radio for a minute or two or five. They would say "Who can we call across the country? Who would be good for a few minutes?" In a way it gave me power, because they were actually listening to me. My goal was to explain the position of Black people and what had happened, and what was happening, and what the solutions had to be in my view. In this way the press was good to me — why I don't know because I've insulted them enough.

One quite big example was when I was invited to participate in a TV show called *Under Attack*, held at Convocation Hall at the University of Toronto in April 1969. A huge crowd filled the Hall, students mostly but also professors and the general public. The organizers knew what I was going to say, or at least the line I would be taking. I'm still trying to raise money for Sir George and I'm willing to take anything at all. If someone calls me and says I want you at this high school in Edmonton and if they're going to pay my way and the money can be sent to them in Montreal, I'll do it. I was just totally committed to fundraising at that point. When I did that show in Toronto I've got four years of experience dealing with politicians, W.P. Oliver, students, large audiences and small, so I'm reasonably polished and knowledgeable and I go into this panel at U of T feeling confident. And they come after me. What I was saying, my basic thesis, was that society as we knew it was corrupt, and our political system as we knew it was corrupt, and that we had to restructure society, and that Black people were used as a source of cheap but readily available labour. That meant we had to be close to where they needed us. You had to have Black communities surrounding major cities, or in concentrated areas within cities, so that you could draw upon this labour whenever you wanted to. And the white working class, contrary to what the unionists tried to say, was in fact a reactionary class with regard to Black people, and that wasn't because they were inherently racist but because racism was built right into the system. I would take positions like that, and the panelists attacked me, and so did the audience in the question period. I was really "under attack." All of my beliefs were put to the test, everything was tested that day, but I had my firm convictions and nothing could change my mind. Maybe I converted some of them, maybe I didn't, but at least I was getting heard. Some of the reports of that program claimed I was advocating world-wide revolution. In a way I suppose that was true, but they missed the real point. If the blinkers are violent, then the message that comes through is read as violent.

Behind my back, in fact totally unknown to me at the time, there are people from BUF consulting with Secretary of State officials to put together an acceptable proposal to Ottawa. A senior man from Ottawa, Larry Heinemann, was very instrumental, along with some of their local representatives. It's interesting that government people are designing a plan to be presented to the government for funding for BUF. I understand that a final draft was ready by the spring of 1969, at least to the satisfaction of the civil servants and the leaders of BUF. BUF was to be a separate organization after all, not an umbrella as originally intended, and there would be representatives from each Black community in the province. This case is being carried by John Munro, the Minister of Health and Welfare, along with Gerard Pelletier, the Secretary of State. But it still has not been approved by the political leadership, the federal cabinet. Well Munro goes public prematurely, and during a speech he says he is giving money to the Black United Front in Halifax so that the Black people there can "raise hell." Hell was raised all right, but not by BUF. People all over the country begin objecting, complaining that this radical Rocky Jones is going to receive government money to attack and undermine our society. Munro had to back off, and W.P. separated himself from me publicly, saying I advocated violence but BUF wanted constructive relations with the government. In June Heinemann and another federal official named Cam Mackie met with the Interim Committee. I was still a member, so I was included. As usual I pointed out that we had no mandate to accept government money, that government money in any case would poison our fundamental purpose, that BUF was supposed to be an umbrella of other Black organizations, and above all we were obliged to go back to another Family Meeting before proceeding with any plan. Denny Grant and Keith Prevost were supporting me in these meetings. But the plan went ahead anyway. That same month, June 1969, Munro and a bunch of his officials came down to Halifax, and they did a tour out to North Preston. With him he brought reporters from outside newspapers, and they gave this visit a lot of publicity. The *Ottawa Journal* claimed that Halifax was "close to a race riot," and called North Preston "a Black ghetto of poverty." The *Toronto Star* also claimed that the situation in Halifax was "explosive," and they added "if BUF doesn't work, the revolution may be much, much worse." Imagine! This whole "threat of violence" thing had been constructed, essentially by W.P. and Gus and their cohort, in order to frighten the government into giving them money. Now it is being accepted across the country. Unless BUF gets the nod from Ottawa, I'm going to launch a revolution!

As I have later learned, the BUF proposal was taken to a cabinet committee by Munro and Pelletier, and they accepted it. But then it had to go to the full cabinet, and there Pierre Trudeau himself had objections. The June 1969 White Paper on Indian Affairs had just been introduced, and Trudeau said that we couldn't be trying to remove distinctions between whites and Indians and at the same time create a separate organization for Blacks. So Munro and Pelletier give their proposal a new purpose. As Munro said when he announced the grant, it was to help solve a poverty problem, not a race problem. This argument was accepted by the full cabinet, because it didn't contradict the government's integration policy, and the money was granted. Not only that, the amount of the grant was actually larger than they had been asking for. They got a budget of $100,000 a year for five years, $500,000! But there were still more problems. The provincial government was now objecting to the whole operation. They wanted a hand in controlling BUF, afraid that if Black people had control something real might happen. A compromise was worked out, that there would be a "liaison committee" with provincial officials to approve BUF expenditures. W.P. accepted this condition, and there was a meeting with the Interim Committee, or some of them, where a vote was taken. I was not even aware of this meeting. Well, the Interim Committee members present voted in favour. This cleared the way, and just two days later there was a formal ceremony at the Nova Scotian Hotel, where Munro makes his announcement. It was August 15, 1969. I was surprised to see that Denny Grant was up there on the platform with him, along with other members of the Interim Committee. I had not been invited. Perhaps I would have declined the invitation anyway, but in fact I never got the chance. I was just side-lined. In September the elections for the BUF Council were held, two representatives from each Black community. They came together and elected a new Board of Directors, to replace the Interim Committee. I was not elected to the Board.

But if I was out of the leadership of BUF, I was still connected to the Halifax community. I think the most exciting community event around that time was Encounter Week, in February 1970. There was a lot of optimism in Halifax, more enthusiasm for positive change than any other time I had experienced previous to that, or after that. When I think of it, it was more like the end of the 1960s than the beginning of the seventies. I was not one of the organizers; it was more or less done out of city hall, but I was consulted by the organizers and I participated in everything that was going on. Allan O'Brien was mayor, and the city brought in a whole bunch of experts who visited places in the community and then had plenary sessions to discuss what they had seen and what their analysis was. This gave the citizens a great chance to give feedback and talk about their community, and what was wrong and what needed correction. It was the calibre of the people invited, the experts, that got everybody so excited. The leader of the pack was Saul Alinsky, undoubtedly the leading expert on community organizing in North America if not the world. He had done organizing work in Black communities in the States already, and on Indian reserves in Canada, so he was quite sensitive to racial issues as well as poverty. We had just gone through a period of confrontations, and a lot of issues had surfaced. I think that people believed at that time that we could solve a lot of problems, and they got so involved in the Encounter series because we hoped collectively to get some answers, some advice from these experts. The city spent a lot of money. They had buses to take these people to different places. It was like having a basketball team or a bunch of celebrities. And they were treated as celebrities too, they were given a lot of deference. And their daily reports were very important to the community. The whole city was really into what these experts were saying about our town. And the experts made it clear that they were going to say exactly what they thought without taking any sides, so people had a belief that they were going to get the real goods or, like the experience of the Black community in particular, get researched but never get the benefits of the research or even any knowledge of what the research has really said. In this instance, they would be talking to Black people during the day, gathering information on a particular issue and discuss it the very same day in the media. This had never happened before, anywhere, to my knowledge. And it was extremely successful, in as much as it heightened a lot of the contradictions that existed, between the wealthy and the poor, the government and the people, Blacks and whites. Out of Encounter people looked at some solutions, and in terms of awareness of the issues in the city, as an educational tool, it was incredible.

I have to credit Allan O'Brien; the Encounter series was consistent with his kind of thinking. I knew him personally very well. He was very supportive of the initiatives we had been involved in with Kwacha, and in fact sat on our board before he became mayor. And we were very supportive of his candidacy; I like to think we were a part of the reason for his success. There are very few things that I can look at that have been the brainchild of the bureaucracy or the government that I can commend, very few, but certainly the Encounter Week would be one. It was much more than therapeutic, because it illuminated the problems and there was a way of looking for resolutions that we just did not have before. Through Encounter we could get direct dialogues. Even persons representing industry felt they had to outline their position on things, which before they didn't have to do, but because of Encounter they had to respond and take positions and it opened the dialogue to such an extent that some people were able to talk to others who were completely different, different economic classes and social classes. You'd have somebody in abject poverty and the other person being the boss of some industrial initiative, and they were both treated equally by these Encounter visitors. In these sessions you couldn't hide behind the fact that you were an industrialist; your policies were there and open for scrutiny and you had to be prepared to defend it or speak to it. I recall Saul Alinsky talking about pushing a weight up a hill and the struggle to do that, and how it required many hands and many backs to move this an inch at a time. It was very graphic, an example of why and how a community has to work together to get something achieved. That was part of his message, "You've got to organize and unite." I can to this day remember, it was so simple a concept, that you need many backs pushing and you are only going to get an inch at a time.

I think the Encounter experience is what inspired the Black community, maybe for the first time, to get involved as a group in municipal affairs. Almost immediately after Encounter Week the city announced that they were hiring a new city manager, a guy from Oklahoma named Robert Oldland. The union movement researched this guy, and found that he is a union buster. Gus Wedderburn phoned some contacts in Oklahoma City, people in the NAACP, and learned that this guy is considered a racist as well. Now we had the ear of the mayor, or thought we did. He was a known supporter of the Black community, a member of the NDP, generally a progressive person. So a group of us spoke to him and we said, "Look, you can't bring this guy in. He's racist, he's anti-union, he's everything we don't want." The mayor refused to do anything. He may have felt that he was stuck with a decision that he couldn't back away from. It was a unanimous city council that had made the offer to Oldland. This meant that we had to organize and show that we were serious, and O'Brien's supporters would either have to be on our side or against us; there was no possibility of compromise on this one. It split the so-called progressive white community because many of the NDPers and many Allan O'Brien supporters were quite prepared to support him just because it was him. He said, "Look don't worry, it will work out okay." So Halifax was quite split among the so-called radicals and progressives. Then it was a question of trying to get to O'Brien again, after seeing the split in his own constituency, and taking the results of our research to him. We actually were able to get letters from Oklahoma City confirming that this guy had a reputation and a record that was anti-union and anti-Black. And Allan O'Brien still wouldn't change his position.

We decided that we would make a delegation for a presentation at the city council meeting. They had some rule or practice that all you could do was put your name on the list, and you could get five minutes to speak at the council, and they were able to limit the number of speakers. We had a meeting, Gus, W.P., Keith Prevost, myself, a number of us, prior to going to city council. This issue united every faction in the Black community. At the meeting I suggested that we would have to go to jail over this issue. If necessary we would have to sit in, occupy the council chamber, take over the council meeting, to get a chance to make our position clear. And I proposed that W.P. Oliver be the lead and go to jail. He had the most stature, and if they put W.P. in jail then the whole of Nova Scotia is going to be upset. We could bring the city to its knees. W.P. almost choked. He wouldn't go to jail and Gus wouldn't go to jail. So I'm saying, "Well if you guys are not prepared to go to jail, well, I am. You're in a leadership position, and right now you need to be right out front and prepared to take whatever it is you need to take." Gus later liked to tell the story that when I said, "W.P. you have to go to jail," Gus is saying, "I damn near fell off my chair!" But he left out the part where he himself says, "I'm not going to jail." I had to be nuts to think they would. Even though we ended up on the same side, to me they showed their true colours. But we did agree to call for a mass rally the night of the council meeting, and according to reports there were over a thousand people outside city hall. We sent in a small delegation to see how the council is receiving us, but they won't budge. Then, according to the reports, 400 of us enter the council chamber. I don't see how you get 400 in there, but it's true that people were standing and sitting on the sides, everywhere. At any rate we go in with as many people as possible, and we're jammed into the council meeting. I think there were more Blacks in there than white unionists, but I'm not entirely sure. So we're in there, and I'm prepared to defer to W.P. or Gus as my seniors. But no, they tell me I should be the one to speak on behalf of the delegation. The entire delegation is on my side, they're agreeing with everything I say, they're cheering. I don't remember my words, but there's no doubt that I'm speaking on behalf of many many people in Halifax that night. The councillors don't actually admit that they don't care how racist Oldland is. They say they made a job offer in writing and the case is closed. Surely they would have known that he couldn't have done the job if he did come. Halifax was a unionized city and the unions were absolutely united against Oldland. Afterwards Gus came over to me and shook my hand and said, "Rocky, you showed true leadership tonight." I appreciated that, even if city council didn't. But after this display of opposition, Oldland himself withdrew his application. He bowed out. I think this whole episode may have been the beginning of the end for Allan O'Brien. It certainly disillusioned many of his followers. He had tremendous support in the Black community and among the leftists, and a lot of that support eroded. For those of us who organized that delegation, the unity did not last. It did not provide a lasting momentum for further cooperation, but there would be some meaningful occasions.

The Oldland Affair, as it came to be known, had another consequence, or so I truly believe. First some background. Joan and I decided we needed a new place to live. We had all these kids, we had all these people coming to stay with us, we were paying rent and the rent kept going up. We knew we had to buy a house. A house on Cunard Street became available, part of an estate, and it had over a dozen rooms and the furniture was already in it so we didn't have to worry about finding furniture. And the price was right. I called Lou Moyer, who was doing insurance, he later became a judge, and I say, "I just bought this house and I need to have it insured," and he said, "No problem." I did not give him any money or anything. "No problem, we've got it covered, come on down tomorrow, I'll do the papers and give me some money then." I say, "Okay, we've got a deal." That was in the afternoon, I think on a Thursday. We had not moved in yet. That same evening someone set that house on fire. It had shingles and they were able to pull up the shingles and start the fire under the shingles. The fire literally went up the side of the house. Fortunately no one was there. The fire squad came and put it out, but it had been quite an extensive fire. So the next day I called Lou Moyer, and I said "My house caught on fire." And he said, "Okay, it was insured." I said, "Well, I didn't give you any money or anything," and he said, "We made a deal, you're insured, don't worry about it." That's how much integrity that guy had. So, the insurance pays for it, we get the house fixed up and we move in.

This house had a small pantry in the back, less than a storey high. It was seven feet outside, and the next level went to the second floor, where the children had bedrooms, and we had our bedroom, and on the third level were rooms we rented to boarders. We'd been living there for no more than two months, the kids were asleep, and we were in bed, and bang, bang, at the door at about two o'clock in the morning. There was a tendency not to answer knocking at the door because of the life that we were living, but we go to the door, and Murray Langford is there and he says, "Your house is on fire!" "What?" We go around the back and sure enough the house is on fire. Well, we rush to get the kids out, and everybody gets out, and the fire engine comes and they put the fire out, and there's extensive damage in the back. Our house was next door to the Legion. Murray Langford was in the Legion and stepped out back for a minute, and that's how he saw the fire. The fire was going up the whole back of the house, right where the kids were sleeping. If he hadn't spotted the fire and woken us up, it would have burnt up everybody in the house.

That fire was deliberately set. It was discovered that they had poured coal oil all over the back, and it ran from the second floor over the pantry roof. We were just blessed. Normally you wouldn't see the back part of our house from the Legion. They never found out who did it. No charges were ever laid. That was two fires, and nobody saw who did it. Now here is something strange. I was under constant surveillance from the RCMP. We knew this at the time and it has been confirmed by documents I got through Freedom of Information. They had officers assigned to me, watching my every move. They were paranoid. In the documents you can see that they classified the "Black radicals" as the number one threat to security, along with the separatists in Quebec. They are bugging my phone, following my car, watching my house. Why wouldn't they have seen somebody starting those fires?

Why do I link this to the Oldland Affair? Feelings were very hot about that in certain quarters, and because I had organized the rally and I had spoken in the council meeting, I was seen as having a certain power, or influence. I could rouse people up and maybe cause some real trouble. Our influence was broadening. We had labour, we had white leftists, we had just ordinary Black people all coming together to stop Oldland. Somebody decided I had to be slowed down. If the Mounties didn't do it themselves, they must or could have known who did it. They were burning barns in Quebec, after all. And another thing. Not long after this, my store in Scotia Square was robbed for the second time, when the Square was closed, overnight. They went in over the wall, robbed my whole store and got out. The place was locked up solid. No other place in the whole Square but mine was touched. And the money they could get from taking the clothes wouldn't have been worth it for any real thieves; it wouldn't be worth the risk or the effort. They stole it all, over a thousand dollars worth of goods. It could easily have put me out of business. And it happened twice! I lost my credit rating; I had to make a deal with my suppliers to pay off $25 a month, because I couldn't cover the whole thing all at once. It took years and years to climb out of the hole. My leather suppliers wouldn't give me any more credit, and that's why I switched from leather to jewelry. The jewelry suppliers hadn't been affected by the robberies, so they were still willing to give me credit and we were able to carry on. It did come close to slowing me down, but it sure didn't stop me. If the Mounties weren't doing this, or collaborating in it, or allowing it by turning their heads, how would you explain it? I know what I believe.

So maybe we didn't get the revolution we thought we could get, through Kwacha and the Panthers, the Family Meeting, the ACLM and the Black United

Front. And maybe that's why writers like Tariq Ali have ignored us. But I think we do deserve attention, because serious changes were made, a real momentum was started, and those changes were genuinely revolutionary. We introduced the discussion of systemic discrimination, an idea that has become orthodox in human rights and race relations everywhere in Canada. We launched a cultural awareness that would grow to produce Black poetry and film and a renewed interest in folk-lore. Blacks in Nova Scotia moved from being a "category," which we were put into by others, by whites, and moved into being a "people," self-defined. People identified as "Black" in a way that "Negro" was never an identity. When I was growing up, our attitude, if we want to admit it, was "white is right." We had pride in our family and pride in our community, in my case the Marsh, but we had bought into the idea that what whites had and what whites were like was the way it was supposed to be. As one significant example, like many other young Black people I used to straighten my hair. Everybody I knew did it. We used to take Gillett's lye, soap and potatoes, and stir it up. And the pot you were stirring it in would be red hot, so you couldn't handle it. And you take that on a comb and put it on top of your hair, and comb it through, and it straightened your hair. And it burned your scalp! The idea was that you would have this nice straight hair. The words that were used were "she has got good hair, quality hair." That meant her hair is like white people's hair. When I became political I used to say in my speeches that Black people had hair that stood up, stiff and curly. It wasn't weak; it didn't just fall down like white people's hair. If you let your hair grow it went straight up in the air and that is strength and power, and we should acknowledge the power we have as a race of people. If we make our hair limp, we are buying into a weakness. Your hair became a symbol, something that declared your pride in being Black. People didn't just walk, they strode in their new Afro, they moved with pride. A real re-assessment was underway. This was revolutionary, believe me, and it set a foundation for more exciting things that would happen in the Black community in the 1970s.

Chapter Seven

COMMUNITY, CULTURE AND POLITICS

My public role changes during the 1970s. I begin to be sought after by established agencies, whereas before I was focusing the debates around them and against them. In the seventies, in fact, I was starting some new agencies or joining new ones, to help them move along. I didn't think of it as being co-opted but as a logical progression given my circumstances.

Education was a huge issue in our community in the sixties and seventies. Officially, segregated schools in Nova Scotia ended in 1954, but you still had de facto segregation, where the community lived around a school and that neighbourhood school would be all-Black. This was quite common in the rural areas, and often the school would only go to, say, grade 7. If kids finished grade 7 before reaching school-leaving age, they would just repeat that grade until they were old enough to quit. In the urban areas you had streaming, so that the academic opportunities for Black students were being limited by the biases of teachers and administrators. Historically, whether urban or rural, Black kids did not get through high school. In Nova Scotia, prior to the 1960s and 1970s, most people could survive without a high-school diploma. The jobs were such that the employers were not demanding that level. But then, either through government initiatives or through employers themselves, education levels for the entry into certain jobs increased, higher and higher. Black students were not keeping pace with those education levels and so they were getting excluded from employment. In earlier times trades were passed from father to son, mother to daughter. You could learn carpentry from your father, and it was other carpenters who decided if you were qualified. It was totally controlled by the tradespeople in the community. Then the government got involved in developing formal apprenticeship programs and formal certification of trades, and for this young people needed literacy. Many were coming from situations where they did not have the resources to gain the needed degree of literacy, and more importantly, the education system was seen as hostile or racist for Black people, so we saw them dropping out of the system at a faster rate and with lower grade levels than their white counterparts. We can see the impact of this in the construction industry. In order to be a certified bricklayer you had to do an apprenticeship and you had to write tests. Black people who had been bricklayers for years could not get that certification. This meant they could only be helpers to "qualified" bricklayers, and yet they were doing the same work. In the practical sense the trades still existed, but in a formal sense they virtually disappeared. So Black people went into the kinds of trades that didn't require certification, like cement workers. These trends, of course, affected the amount of money you got paid, and the quality of life for the family.

In Professor Shepperson's seminar at Dalhousie we would have discussions along these lines, and we carried them on in the kitchen on Pepperell Street. We were always debating, where do you start to make the change, do you try to change things at the elementary level, or the secondary level, or the university level. If we weren't getting people into university, we wouldn't have the kind of leadership we needed as a community. We also recognized that because of streaming, Black students were not in the university preparatory program. They could never get into a university even if they finished high school. I was a rare exception, very rare, given my slim qualifications.

There was a moment when all this discussion became focused, and turned into action. In October 1968 I talked Jim Walker into going duck hunting with me. He'd been part of these discussions, and I felt it would be a bonding experience, to strengthen our friendship. Although he'd never been hunting before, and I think was a bit cool on the idea, I sold it to him as a kind of camping trip. I lent him one of my guns, and even a pair of waders because he didn't have anything of his own. When we got out there and we're unloading my truck he says, "Where's the tent?" "What tent?" "Well you said it was going to be like a camping trip." "No, no," I said, "this is survival quality stuff. We have to build a lean-to to sleep in, we have to build a duck blind." He likes to tell the story of our hardships. It was so cold we actually zipped our sleeping bags into a double, and brought my Lab in with us to stay warm. But it was during that weekend in the woods, when we had time to talk and think and debate, that we reached the conclusion that the best place to start would be at the university entrance level, and we came up with the idea of a special program for Black kids who had dropped out of school, to upgrade their learning skills and their qualifications and even, hopefully, to allow some of them to get into university. There was a syndrome in operation, with low teacher expectations for Black students and Black students shaped their educational ambitions within those expectations. We were hoping to design an intervention into that syndrome so that some kids would be able to improve their education and show their abilities, and it would become self-perpetuating if parents and teachers recognized the potential for all Black students. At the time we were thinking of it as a surgical strike, not the establishment of a new permanent institution.

We weren't sure what kind of reception we'd get, from the community or from the university. We started small, getting a room in the Student Union Building to hold night classes. In a way it was like a continuation of what we had done in Kwacha, and in fact several Kwacha people came to our sessions. We helped them with homework if they were still in school, and we presented classes in Black history and culture just like in our freedom school. We invited Jules Oliver to join us, so there were basically the three of us plus occasional others doing the tutoring and teaching. This was in October 1968, just before Stokely came and more than a month before the Family Meeting. In our evening sessions we were passing on some of the things we were reading in Shepperson's Africa and the Diaspora course, and stuff from Jim's research on the Black Loyalists. Not long after we started we found out that Sylvia and Paul Norton were starting a similar group, focusing particularly on Black culture. They had Fred Ward, an African American poet and later novelist, as part of their team, so they were more involved with literature than we were. We all got together for meetings and planning, and it was out of this mixture that we decided to approach the university and ask for a full year, full time program for Black students. Sylvia enlisted the support of the grad student association, who came on strong in our support. I'd even say they left us behind. "Wow this is a great idea. Let's do it!" And the faculty association soon came on board, with leadership coming from a history professor, a South African of Indian descent named Bala Pillay, and from the dean of Arts and Science. With this kind of backing the Dalhousie Senate voted in favour, and the administration was convinced that it was a viable idea. They agreed to finance us for a trial period of two years.

But it wasn't just Dalhousie we had to deal with. All along we had the intention that this should be a community program, adopted and controlled by the community. We held a community meeting at the North End Library, in December 1969. Over a hundred people attended. We described the kind of program we had in mind, and we got their enthusiastic endorsement. Within a couple of months we had 82 applications from Black students, showing the degree of interest there was out there. But the issue of university control or community control came up almost immediately. Our attitude was that the Transition Year Program — now that it had its proper name — would be "at" but not "of" Dalhousie. They would provide us with the facilities and we would run the program. A community committee was set up, intending to make the major decisions. Lem Sealey, a central figure in getting the community's support, was on this committee, and Donna Byard (later Donna Sealey), and Frank Boyd. I was on it, and so was Sylvia Norton, so there was overlap with our original founding groups. But the university considered us as strictly an advisory body; Dalhousie had to have the final say.

The applicants were interviewed and selected based not only on their potential to do university studies, but their commitment to go back to work in their communities, to educate others. In fact the university gave us control over selection. For that first year's intake we chose 27 students, and this included Mi'kmaq students. When we first started to talk about the Transition Year Program, we were talking about a program just for Black students because for Aboriginal students there was already a program in Saskatchewan. But it was made clear to us that politically we would not get funding for a Black-only program. And, especially important, the Natives were eligible for independent funding of their own through the Department of Indian Affairs. There was also a lot of pressure for us to include whites, but we held that line very strongly: if we opened the program to white students, eventually whites would take over and there would be no Black or Aboriginal students whatsoever. Our program emphasized Black history, Black culture, Black music, Black literature. It would have destroyed it to have white students in there. We said, "Look, if you want a program for poor whites, go ahead and start your own. Ours is for Blacks." And, as it turned out, for Blacks and Natives.

The Natives weren't really supportive of the program at first. When we started trying to put it together we didn't have any Natives to bounce things off of or help us. The Union of Nova Scotia Indians was being organized at the same time as we were organizing TYP. If they had been part of the planning from the very beginning, we might have done things a bit differently. It is later that they get involved, after the concept is established. It was very paternalistic on our part, because the Union of Nova Scotia Indians were presented with a brief and a program that was already designed, though we did add Native Canadian history to our proposed curriculum. And so they were approached and we asked them if they wanted to send any students to Dalhousie, to TYP. And they explained that they had a program in Saskatchewan, but they would look at sending students here, since it was closer. So they were basically an afterthought. When they made their decision, at least they were able to select their own participants.

We opened our doors officially in September 1970. I must say Dalhousie was very supportive with resources. We were given a house on LeMarchant Street for our exclusive use, tucked right against the new Library building. We had a couple of classrooms there, and offices for those of us who didn't have homes in other departments. Three full-time faculty members were seconded to the program, and as far as I know their own departments paid their salaries for one course each, because there was no budget for them through TYP. Department chairs must have gone along with this. The regular faculty who taught in TYP sought the program out because they wanted to work with those particular students and do something in that program, and as such they had a certain political perspective. We had a senior professor from mathematics, Arnold Tingley. He was certainly not what one would consider left-wing, but he was completely committed to the program, he was committed to the students, he wanted to make it work. He had the students' welfare at heart, and he used his influence in the university to protect the program. We had an African American professor, Roy Overstreet, who taught science in the program and was equally committed. This was different work, and you might say more difficult work, from what they were used to in their home departments. Bala Pillay was our first director, paid for by the History Department. He didn't do any classroom teaching, but his administrative work took up a lot of his time. So all these people were making a sacrifice of their time.

Then there were some people employed directly by TYP. Fred Ward, who had been part of our organizing committee along with the Nortons, taught African and Diaspora literature, and Marty Sonkin taught remedial English skills. Marty was a white American who had trained with the U.S. military intelligence corps. There's no doubt he cared for the students, but he didn't socialize with us very much. And then there was Jim and me. We were paid $1,000 each for the entire school year. I think that must have been the rate for a teaching assistant, though we had responsibility for complete courses. I'm guessing Marty and Fred were paid the same as us. Jim taught Native and African Canadian history, and I taught African and African American history.

We had a lot of preparation to do, but the Shepperson course material came in handy. I really had a good time in class. I had the students reading Frantz Fanon and C.L.R. James, W.E.B. DuBois and Booker T. Washington. We had some great discussions and I really enjoyed every class.

So on the teaching faculty we had two African Americans (Overstreet and Ward), one white American (Sonkin), one African Canadian (Jones), two white Canadians (Tingley and Walker), presided over by a South African Indian (Pillay). We also had our own full-time secretary for the program, Valerie Brown, who was English. What a mix, and it was exciting, it was interesting, it was fun, and it worked. Before the beginning of term we all met and set up the curriculum, how many hours of this or that, what we wanted our courses to accomplish. There was no apparent interference from the Dal administration. We had regular meetings to discuss our courses and the students, just among ourselves, but we were never inspected or challenged about what we taught or how.

Because of the funding from the Department of Indian Affairs, we were able to rent an entire house for the Mi'kmaq students. They were coming from different parts of the province, and we thought it would be better for them if they were able to have a place where they could all live together. For some of them it was their first time in the city. I can't say whether it was a good idea or a bad idea, but they liked it that way and certainly nobody ever complained. We had some great parties in what we called the Indian House. Black students would end up there, staying overnight. I saw mornings when I had to go to the Indian House and drag them all out to get to a class. "You guys gotta get your ass up." The students told some amusing stories. When they came into the program, especially in those early years, they came with the same stereotypes and impressions of each other as were held in the larger society. The Aboriginal kids saw the Black kids as being from the ghetto, maybe threatening and violent. The Blacks had stereotypes of Indians as shiftless and drinkers. So both groups came not really knowing each other but being influenced by television or whatever they had heard. It was interesting to see how the two groups grew together and began to understand and respect each other. That part of the whole experience was just so worthwhile to watch and participate in. To see that transition, to see how these students grew, was very positive.

So these kids are all coming in with different backgrounds and in fact different levels of education and academic ability. But there's no doubt that it turned out to be a great success, and many of those kids went on to make major contributions to their communities with the help they got from their

TYP experience. Among the Indians there was Bernie Francis, a blue-eyed blond but as much Mi'kmaq as the rest of them, who ended up as a professor at the University College of Cape Breton. Russell Marshall became a chief, Joyce Gehue became head of the Mi'kmaq family and social services, Linda Julien became a teacher in the regular school system. Among the Black students from that first year we have similar stories. Louie Gannon joined the Y, continuing to work with youth. He became their director, and later director of the Black Cultural Centre. He often comes to me and says how TYP opened his mind to so many new ideas and opportunities. Louie Dixon also worked with youth as a basketball coach and manager. Irvine Carvery became head of the postal union in Halifax, was elected as a trustee and was eventually made chair of the Halifax Regional School Board. For years Irvine was president of the Africville Genealogy Society, fighting on behalf of the former Africville people and successfully negotiating with governments for compensation. Maisie James got a graduate degree in education and went on to teach in the school system. And then we had Ernie McLellan. He came from Lincolnville, without ever finishing public school. In our naïvete we thought that didn't matter, and we put him in with the other students and involved him with readings and discussions that were essentially at a university level. Not surprisingly, when the end of the year came he could not pass the exams and could not enter Dalhousie as a regular student. In the university's eyes, Ernie was a failure. But as far as we were concerned he was one of our great successes. Through a lot of encouragement and patience on the part of faculty and other students, Ernie learned an incredible amount. Although he did not use what he learned to get a university degree, he did use that skill to move himself forward in the union movement when he went out to work. He became an active trade unionist and a bus driver in the city of Halifax, which is a good, well-paying job. I've spoken to Ernie about the value of TYP to him. I was feeling, maybe we didn't do this guy any favours, and he explained that he was just absolutely thrilled to have the opportunity to come and he grew immensely. He told me, "You know it was the most fascinating experience that I ever had." He said that if he hadn't come to TYP he'd likely have ended up working in the woods part-time, not having any kind of a future. He learned things that there is no possibility that he would have ever learned in Guysborough and Antigonish Counties. He said he would be forever grateful that he had the opportunity to come up to Dalhousie and change his life.

Despite these, in my mind, absolutely great accomplishments, TYP was always under threat. After that first year, when we had virtually complete control, the Dalhousie administration stepped in and said they wanted to set the curriculum and say who passed. This is a Dalhousie program, they said, and Dalhousie must be able to have control over what goes on. That is one area where there was conflict and the other was the role of the advisory board. When the program was set up the ideas came from outside of the university, and people within the university who were sympathetic helped put the ideas together in a manner that would be acceptable to the administration and used their influence to get the program accepted and to keep the funding. However, the administration and some profs did not believe that a community group should control a university program. They did not see that these community people should have a direct role in recruitment, setting recruitment standards, evaluation, setting evaluation standards. The university maintained that this was a role for the university because it was Dalhousie's reputation at stake, Dalhousie resources to make the thing go. But, strangely, they did leave us alone for some time longer. When we were recruiting the second in-take of students, in the summer of 1971, I did virtually all of the selection, with Louise Young after a bit. We went to all of the schools, we selected the students, we did the interviews, we accepted whatever students we wanted to.

At the same time that community committee, the ones Dal thought should be advisory only, were staking their own claim to control the program. By this time people from BUF were on this committee too, and they wanted to wrest control back. Some of the people on the committee wanted me out. The idea is to get me out of TYP, because by then I have the students looking at these radical materials and I was spoiling young minds. As it turns out, surprisingly, I have the support of the faculty members on TYP staff, in particular Pillay, who is not prepared to allow these people to come in and get rid of me. I would not have had any power, internally, to make any decisions; the decisions were made by the faculty and they would have been listening to Pillay, Tingley and Overstreet. Other members of the community committee, such as Dr. Lem Sealey, were wanting to keep me on. They fought off the attack by these people from BUF. And while I became a focus of their discontent, I really think that the basic issue was not me as an individual but the issue of who should control this program.

Well, the university administration won, of course. They held the purse strings and they could say who could enter the university after passing through TYP. In our original thoughts, university entrance, while strongly desired, was not the be-all end-all of the program. Look at Ernie McLellan, and lots of others who gained tremendously from TYP but never sat in a regular Dalhousie classroom. But Dal was thinking of this as university preparation exclusively, and they tracked the rate of university entrance and the success of those students once in university to determine the value of the program. After the second year, Dal upped the entrance requirement to grade 12. They took away the potential for so many prospective students, and they changed the program. It was an incredible shift from the first two years of the program. Now I don't think that TYP was actually able to hold the line and only take grade 12. But this again is part of the conflict between the university and the advisory committee. After the second year, in 1972, Bala Pillay resigned as director. Dr. Ted Marriot was the next director, and there were a lot of things that he did not understand about either the Black community or the Aboriginal community. But he did have a belief that this was a good program and it should be continued. It was quite paternalistic in that he shared the belief that the university should run it and control it, that people from the community didn't know about the university.

That same summer of 1972, as Bala Pillay was leaving and standards were changing, relations with the Mi'kmaq came to a head. There had been some complaints from the beginning. They said the Department of Indian Affairs is giving a certain amount of money to this program because there are Indians in it, not for a program for Black students. Their point was that they were subsidizing the Black students. The Union of Nova Scotia Indians also complained about the lack of progress by Indian students. Many of those students came from rural reserves where they didn't have the highest academic standards. With the Aboriginals we weren't getting the grade 12 students, which was what Dalhousie now wanted. In the beginning we take students who didn't have the academic skills and they did have a hard time doing the work. We believed they had the potential, and that was why they were selected in the first place. The Union interpreted the fact that they weren't passing these courses very easily was because the program wasn't relevant for Indians. The Black people are doing better and therefore it is not a program for Indians. They weren't looking at the fact that the Indians were coming from rural areas, their first time in the city some of them. For the Union TYP was doing something wrong in regard to the Aboriginal students. Add to that the fact that the Union were not involved in the creation of the program. They didn't go through all the time and effort to get the program going; they didn't see it as their program, not at all. So then, before the new term began in 1972, they pulled the Mi'kmaq students out. This was a bad decision in my opinion, and it wasn't one that lasted, but it was another factor in the turmoil that was TYP and is part of the history of the program.

There has been a lot of debate over whether TYP is a success or a failure. One way to look at it is the Black or Indian students who went to university in the 1970s, any university in Nova Scotia, came through TYP, almost all of them. Our program had imitators, universities in Ontario especially, who set up their own versions of TYP. Right in our first year representatives from the University of Toronto came to us to see how we were doing it. They set up a program that was not specific to Black or Indian students, and their students had to pay fees whereas ours did not, but basically they followed our format.

But I think that the best measurement of our success is that our students' consciousness is being raised, significant issues are being debated, and TYP students are taking a message back into the community. "You can go to university and this is what it's all about." They have become critical of the system, and there is a large intellectual body, by the mid-seventies, who are politicized and focusing on the concerns of young people. The agenda is being determined by them, and education comes to the front because the leadership, the real leadership, is coming from the young people themselves. The people that come through TYP are the ones who become chiefs, they're active in the Union of Nova Scotia Indians, they become the leadership. Certainly we had some influence in creating that groundswell. An incredible momentum was put into play, as Black consciousness spreads across the Black communities all over the province with TYP students going home. It leads to a real shift.

I stayed in the program for ten years, from 1970 to 1980. It was a very exciting project and it was really fulfilling the need for Blacks to get into the university. I certainly didn't stay for the money. I don't think the salary ever got raised from its original $1,000 a year. It was never a financial consideration for me. I was able to be part of it as a lecturer and to run interference to deal with faculty if necessary when there was problem, and I was able to be a resource to students for their own issues in life. I did not always approve of the various "reforms" that were introduced, taking TYP further away from our original idea. But it was worth it. The students were most appreciative, the community was appreciative, people supported that program, and I felt for the longest time that I had to stay just to make sure that it was so well-established that the university couldn't get rid of it. Its survival for all these decades proves that it is needed.

Of course TYP was not a full-time job. We still had the Nile in Scotia Square, and we opened the Blue Nile in the MicMac Mall over in Dartmouth.

Although I was still paying off my creditors, after the burglary, that still gave us enough cash to come and go on, along with the rent from our boarders and whatever I could pick up at cards and pool. Somehow we managed to survive. But my greatest passion in the early 1970s, besides TYP, was the Black HERO project, the Black Historical Educational Research Organization. This project comes out of my interest in Black history and the fact that everything pertaining to the history of Blacks in Nova Scotia was something documented and written by outsiders. I didn't get a sense that I was getting a true history of my own community, and there were things that I knew that weren't written down. Marjorie Whitelaw was an influence on me at that time. She was at CBC Radio and she was really quite interested in gathering oral history. I had talked to her about how to collect the history of my own community. And Dr. Helen Creighton was doing oral interviews, collecting ghost stories in the province, and she also gave me some guidance. Through them I became convinced that we could get the history of the Black community of Nova Scotia through interviews. Now the problem we had was first of all financial, because we were thinking about a huge project and no one seemed to have any knowledge of how to do it. I went around and I talked to a lot of people about how to put a project together to collect the history of Blacks in Nova Scotia.

I figured we would need at least 15 people, and I then applied for a Secretary of State grant, Opportunities for Youth (OFY), for the summers of 1971 and 1972. Bala Pillay lent his name to the project, which gave us access to Dalhousie resources, and Dalhousie provided a room so we didn't have to pay any rent. OFY provided the salaries and some other expenses. Then the tapes were provided mostly by CBC, leftover, reusable tapes. So that was the physical side looked after. I was quite arbitrary in recruiting staff, people who I thought would be good at collecting information, and I picked mostly TYP kids, including my sister Luella. I wanted people who had the skill to write a little bit of the historical background, and they had to be trained in a hurry. Before the students went into the field we had a training program where I lectured on Nova Scotian history, though I certainly wasn't an expert, but I was what we had. And we decided that there were key events that we all had to know about in order to have timeframes when we were doing interviews, like for instance the Mice Epidemic, the Halifax Explosion, the Flu Epidemic, the Year that Marcus Garvey came. I had to find out this information and give it to them. Then we had areas that we thought we wanted to know about the community, about home life, work life, religious life, medical remedies, military experience, songs and spirituals, and stories. We then made up a form, an outline of all of these headings and topics, not to be used verbatim, but just a guide to the areas we wanted to cover.

Histories are always taken from the literature, memoirs and the writings of literate people. Well we come from an illiterate people, so our writings can't be used to write our history. So all of those histories are based on the writings of outsiders about our community, and what I envisioned was for our people to tell our story. We would just take what the people said, record it and then present it, in their own words, with as little editorializing as possible. Our target was persons 65 years or older. People responded so well that they told us things that you wouldn't tell in public. "You know, I have three sisters, but one of these isn't my real sister, she is so and so's kid, who my mother took in when she was a baby because so and so got pregnant by so and so." The community just opened up to these young people who were asking the questions, and we ended up with some information that I felt we had no right to divulge. One thing I wanted to do was be able to do a genealogy of Nova Scotia, and you can do that with these recordings, known as the "HERO Tapes." I could tell you everybody who is related to everybody and what everybody's genealogy is for three generations. The HERO Tapes can tell you stories of the Black men who went down into the mines, and how they survived with the blind horses and all of that. Every aspect of Nova Scotia life in the Black community is covered in these tapes, every bit.

We were real amateurs. Here I am trying to train researchers to go out in the field and I've never been in the field myself. Here I am writing the questions to ask, saying these are the important questions that we've got to have, and the important information that we have got to get from our community, and I have no training as a sociologist, I have no training as a historian, I had no training at all; I had to come up with all of this stuff out of my head. We got the old, used tapes from CBC and some from CJCH, and then when we get most of the students recruited, I said you've got to bring your own tape recorder with you because we couldn't afford tape recorders. Most of them didn't have one, so we scrounged whatever mobile tape recorders we could get and they would take tapes and off we would go to Guysborough County for instance. Well many of these places didn't have electricity. We've got students doing interviews and the batteries are running out. You are in the middle of the thing and the battery goes dead. We had to combine cars, to get somewhere. We had a car for the project but we had eight people, so we couldn't all get into a car. We had to bum rides. We had to get the community to put people up. When we were going to Cherry Brook it was nothing, because our students could go to Cherry Brook and go home, but when we were going to Liverpool or Yarmouth we couldn't afford to stay in hotels. We had to go down to those communities, meet the people and get the people to agree to put the students up and feed them while they were there, and open the doors for them to go around to the community. So there I was, I wasn't even doing interviews. All I was doing was organizing, saying, "Listen, I've got students coming, will you take this one?" "Okay you two, I've got this setup." Then we get a tape out in the field, and either mail it back or bring it back or somehow get the tape back to the office. In the office we've got people who hardly have any skills either. They are listening to the tape, we've got poor quality tape, plus we've got people who are talking with different accents or almost dialects from different parts of Nova Scotia, and using words that young people don't know the meanings of. The typist doesn't even know what it is that the person is saying. And then after they transcribe this tape, we had to reuse the same tape over again for another interview, so some of the tapes would have half of somebody's interview and half of somebody else's on it. In this way we did 350 interviews over the two summers of the HERO project. It is an incredible number of hours of interviews.

I had a set of the tapes that I gave to the Black Cultural Centre and a set to Dalhousie University Archives, to make sure the best I could that this didn't get lost. I also had a 20-year freeze on the Dalhousie tapes, because I didn't want people using this material when these people are alive, and all of a sudden we had lawsuits all over the place. But if a person is dead you can use their stuff. They were 65 or older, and in 20 years most of them would be dead. But, and this is another incredible part of this story, I had all kinds of people who were still alive 20 years later. At one point I was trying to have the tapes digitalized, because the tapes and the transcripts we had were in such poor shape. Dalhousie offered to do it, but they needed to have ownership of the tapes and I didn't want that to happen. I wanted them kept in the control of the community. They are an extremely valuable resource for our community, and they should be available to community members and researchers. I sure would like to see them done before I am dead.

Besides all this I was still a student at Dalhousie, doing my BA in History. I finally finished my BA in 1974, which I started in 1968, so it took me longer than for most but I was doing a lot of other things. Then in 1975 I started my MA. I really enjoyed the study of history doing my BA. I enjoyed the reading and everything, and then when I was doing an MA, I really enjoyed that too. I liked the debates and trying to figure out the meaning of things, the different interpretations. One thing I thought was that I could link the HERO project to my MA studies. What I really wanted to do was use the graduate program to be able to hone my skills and get good knowledge and background to be able to complete the work on the HERO Tapes. That is what my intention was. Then, after I'd been in the program for two years, I got into a dispute with my supervisor and I dropped out. That was in 1977. I wouldn't say it was time wasted, but in the end I did not get my MA degree.

During that time, the mid-seventies, Joan and I sort of came to terms with BUF. We decided to give it another kick at the can. BUF had become an institution instead of a movement. After all the hype over the funding issue and the radicals taking over, Jules Oliver was named as the first executive director in the spring of 1970. I really thought that we would be able to organize the Black community so that people would be focused and progressive and do things in the community, and that didn't happen. I was not successful. I say "I" because I take a lot of personal responsibility in terms of being able to get other young people to adopt the philosophical stance that I had adopted and to make commitments to change things. Some of the people in BUF were using the Black struggle as a means of attaining personal goals—prestige, jobs. And they were in effect exploiting the Black community. They became dependent on government financing, so the disappointment was that we were not able to create an independent organization that was supported by the community to look after the interests of the community. Some of the brightest people in our community then became government workers by extension. We lose our independence; we just don't have the ability to confront the government. BUF became as its name suggests, a BUFfer; it stood between the people and the government. And on many occasions, people would approach government with a problem, the government could righteously say, "Look we are funding BUF. You've got an organization who can look after this, and we will deal with the organization. So go see BUF, you don't need to come and see our workers, you don't need to talk to the deputy minister or the minister, go see BUF." So BUF is actually a gatekeeper. It stops people from moving directly to confront the very persons, organizations or groups that are oppressing them. And it shouldn't be; the people are victims here.

Yet people still had faith, or hope, that BUF would fulfil its promise. I think this was especially true of the young people. There was one significant moment in the fall of 1972 when a group of young people, students and others, actually occupied the BUF headquarters and refused to leave until the BUF leadership made some commitments to address real problems and issues and became more transparent. They did this more than once, in fact. They were feeling alienated and not part of the decision-making. I was actually blamed for this in the press. "Black activist Rocky Jones has organized a sit-in at BUF." But I didn't even know about it until it had started. I did go down to the BUF offices to express solidarity with them, but I didn't stay and I didn't make any speeches. I think it happened because they believed that BUF was important. They were looking to BUF for leadership, and there was no other provincial organization other than the African United Baptist Association (AUBA). The circumstances and the rhetoric surrounding the creation of BUF led people to believe that it would be a catalyst for change, an organization that would fight for any and all of the causes that came up in the Black community. There was such hope and optimism that they'd be able to get something done at long last.

After Jules left to join the civil service in Ottawa in 1974, Art Criss became director of BUF. In his early days Art was really proactive in the community in terms of housing projects, home renovations, attempting to get people into jobs, trying to get government grants such as Local Initiatives Projects (LIP). BUF becomes pretty relevant, though Art was very dictatorial in his leadership style. I went back on the board, and Joan went to work for BUF as outreach coordinator, a job she more or less defined for herself. I also did some contract work for BUF in Southwestern Nova Scotia, analyzing Black leadership and community dynamics. In the end I didn't submit my report, because I was afraid BUF would use the intimate details to try to control those communities. Our renewed relationship with BUF didn't last. There were progressive people working for BUF, such as David Woods who was a youth worker, but generally as an institution it was disappointing. Basically, BUF had no power. Once you're paid by the government, you need your salary paid and you can't criticize your employer.

Another organization that started out with great optimism was the National Black Coalition of Canada (NBCC), founded in October 1969. It had been talked about during the Black Writers' Congress in Montreal and the meeting at OISE in Toronto. People were aware that we needed a more united voice, a united front I guess you could call it, to deal with the federal government and the things that were happening with Black people all over. There were two major meetings to set up a national coalition. At these meetings there's a lot of tension between the people from the West Indies, who seem to think that they're representing the interests of an island, and the others are people whose families have been in Canada for generations and seem to be representing what they consider to be the interests of Blacks all over Canada. It is very difficult, but the NBCC does get formed. It was the only national organization that eventually did allow for all of these different factions to meet under one roof. The NBCC attempted to bridge the gap by having awards that would honour different people, carefully selected from different islands or different backgrounds, to say that we acknowledge that you performed a valuable service to the Black community. That was a way of trying to heal the rifts that were out there. As far as being a political voice, our articulated objective was to be able to speak on behalf of the national Black community. The government was always aware, obviously because of their informants, that the NBCC was a paper tiger and that the NBCC was never able to have the power necessary to make change on behalf of the national Black community. It didn't work for us. And although the association continued on for years and we had many, many meetings, I don't think we ever got any political power through the NBCC.

In thinking back on it, there was no possibility that the NBCC could really deliver. The Black community of Canada was so fragmented. Howard McCurdy and I were at that time, in the late 1960s, gaining the kind of personae that people could potentially fall behind, but neither one of us could draw the West Indian community. We could go anywhere in Canada and the Black community would turn out in droves and come to our meetings and listen to our speeches, but when it came to political action, people divided depending on what island they came from, and there was no West Indian who could unite them. It was our downfall, that tribalism. The politicians are aware that the votes are in Ontario and Quebec, and by the late sixties the West Indians are the numerical majority in Canada. The politicians play to that reality, and they're the ones who get appointed to boards or commissions or whatever it is. They're the ones who have to deliver to their constituencies, and their constituencies did not include Buxton or Amherstburg in Southern Ontario, or Amber Valley or the small areas out west, or Nova Scotia for that matter. We're not even players in the politics of Canada. We don't have the numbers, we can't elect members of parliament, we can't influence the vote, so they don't play to us. There's no way to have a national consensus, not only because of the tribalism but because we are coming from different political positions. We've got cultural nationalists, Marxists, stone-nosed Tories; our ideologies are from one spectrum to the other, and the coalition contained athletic clubs, church groups, political activists, cultural and community organizations, and we're all trying to get into the same organization. And there was another split, between the people from Quebec and the rest of Canada. After several years of meandering there was an attempt to revive and redefine the NBCC. At a meeting in Toronto in May 1979, one of the Quebec members actually attacked Howard, I mean physically, and there was a real punch-up. The Québécois separatists thought Howard, and probably the rest of the Anglos, were ignoring their genuine concerns. Despite this there was a brief revival of the NBCC, led by Wilson Head, who converted it from a coalition of existing organizations to a direct-membership organization. So Wilson's efforts succeeded, to some extent, in overcoming the worst effects of the tribalism, but the internal difficulties prevented anything lasting from happening. The NBCC only went on a few more years, though some local organizations calling themselves "chapters" of the NBCC continued to exist. I feel a sense of disappointment that we couldn't make the NBCC work, and there's been nothing since except government-sponsored organizations that purport to be Black.

Another thing that contributed to the feelings of disunity and even resentment was the World Black and African Festival of Arts and Culture (Festac) conference in Nigeria in 1977. This was the second world festival; the first was in Senegal in 1965. The idea was to showcase the different places where African people had gone, in Africa and in the Diaspora, and to show them where they were at and to bring them back and connect them together in the mother country. I really wanted to go to Lagos in 1977, but the Canadian contingent was organized and controlled by central Canada, and by persons who came from various islands and other places around the world and who identified with their places of origin. I continually raised the issue that the recent immigrants, although they had their place in Canadian society and certainly their stories were important in understanding Canadian society, the other story which had to be told is the longstanding story of Blacks who had lived in Canada for a couple of hundred of years, and that's the Ontario settlements, the Western settlements, the B.C. settlements and the Nova Scotian settlements. And those people and their ideas were not included in Festac. Their stories weren't included because they weren't part of the numerical majority of the Blacks in Canada. I saw it as very destructive to continue to go away to a festival in another country to say this is what Blacks in Canada are all about and to exclude all of our own stories.

While all this turmoil with the NBCC and Festac was going on, there were two national conferences on Black Canadian Studies. It's hard to imagine, but it does show the interest people had in strengthening the unity among the different Black communities in the country. The first conference was held at the University of Windsor in 1978. The whole thing was the brainchild of Professor Tom Posey, from Windsor, an African American. In a planning meeting in Winnipeg we had people from all over Canada, the West Coast, the Prairies, Upper Canada, Quebec, the Maritimes, primarily people with Canadian ancestry going back several generations. There were a few African Americans, like David McKinney from the University of Guelph, a West Indian or two from Montreal and Toronto, and Gil Scott from the Secretary of State, which was funding the show, was West Indian. But for a change West Indians did not dominate numerically. Jim Walker was our sole whitey. The conference we planned was fundamentally academic, which was what Tom Posey wanted, though when we got to Windsor there was a mixture of academics and activists. The call went out nationally to come and present papers, or just attend. I took a group of TYP students with me. At that moment the program's funding was under serious threat. I wanted the kids to experience the conference, but I also wanted the conference to experience the kids and to generate pressure to have the program continued. Whether this contributed or not, the program did survive.

The book of papers from this conference, edited by Vincent D'Oyley from the Ontario Institute for Studies in Education, includes one I wrote on the Maroons in Nova Scotia. I had written it with the assistance of Jim Walker and my sister Lynn. If you look down the table of contents of that book you'll see the who's who of Black Canadian intellectuals at that time. People came from universities all over the country, most of them West Indians. In fact I did not present that paper orally; I just submitted a copy to Professor Posey because there was no transcript of my actual remarks. At the conference the discussions were basically about West Indians, about their problems with immigration and adapting to Canada and so on. Just as we were getting our act together, getting some attention from the public and from the government, the agenda gets shifted from our issues to immigration. So when I got up to speak I put aside my prepared paper and just talked off the cuff. I wanted to analyze the struggle of the Black Canadians, a continuation of the analysis I was then putting forward generally. In this presentation I decided that I would be totally honest, and in essence I said that we are the victims of skinocracy and this island mentality, that people were bringing to the struggle their beefs directly related to their birthplace. In this whole political arena, where you had Black people from the Caribbean and Africa, talking about their needs as people from the Caribbean and Africa, the politicians in Ottawa or Queen's Park or whatever were responding to the needs of the recent immigrants, and these people had the ear of the politicians because they had the numbers of votes. I went on to argue that although these people were Black they were not sensitive to the needs of the African Canadians from Nova Scotia or the Maritimes. The money and programs were focused on central Canada, because they had the clout to do it, and indeed they discriminated against the Canadian-born, what we would now call indigenous Black Canadians.

Well, it raised a few hackles, and I was quite prepared to debate my position and change my position if I could be shown it was wrong. But my analysis at the time certainly confirmed that I had more in common with a poor white from Halifax than I had in common with the West Indian, because his needs were so much different from mine. It was the first time I had arrived at the position square enough that I could articulate it and defend it. My analysis and political positions were derived from my experience and not from readings or academic discussions. It was taking a practical experience and analyzing it and saying this is what I think about it. This was my position of how Black people interacted with each other and how the indigenous Black people across the country were getting screwed, and it is true to this day.

As soon as I had finished, Clarence Bayne from Montreal jumped up onto the platform. He's saying how hurt he was at my betrayal, that he had worked on behalf of all the Black people in Canada, that my attitude would undermine any opportunity for Black unity. You would have thought I was crucifying the very image of Christ on the cross. It was really something. And then Howard McCurdy got up on the platform. He had given a paper the morning before, and he said, "Yesterday at lunch somebody came up to me, from this audience, and said 'That was any interesting talk you gave, sir. Tell me, what *island* are you from?' I stand with Brother Jones!" Howard was a serious scholar and a national leader, and would later become a Member of Parliament. His endorsement meant something. I thought at the time I might have done what Clarence said, and damaged the possibility of unity, but it turned out that many people agreed with me, or at least saw my point.

I think that the Windsor conference was extremely important. It was the first national conference, and it raised an important issue for debate. And I think that because it was raised in that fashion in that forum, people did look and say, maybe we are a bit insensitive. It came back to me many times since that, although maybe people didn't like what I said and they didn't like how I said it, what I said had truth to it and they would try to see if it were not possible to address that as a problem in the community. And I think they did. It wasn't easily solved but I think that the West Indian scholars in Canada paid more attention to the indigenous Black community and tried to incorporate the thoughts of the indigenous Black people into their work, or tried to involve them in their conferences or in their discussions. I do think that happened.

There was a follow-up conference the following year, 1979, at St. Mary's University in Halifax. It was organized by Professor Bridge Pachai, a South African of Indian descent who was then teaching at St. Mary's. He later became director of the Black Cultural Centre and eventually the Human Rights Commissioner for Nova Scotia. This conference wasn't quite so blue chip as at Windsor, but it did bring people together and they shared a lot of their research. A book came out of that conference too, edited by Professor Pachai. I recall the different people arriving at the Lord Nelson, people I'd never met before from McGill or whatever, and as I was speaking to those people I realized they had no understanding that there were Blacks in Nova Scotia who were born here, and they were surprised that I identified as a Nova Scotian. And I remember thinking, they come here and they still don't know that we exist. So even by then, we hadn't got the message out with the scholars coming to our town. They knew by the time they left, that's for sure. The Halifax conference was in a way more grassroots than at Windsor. The people living here felt involved, felt that they could go to the sessions and partici-pate, whereas in Windsor it was more confined to those who were academic or political. Although I did a lot of speaking, I didn't give an actual paper. Instead I presented Jim's paper, because he wasn't able to attend himself. His son was undergoing serious surgery in the Sick Kids' Hospital in Toronto. I really do believe that those two national conferences contributed immensely to a national consciousness among Blacks in Canada. We realized that we are a community of communities, and we had a lot more in common than it looked like at first. Racism doesn't care where you come from, just the colour of your skin. Those conferences also contributed to making Black Canadian Studies academically respectable.

And as this was happening, in the 1970s, Black Canadian culture was start-ing to move onto the stage. One of the best things BUF had going was the Cultural Awareness Program (CAP). They did workshops with the young peo-ple on Black history and culture. This was a gradual build-up over the decade, and by the mid-seventies there was a lot more material that was indigenous than there had ever been before. The consciousness-raising that was in the sixties is bearing fruit in terms of the cultural productivity that is beginning to happen in the schools and in the community generally. I had my own hand in that, in a sort of way. In the summer of 1978 Sharon Ross and I co-hosted a CBC Television show called *Black Insights*. That comes about because of a national policy that the stations had to have so much local cultural content. CBC Halifax hadn't filled their quota so they were looking to do something and they approached us, Sharon Ross because she was a very beautiful woman and intelligent and articulate, and me I think because of my political stance. They thought between the two of us we had the chance to attract viewers. Sharon later went on to a very successful career with the Secretary of State in Ottawa. I do believe *Black Insights* was the first time that Black people had a chance to set their own agenda for a mainstream television show, maybe in Canada, certainly in Nova Scotia. We would sit around and pick topics and decide to tackle issues, and go out and interview people and talk about housing, talk about education. We did some very controversial things. We had an episode on Africville, one of the first attempts to look at the situation from a Black Africentric point of view, saying that mistakes were made and people suffered, saying it was wrong and racist. We also did a history episode where we were able to show the movement of people from the American South along the coast and up into Nova Scotia, and then moving from here to Sierra Leone, even showing the ships. It was graphically really something. It was an exciting series to do because we had the benefit of the professionals at CBC to help us put it together. We came up with ideas and they helped us script it and did the background graphics for it. It was a really high class CBC production. I believe we had ten episodes of an hour each, over the whole summer. It was very successful as a show but they wouldn't keep it. The viewers just loved it; we had excellent feedback.

One key moment of that period was the visit of Harry Belafonte. He was giving a performance at the Rebecca Cohn auditorium, it was at Easter time in 1978, and I went backstage and invited him to come and meet some of the young Black kids in Halifax. So he came over to our house. We were living by then on Windsor Street, near the Forum. We put the word out to TYP students, any old Kwacha types who were still around, some other young people including George Elliott Clarke, and invited them to come and meet Harry Belafonte. We phoned a whole bunch of kids and they came in hordes. George, it turned out, was busy writing a poem, but anyway our house was full. It wasn't just the kids; older people came too. We had two rooms that could open into one big room, and the people sat on the floor in a circle around him. He didn't sing, he just talked and answered questions. He said he was grateful to be invited. It was very exciting. He explained what it was like to be in show business in that era, what it was like to be a singer, what he had to go through to get to where he was. He talked about socialism and race relations in the States, and he talked about the struggle in Africa and different parts of the Diaspora. He stayed for at least three hours. Joan cooked up a chicken curry and fed everybody, as per usual. Everyone wanted their picture taken with him. I must admit that I didn't have a sense of how significant it was. When you look back at it, to be in Nova Scotia and to have an international star like Belafonte just come to your house and sit around, eat chicken curry and talk to everybody and explain things, it was absolutely amazing. He was so good for us, because he was able to explain things that we didn't really know about because he was so very aware.

In some ways the Belafonte visit is symbolic of the increasing influence of international Black culture in Nova Scotia during the 1970s, like singers and movies — James Brown, Aretha Franklin, Richard Roundtree, Sidney Poitier and of course Belafonte himself — just as Stokely's visit was symbolic of the political influence of Black America in the sixties. Although Harry talks politics in our house, he is a cultural figure. The political figures are sort of moving off the stage. The Panthers are gone. All of those figures are out of the spotlight, or they are certainly dimmed. People are beginning to be influenced a lot by cultural things. It was a period of self-reflection, when we look back at ourselves and our own history to draw inspiration. It wasn't just African American. Reggae and Bob Marley were very big. When you think of the shift from the political figures to the cultural figures providing the voice, Marley was one of the most important. Obviously there was a political message to all of this that cannot be disguised. But the inspiration is coming from cultural icons. And people are connecting with Africa too. In the sixties we wore our dashikis, but by the seventies it was not uncommon to have people going to full African dress for special events. We've got Nova Scotians going to Africa, and they come back bringing gifts, and the African students who come here are going home and sending things to us, so we have more access to traditional African clothing and people begin to wear it. Although African independence was very thrilling in the sixties, by the seventies African politics had become tarnished with one-party states and military coups. But that didn't tarnish African culture.

As you go through the 1970s and after, the community is gaining all this new information and it allows us to generate new information for ourselves. When I look at who is creating this new cultural expression, I'm thinking of people like Walter Borden and Maxine Tynes. Walter is very active in the theatre beginning then. He was a gifted writer and a really great actor. He is well known around Canada as an actor, but his poetry was brilliant too. Sylvia

Hamilton's works come out later, but she is still a product of that time, and the same for David Woods and Ken Pinto. And later again our own George Elliott Clarke, Canada's pre-eminent poet of any colour and not just a representative but the main scholar of what has been called the Black Renaissance. The artists who are creating things are homegrown, even though there is the international influence on them. We are developing an artistic mass, perhaps not a critical mass quite yet in the seventies but certainly there is a mass, people who grew up in Nova Scotia and have now matured to the point where they are creating the literature and the art that will eventually shape the ideas in the community. There are a lot of cultural things happening, and that is an expression of our politics. This is more clear in retrospect than it was back then. There is no question when you look back, the seventies were filled with cultural movements, and an amazing cultural energy. This is the source of so much more that happens in our community and our culture. We were beginning to grow up.

In my own case I went into mainstream politics toward the end of the seventies, though perhaps you couldn't call the NDP "mainstream" in Nova Scotia at that time. My involvement with the NDP was a very important part of my life, but it was always something of a love-hate relationship. I first came into contact with left-wing politics when I was a kid growing up in Truro. Right at the end of our street there was a man who owned a grocery store, Harvey Curtis. He extended credit to our family and basically to the community. You went up to the store and you had no money, so he would make up an account for you and whenever you had money you could go and pay him. He was a good and important part of the sustenance of our community. Then election day would come, and Harvey would be running for the CCF or then the NDP. I recall people getting dressed up to vote, a car coming by and the men getting their drinks and women getting chocolates and nylons, but they weren't getting them from Harvey and Harvey wasn't getting their votes. I was told he was a communist and communists were bad and they wanted to destroy our country. But I knew there was an inconsistency about what people were saying about this man come election time and what they thought of him between elections. I never understood how people could turn against someone who was so good to them. It made me question how politics worked, but I didn't have any kind of analysis. It just didn't feel right, it didn't make sense. When I did become political I embraced the NDP as the closest party to the things I believed in, the most likely to implement some of the things I wanted to happen. I never believed the NDP was a revolutionary party or even all that progressive, but they were the least evil of the mainstream parties. I think

Harvey Curtis represented to me what I believed to be a New Democrat: you are helping your neighbour, you are doing what you can, and you are there for the people all the time and not just for elections.

When I came back from Toronto in 1965 I joined the NDP, and eventually served on the provincial and federal councils of the party. When I went to conventions in Ontario, representing the NDP in Nova Scotia, it was very clear to me that the Golden Horseshoe was the axis, the centre of power, and the world revolved around Upper Canada. At the NDP conventions it really played out that way, where you had the large unions, with an incredible amount of experience and influence, and you had the people from the West, also with experience and influence, but the bulk of the votes were in Ontario. The issues that were important to Nova Scotia just did not make it through the resolutions committee; it was very prejudicial, not only geographically but also racially. There was virtually no understanding, no sensitivity to the struggle that Black people were going through, it just wasn't there. The NDP in my opinion, except for their rhetoric, was the same as the Liberals or the Tories, it didn't make any difference. Now I was one of those at federal council who was able to stand up for Nova Scotia, with very few votes to support me, and make arguments on the convention floor. But it was really difficult and not at all inviting. That almost disillusioned me to the point where I wouldn't belong to the NDP, but there was no alternative; if you wanted to do anything in terms of electoral politics that was the only game in town.

Provincially, under the leadership of Jeremy Akerman beginning in 1968, the NDP realized that they could not form the government or even the opposition. In the 1970 election they got only two seats, Akerman himself and Paul McEwan, both from Cape Breton. The players in the party who really want to do things in terms of straight electoral politics are prepared to put elections in front of ideologies. The NDP is split between the intellectuals, who are determining most of the agenda, and the lunch-pail members, who are less articulate but sticking to their leftist principles, and they are the bulk of the voters in industrial Cape Breton. So you've got a continual built-in tension between mainland Nova Scotia and industrial Cape Breton. You also have rural Nova Scotia down the Valley, which is another area where you have a more educated population, more inclined to be sympathetic to the ideas of the intellectuals. The party is becoming more conservative as we move into the seventies, hoping for some success at electoral politics. You couldn't have it both ways. You couldn't have a radical platform and a radical position and at the same time go to the community for votes because the community would not be that radical. That meant that they had to water down the rhetoric and water down the programs to make it appealing to the largest number of people. So the party became more and more conservative and its popularity did go up, and that drives the momentum; it keeps the party moving to the centre. In the 1974 election they got three seats, and in 1978 four seats, all of them in Cape Breton.

The NDP needed to have an executive assistant to the caucus, and I got that job in 1978. My hope was to keep the party on the left, to encourage the more progressive members and have more influence in the party overall than I could as a member of provincial council. I could get certain resolutions on the agenda and get them debated and try to make them policy. Then Jeremy's executive assistant left, and he offered me the position as executive assistant to the leader. There were rumours of a moral issue about the Liberals at that time, and he wanted to launch a major assault against them. He thought I could be useful in this attack, while I thought the move would give me even more opportunities to make some practical changes in the NDP. Jeremy and I were about the same age, and although we never became close friends we did have a good working relationship. I wouldn't go so far as to say that he adopted all my suggestions, but I did feel I was having enough influence to make it worthwhile. This was full-time work, and it was in this period that I gave up both the stores and left TYP. There just wasn't enough time for everything, and the NDP was giving me a living wage. I was in this job as Jeremy's assistant when the party made a move on Paul McEwan. Paul had made some sort of a remark about Trotskyites in the party and it hit the news stands, and there were some allegations that he was charging his constituents for his services as their MLA. There was a meeting held in Truro in June 1980 to vote on whether to expel McEwan from the party. I believed that to get rid of McEwan would mean sacrificing Cape Breton, or at least part of it, and there was an election coming up the next year. The area Paul represented, around the Pier, was heavily influenced by Black people, the only riding where that would happen at that time. I was supportive of having him stay. This thing with McEwan polarized people all over the province. There was no wishy-washy position you could take; you were either for him or for the people in Halifax who were leading the attack against him. I took the position that they shouldn't go after Paul, so I was now an outsider living in Halifax. So we fight that issue on the floor of the provincial council, and Paul loses. The vote went against him, and out he went. Sure enough in the 1981 election we lost Paul's seat.

But actually before that, in May 1980, I ran as the NDP candidate in a by-election in Halifax-Needham. I was approached by the constituency organization there, and I agreed. I had the support of caucus, but there were a lot of the establishment of the party who didn't want me. They set it up so that I had to have a contested nomination. I went out and signed up all kinds of people. I was ready for the vote. Then when the night came, the people who were going to run against me didn't show. Nobody would run, so I got the nomination by acclamation. I had campaigned on behalf of other people many times, but this was my first time campaigning for myself. It really was fun. I had a bunch of people from the neighbourhood helping me out. Then election day comes and these guys are supposed to pull the vote, get our known supporters to the polls, offer them rides. I'm waiting, and they aren't showing up. These were people I'd befriended and done things for, and here they were driving these big cars working for the Liberals! I will never forget it. I said, "Jeez, you were supposed to come and give me a hand," and they said, "Listen, what they offered us for this day, we couldn't turn it down. We are sorry Brother but we just couldn't do it." I remember the tears running down my face. I related it to the 30 pieces of silver. These same guys who I was working with to set up playgrounds and do things in the community, and we had all of these discussions about how the community needed to be protected and the things we needed to do together, and then come election time, for the money, they did this. As it turned out I lost my deposit. I got 700 votes. I did increase the popular vote, but it was just a disaster. Edmund Morris, the Tory, won narrowly with 2,618 votes to 2,592 for the Liberal Dan Clarke. I just ran the once. They asked me again and I said no, I would never do it again. It was just too painful.

Jeremy resigned as leader, and there had to be a leadership convention. Alexa McDonough was running with the support of the Halifax intellectuals. There was the feeling that we had to have a mainland leader to attract more votes, and Cape Breton would stick with tradition and continue to vote NDP. In my analysis, the party was prepared to give up the seats in Cape Breton to gain strength on the mainland. I had positive feelings for Alexa. After all her father, Lloyd Shaw, had been one of the main supporters of the Nova Scotia Project. But personally I supported Buddy MacEachern. He was a lunch-pail Cape Bretoner, and he stood for a lot of the things I stood for myself. During the campaign Buddy and Alexa used to get into it, at least in their public debates, creating some bad feeling. Well Alexa won in a landslide in November 1980. My fears about Cape Breton turned out to be correct. In the 1981 election the NDP lost all of its Cape Breton seats. The only victory was Alexa's own seat, in Halifax Chebucto. This was the first time the NDP ever won a seat on the mainland.

I was still executive assistant to the leader. Right after Alexa took over she calls me into her office. She said, "I'll never forgive you for what you did." I said, "What did I do?" She said, "Oh the things that Buddy MacEachern said about me publicly." I said, "Well Alexa, Buddy is his own person. I don't control what Buddy says, whatever he said, he said". "Oh," she said, "you can't work here, I'll never forgive you," on and on. This was almost at Christmas. I said "Alexa, I have five children. We are coming into Christmas and you are telling me that I'm fired now?" "Yes," she said, "you are finished, I can't forgive you." I said, "Let me tell you. I'll stay until after Christmas, then I'll be gone. I'll leave right after Christmas," and she agreed. There was no termination settlement. My friend Blaze McDonald, a labour lawyer, said "Look, let's sue the party. There is no legitimate reason for you to lose your job here. At least you'll get some money out of it." I said, "No, I can't agree." At that point I was the only Black person to have any real stature, a public face, in the NDP. If I sue them, what message am I sending to Black people in this province? I think that the NDP is the only party that will at least open its doors to Black people. Even though they are like this, and Alexa has taken this position, I still don't want to destroy the party. To try to punish Alexa for what I consider to be unfair, I would be punishing the party. Blaze said, "If you want I'll take the case and I'll do it for free, don't even worry about it." I said "No, I'll get through Christmas and go on about my business." That was Christmas 1980.

I was very dejected. I had been an active supporter of the party for over 15 years. I knew we had a long way to go and we had internal things to settle, but there were areas where we were gaining ground, bringing important issues to the public. I had put my trust in these people, so it took the wind right out of my sails to see them all going on, including Alexa, like nothing had happened. It meant nothing to them. I was totally dispensable, just another nigger to discard. It didn't matter if my family survived. It didn't even matter if we had a Christmas. But I do think I was right not to attempt to destroy the party. Eventually I rejoined the provincial council and was elected to the executive, still hoping things will go on the way I always hoped they would in the NDP.

Chapter 8

TURNING
TO THE LAW

No NDP. No shops. No TYP. In short, no job. I drifted for quite a while, and I did a lot of thinking, and re-thinking. In the sixties, my political position was that you had to work from outside the system if you wanted to apply pressure to change the system. As you were attempting from the outside to restructure the system it would respond, to violence, for example, or the threat of violence. But as time went on, into the 80s, I became more aware that in the Canadian context, it was unlikely that a revolution would happen, that people would actually rise up and overthrow the government and restructure the society, at least not within my lifetime. That was not only true of Canada. Through the sixties and early seventies there was a great belief in a global revolution coming. That idea had begun to fade, but people realized that there is still need for change and reform. I began to think that if you can't get a complete restructuring, then it was important to get positioned to be able to make influential decisions without compromising your principles and your beliefs. There were institutions that existed within our society that would allow some progressive change to happen if you go there and you pushed, and the law was one of those areas where decisions were being made that had an incredible impact on the Black community. And those people who were making those decisions, the judges and lawyers, were not part of our community by and large. I was developing a conviction that the law is a route, an instrument, that is relevant in terms of the changes that had to be made. This was not at that time a decision for myself personally to go into law as a profession, but I certainly had a growing belief that the law was relevant.

So there I was at loose ends with these kind of thoughts in my head, when one day as I was walking down Gottingen Street I got into conversation with Vince McDonald, a friend from Cape Breton who was the district director for Corrections Canada. He is asking me what I'm up to now and I said not much of anything, and he said, "How would you like to come to work with me, with ex-cons?" I said, "Well, that's something to think about. What would I be doing?" And he said, "I don't know yet, that would be up to you. I've got some money in my budget and I could pay you. This would be on contract, not a permanent job." So I reported for work and they give me an office, and Vince says "Now you'll have to define your job. I've got the budget to work with prisoners but we don't have a program. We do know that we want them to be able to find jobs and be ready for work when they are finished their sentence." For the next couple of weeks I just talked to people, exploring ideas, and then I went back to Vince. "What everyone is telling me is that we've got to have some sort of employment program, and we have to find a way of letting the guys out of jail, on temporary passes, every once in a while to get them ready." In the early 1980s, Corrections had a mandate for rehabilitation, that the prisoners had to be able to integrate back into mainstream society. Vince was totally supportive of almost anything I wanted to do, so I set up this program called ROPE, Real Opportunities for Prisoner Employment. I was in charge of it, and I hired Gilbert Daye as my staff. He is Buddy Daye's son, someone I've known for years and I knew would be reliable.

One of our first projects was Good Wood Fuels. The idea was that prisoners would be let out to cut down trees in the area around the prison. They would learn to work chainsaws and cutting up wood, splitting it, loading it onto trucks. We put in a proposal and got funding for the project, including a truck to pick up the wood and take it around and sell it as firewood. After getting out of jail they would come and work for Good Wood, and eventually they would get control of the corporation, running it themselves. It was very successful, and it continues to this day. Another interesting program was Straight Ahead Productions, a wood-working business making lawn furniture. We set up a little store on Gottingen Street to sell the things they made, and we also had space for a life-skills course, and the guys could take high-school courses if they were interested. For each of our projects we could apply for funding, in addition to our core funding, which was for me and Gilbert, and then for Marilyn Heal, our secretary. We kept growing. We were still in the Corrections office, but we needed to move out because we were getting more staff and more projects and we got our own office on Gottingen Street just down from

Corrections. It ended up there were five of us, plus Marilyn, and we were going out talking to employers and explaining what our program was about. The response was very good, and a lot of employers agreed to hire our guys. And we had projects of our own where they could be employed. By then we started getting known in the joints, because the prisoners began to know that ROPE would help them find a job when they got out.

We went further than that. I wanted to offer a wilderness experience. I had this idea that if we took the hardest and toughest of the criminals and got them out in the wilderness, then we could get through some of the barriers and maybe reach inside and do some work with them there. We got the government to buy us seven sets of survival things, life jackets, bed rolls, individual cooking pans, little lamps, tents, a complete outfit. So we could take guys out of maximum security, and the authorities by then had that much faith in us that just with my signature I could sign somebody out. A lot of parole officers couldn't do that, but as director of ROPE that is what I did. We hired a leadership expert to set up the program, and Johnny Canoe was our wilderness-experience guy. There was no security on these trips, just us. I've seen times when the boys were a little testy, but we didn't have any open rebellion. The deal was there was no such thing as going AWOL, because if you ever went back to prison, anywhere in the system, somebody would find you, because you were going to ruin it for the next guy. This was the only program available where long-term prisoners could get out for a break. You had to go back when the program was over or the boys would deal with it. This was our insurance.

We worked with the Black Inmates Society and the Indian Brotherhood, but most of our boys were white. The interesting thing was, there was so much racism in the prison, but when they came into the ROPE program they had to leave that at the door. In order to be racist you have to have the power of the institution to back your play, but when they came into our program there was no power in the institution for that kind of thing. They had to leave that and deal with people one on one as individuals, and we really made it work. We promoted the idea that you are indeed your brother's keeper. If you come into the program and your buddy can't read and you can read, then you have a responsibility to try to help him to learn to read, if he so desires. So whatever skills and resources you have, you have a duty to make those skills and resources available to the other people in the program. It allowed people to develop very quickly.

The whole time at ROPE was very exciting for me, seeing how people could grow past their difficulties. But there was one especially exciting adventure that

Gilbert and I had. There was a facility in Halifax called the Carleton Centre. It was like a penitentiary in the community, or a kind of halfway house, for prisoners nearing the end of their sentence. The director was Jack Stewart, and one day Jack comes to me and says, "I've got a favour to ask you. There is a guy in Westmoreland, and I want you to come up with me and speak to the authorities there and get him out so he can come down to the Carleton Centre. The authorities have a lot of faith in you, and if you can vouch for the guy he'll have a better chance of getting out." I said, "I've never even met this guy. What is he like?" "He is a good guy. He sees himself as a real gangster, but he is basically good. He has a long record. In fact he is about 50 years old and has practically spent his whole life in jail." So I said okay. Jack had an appointment at the Dorchester prison right next to Westmoreland. We arranged to meet him at Dorchester and then go together to Westmoreland to try to free the prisoner. The next day Gilbert and I go up to Dorchester in New Brunswick to meet Jack, and they give us an ID card with our names and pictures and offer us a tour of the prison. I had been to Dorchester before, but I had never been inside in the way we were about to do it. You put your belongings on a conveyer belt and they x-ray it, and you go through the machine that x-rays you. Then you go through a gate and the door closes behind you, and then there is another door, and once you are through that door it closes behind you and you hear a clang. By then you are in an area where there is a guy looking through glass, and behind him are all these guns, and he is in this locked room controlling opening and closing the doors. So they open the doors and the doors slide behind us and suddenly you are in the actual prison.

Our guide is taking us down to where they make the mail bags, to see how it is done. As we are walking by we hear, "Nigger, coon, cheeka boo, boo, boo…" I'm looking at Gilbert thinking, this is a fine place for us. There is just us and all of these white boys. Our guide is taking us deeper and deeper into the prison, and I realize that you can't see the gun tower from here. Now if I can't see the gun tower, he can't see me, and I'm thinking, wait a minute, I'm in a hostile environment. So we get into this room, and we are both wearing suits. I'm saying, "Damn why am I in this suit? Jeez these guys think I'm important. They might take us hostage or something." Well we get into the room where they are making the mail bags, and as it happens a good many of them are from the Halifax area. Now they don't want to be too friendly to us, but the biggest commodity in the prison is news. So here we are fresh from outside, from Halifax, and they want to talk to us. The racism is so pervasive, and I understood why they didn't want to seem friendly to two Black visitors.

So I stood in the middle of the floor, and I just started talking. I said, "I saw so and so the other day, and this guy is in bad shape. We were playing poker the other night and he lost this and he lost that and this happened and that happened." And the guys are inching closer because they know the people I'm talking about. And Gilbert is doing the same thing. Now they are starting to ask questions. They want to know about their family. "Have you seen this one? Have you seen that one?"

While we are in there the bells go off, everybody drops their work, and they all leave. We don't know any different, so we leave at the same time and walk back across the yard to go to the administration building. Well it is mealtime, and we are out in the middle of this yard and there are all of these cons, 500 people, and they are loose and we are in the middle. We are saying, "What have we done to ourselves?" So we are out there and we are really nervous, but I'm doing what I have to do to get through this mess. When I get to the administration door, out comes a good friend of mine, Bobby Moore from Dartmouth. He is in there doing life. Bobby says, "Man, what you doing here?" I said, "I've got this job and I'm supposed to be working with prisoners." He said, "Oh, well look it's noon hour. Come see me after lunch." I said, "Where?" He said, "The warden's office. Just tell them you are coming to see me. There is nothing to it, don't worry about it." So we go down and have lunch and afterward I tell Jack, "Look, I want to go and I have a meeting with one of the inmates." "Who is it?" "Bobby Moore." "Well how do you know Bobby Moore?" I said, "Well he is a good friend of mine." It turns out the guy ran Dorchester. Bobby Moore was one of the heavies there. So I go in and see him, and we started talking. He says, "What can I do for you?" I said, "Jeez man, you've got to do something to loosen this place up. I'm on your side, I'm not going to hurt anybody. I can open doors, I can get some guys out." He said, "Okay, when are you coming back?" I said, "Two weeks," and he said, "Okay I'll do what I can do." And now I had an ally and a protector on the inside, and a very useful channel between ROPE and Dorchester.

Anyhow we go over to Westmoreland. Jack had it set up for me to spring this guy named Bob Ebby, so I had to have a meeting with him. I tell him, "Jack Stewart asked me to come and speak at your hearing, to see if we can spring you." He says, "Yeah, like I need your fuckin' help. I make my own fuckin' way in this world, you know." Nasty son of a bitch. I said, "Well listen, you want my help that is up to you. I don't even know you, I'm just doing this because I've been asked by Jack Stewart and I owe Jack." He said, "I don't give a fuck about you Black fellows coming around here. I don't give a shit. I rob banks for a living, I'm no fuckin' petty two-bit criminal. I rob fuckin' banks, that's what I do." So I said, "I don't think you are going to be robbing too many fuckin' banks in Halifax. We've got some stuff to do and Jack Stewart believes that you can do it and I have a job to do and we can work together." Okay, so I went to the parole hearing and I spoke on his behalf. I said, "He comes to me highly recommended by Jack Stewart, and I'll give him a ticket into our program and I'll keep him with me every day. We'll give the guy a shot and see what happens." They actually let him out to leave with us that day. First day I'd ever met him, he gets sprung, and we bring him back to Halifax. As it turned out he was the first person we enrolled in Straight Ahead Productions.

The ROPE program worked very closely with another program in Ontario, called HELP. It was run by ex cons, a self-help group set up by Tony McGillvray. He had a background similar to Bob Ebby's, a hard guy, just in and out of prison from the time he was old enough to be put into a prison, and foster homes before that. They also were into programming to make people responsible for their own actions and trying to help the inmates get turned around and able to deal with being in society. We travelled to Kingston to visit the HELP program, and we ended up having quite a close association with Tony. He said ROPE was one of the most successful rehabilitation programs that have ever been offered in our federal penitentiary system. An incredible number of people went through it, a lot of jobs created, a lot of people got a fresh start because of it. We must have averaged a couple of hundred people a year, over a thousand while ROPE was operating. There is one guy I placed at the Victoria General Hospital. I just saw him recently. He is still there, a full-time employee looking after their heart machines, computerized machines, that's how good this guy is, and he was in jail. Another guy was a lifer who became a draftsman with ROPE's help. One time I was in Whitehorse, in the Yukon, and as I was going down the street I heard my name. A guy comes up to me and says, "Rocky, you don't remember me. I went through the ROPE program. You guys saved me. If it hadn't been for ROPE, I wouldn't have been up here working." So I met a lot of cons who said that our program really made a difference.

In 1987 the federal government began to change their orientation drastically from rehabilitation to behaviour modification, and as such they weren't prepared to spend money on our kind of programs. They did offer us the opportunity to do contract work or become parole officers. Vince McDonald said, "We're sorry. This is what happened: The funding isn't coming down, but I would give you a contract and you could open a halfway house, or go work in halfway houses." I put the option to my staff, to make up their own minds.

I had no desire to be a parole officer or to be responsible for people in that fashion. I didn't want any part of it. I was on the loose again.

Now, and just at the right time for me, I was offered another contract by BUF. At this time BUF is in a state of flux. Hamid Rasheed (formerly Art Criss) had been overthrown as executive director and moved out in the fall of 1983, amidst accusations of misuse of funds. In fact the provincial government suspended their funding for about a year because of these alleged "irregularities." Then Captain George Borden was seconded from the Department of Social Services to serve as interim director. George Borden comes as a representative of government, supported by government and funded by government. So when he comes in to take over there is a certain reaction, but he brings with him the credibility of having been in the armed services, and being part of the Borden family, so he does have acceptance in the community. He is the ideal candidate in the mind of the government, to be used in this absolute take-over of BUF. In effect Edmund Morris, the Minister of Social Services, is the real person in charge, and he is the same man I ran against in the 1980 by-election. And it is during this time of Edmund Morris and George Borden that I was appointed to the BUF board! Only in Nova Scotia! Whether the minister himself had a hand in it I don't know. If so, perhaps he thought I'd be neutralized as an appointed board member. While George Borden is at BUF, there is rebellion in the staff. People are concerned because there were accusations that someone was taking material out of the BUF offices and hiding it. George resigns in the midst of all of this and is replaced by Rick Joseph. He was coming from the government too, but not seconded. He was appointed as executive director in his own right. I personally didn't know Rick Joseph before his involvement with BUF or even who he was. He was not a community activist.

So there I am on the BUF board, participating in some interesting discussions, and the Marshall Inquiry is being set up. In 1971 Donald Marshall Jr., a 17-year-old Mi'kmaq from the Membertou Reserve in Sydney, was convicted of murdering his friend Sandy Seale, who was Black. After serving 11 years of a life sentence Marshall was found to have been wrongfully convicted. An RCMP investigation found that a particular police officer had been using intimidation and perjured evidence. In spite of this report the Nova Scotia Supreme Court decided that there was no miscarriage of justice. "There can be no doubt that Donald Marshall's untruthfulness through this whole affair contributed in large measure to his conviction." Well this provoked a huge outcry, from the Mi'kmaq and from the Black community, including myself. We demanded a public inquiry, and we got one, the Royal Commission on the Donald Marshall

Jr. Prosecution, chaired by Judge T. Alexander Hickman from Newfoundland. My research contract with BUF came in 1988, and by this time Jerry Taylor was the executive director and Yvonne Atwell was the research director. With Jerry and Yvonne, BUF was more progressive than it had been in a long time. My job was to examine five cases involving the death of Black persons, and this was to be presented to the Marshall Inquiry as evidence of the situation for Black people in Nova Scotia and in the justice system in particular. Since the victim in the original Marshall case, Sandy Seale, was Black, BUF, as the supposed voice of the Black community, was given official standing at the inquiry. I was later given another contract to write a critical commentary on Volume 4 of the Commissioner's Report, *Discrimination Against Blacks in Nova Scotia: The Criminal Justice System,* which had been written for the Commission by Wilson Head and Don Clairmont.

When I did these reports, it became very clear how the legal profession treated us. It was extremely important that the story and the position of Black people be put forward. There was a lot of agitation about Black people being left out of this inquiry, so Tony Ross was hired to represent our interests at the public hearings in the Lord Nelson Hotel. He was there being paid every day to go to these hearings, and everyone expected that Tony would give a report on behalf of the Black community and BUF. Then Jerry Taylor said to me, "You've got to be the one to present our position to the inquiry." What I presented was like a political speech, including a historical overview of the Black settlement of Nova Scotia. I was pointing out the exclusion of Black people in the justice system, and speaking to the need for inclusion. I don't have it written down anywhere. I just spoke about what I knew, including what I'd found out during my BUF contract. It was a big room, filled with people. Instead of having the chairs in a row, they had tables for people to sit around. There were a lot of academics. I was sitting at a table with Richard Devlin, Wayne MacKay and others, all from the law school. The crowd was very mixed racially, a lot of Aboriginal people, a lot of Black people and obviously a lot of white people. Judge Hickman had just an incredible and powerful presence, but by the same token he was a typical Newfoundlander with that really likeable way about him. That allowed him to move from being a Supreme Court justice to just being a good guy, a regular Joe. The day I spoke there was a panel of others also giving speeches, but I was the only one representing the Black community. It was very exciting because there was a lot of apprehension about what I was going to say; the room was quite electric. The Black people were really encouraging. You just had that sense that they were there to encourage you. There was an incredible acceptance to this particular speech. I've spoken at a lot of places, but that was a real highlight, excellent response.

As I was sitting at the table with those people from Dalhousie Law School, we began to talk about the idea that there were not enough Black or Aboriginal people attending law school. And I was starting backwards, I was saying there are not enough Black judges here, and the point was made that you can't have Black judges if you don't have Black lawyers, and there are no Black lawyers, or very few. So we said we should start a program for Black lawyers, a special program to get into the law school, modelled after the TYP. We then set up a committee, including my sister Janis, myself, Richard Devlin, Wayne MacKay, Maxine Tynes, Dean Innis Christie and some other people from the law school who came along. It was really Richard Devlin who was mostly involved from the law school. And we wrote up a report called *A Proposal to Increase the Access of Blacks at Dalhousie Law School.* In this original proposal we were talking strictly about Black people. While we were working on this project, it was the same thing that happened with the TYP: It started off as something we were going to do in the Black community, but it was made very clear to us that it would not fly if it was a program strictly for Blacks. Because of its genesis in the Marshall Inquiry and Donald Marshall was Mi'kmaq, and with funding considerations on top of it, we had to include the Mi'kmaq community. We didn't have a problem with that, though we didn't have anyone from the Mi'kmaq community involved in setting it up from the beginning. After our TYP experience, this meant that politically we should do some back-tracking to get the Native community on board. So we went back and changed the terms of reference; we broadened the idea of the program and that's what eventually got funded. Now this is worthy of discussion, because the Black community was not, and in my opinion still is not, seen as legitimately in need of special funding. The government is not prepared to fund these special programs for Black people, unless they are getting money from Indian Affairs or they are getting help to fund it at the national level. Obviously we are not a priority. Even though we are initiating these programs, we are actually treated as the add-on. In the end the program was approved by the law school as the Indigenous Blacks and Micmacs Program, or IBM. "Indigenous Blacks" meaning African Canadians with ancestral ties to Nova Scotia, and "Micmac" was then the accepted spelling for the province's Aboriginals. We weren't hurt by the fact that in Judge Hickman's final report he recommended that support should be given to Dalhousie's proposed special program to recruit qualified minority students interested in a legal career.

Once the program was approved we began recruiting suitable students. As I was encouraging other people to enrol, they began challenging me: "If this is so important, why don't you do it yourself?" I took the same position with this as I did on fostering and adopting Black children. I realized that if I was going to make an argument that anybody could do this, I had to be prepared to put my money where my mouth is. I had no expectation that my application would be successful; it was something that I had to do. So I didn't even put my mind to going to law school as a desire or a possibility. I put in my application and went out to B.C. on a fishing trip, where I was offered a job as a guide at a fishing camp. I was leaning toward taking that job. It was a long way from home and my family lived in Nova Scotia, but I was seriously considering relocating. And then I got a notice telling me that I had been accepted. But law school was starting in September and I was on a trip that I wasn't prepared to cut short. So I put it up to fate. If I can still get in when I get back to Halifax, okay; if not, then that is the way it is going to be, but I certainly wasn't going to cut my fishing trip short. I found out the opening would wait for me, so I stayed out West and completed my trip, and turned down the job as a guide. I've often had second thoughts: that might have been a nice career move for me.

So there I am in the fall of 1989, almost 50 years old, and a freshman again. When I came into the IBM program I was with the first group, and the law students themselves didn't understand what the program was about. They thought that we were getting a special consideration at the exams and that sort of thing. I think as well that there was a sense that people in IBM were taking up spots that rightfully belonged to other people. So there was a certain disdain for IBM students until I think the first set of exams were written, and they began to understand that the IBM students went through the same apprehension as every other law student. We had to continually explain that we had a leg up to get in but we don't have a leg up to get out. Then the students in the law school became more open toward us, but like anywhere else in Canadian society we had detractors. The law school did in fact have a lot of support for us, with tutors available to give us extra help. Now it is true, for those of us in that first group, we were not necessarily the best scholars in the world. Many of us were older students, and even the younger ones were not fresh out of school. We had all been out working and were going back, as opposed to students who had taken high school, their BA and then law school, so we had different challenges. Of course some of the regular students were older and had to look after families and so on, and had the same challenges we had. The profs, generally speaking, were very supportive; they really went the extra mile. I'd say by my second year I had a sense of belonging at the law school.

My favourite class was on the Charter of Rights and Freedoms, where we looked at a lot of contemporary issues, community issues, Aboriginals, sex, race. I loved that material and I shared the prize as top student in that class. The class I had most difficulty with was property and contracts, and this is ironic because later on I would make most of my living doing property law. I think that Black people grow up in a communal environment and property and contracts are a foreign concept. When you grow up in a Black community, the community has most of the rights to start with and you as an individual have to fit into that community structure. But when you do law it is the individual and the individual property rights that are the most important. It is a reversal of your whole mindset and it takes a long while to figure that out. I had to understand that in terms of the law you put the individual on top, and it is with the individual's rights that you start your analysis. The Aboriginal people too were arguing that what they were being taught was so individu-alistic and not part of their tradition, and they wanted to have some classes looking at Aboriginal concepts of law and ownership and distribution. They still had to pass these other courses, but they were making representations to the law school that they needed classes to examine their communal way of life. It is a whole different way of thinking. Nevertheless it was extremely thrilling for me to be in an environment like the law school. Financially, we got our tuition paid and there was a stipend of maybe $500 per month. Plus I won a couple of prizes that helped with expenses. I won the Goldenberg Prize, which paid $1200 or $1500 for getting the top mark in a course, and there was the G.I. Smith memorial prize, which was more of a bursary.

The way that law school works is different from other disciplines. You have what they call cans, which are like crib notes. You go to a class, you listen to a prof, and you synthesize what they said and pick out the most important points, and you also read the required readings, and you condense that. In the end you have the readings condensed and the prof's position on the readings, and of course the best notes are written by the top students. Now law school is extremely competitive. Some students actually tear pages out of some of the readings that are on reserve in the library so that other students can't get the answers. So these cans, or notes, are jealously guarded and they are not passed around, except in your little study group. You are set up in a study group with four or maybe six people. Suppose you are very good in contracts, so it would be up to you to bring in cans on contracts and property, and someone else on another course. And you share your notes and discuss it. Well I had access to the best cans in the law school at all times. I am an outdoors man, and so I was able to take the smartest students in the law school and say, if you help me I'll help you. I'll take you out canoeing and fishing and show you Nova Scotia; you show me how to do this law work. I was able to have the assistance of some of the smartest students at the school. My group was called the Outdoor Enthusiasts. We went out, we camped, chummed around and it was very exclusive. A lot of people wanted to become part of the Outdoor Enthusiasts but you had to be very special to join. I just happened to have two of the top students in the whole school in our group, so that was very, very good for me, considering that I was a little older and not quite as fast, and I didn't come from a tradition of doing law in my family. One of those top students went salmon fishing with me and I was able to get him into a salmon, and I'm sure to this day he knows that he owes me! When the time came for me to graduate, in 1992, I was elected valedictorian for the Dalhousie Law School. I think the reason I was elected was that the student body wanted to endorse the program. They wanted to say as a body that this was something good to do and they supported it. I'm not playing down whatever I may have done personally, but I think that election was more about the general politics of the law school and the acceptance of the IBM program.

Since that first group of IBM students we are getting more and more Black people who are not from here. It is not just for Indigenous Blacks and Mi'kmaqs; the program has expanded so that the people are African Canadians and they can very easily be the sons and daughters of the Black elite in Montreal and Toronto. They are not going to stay in Nova Scotia. More and more, the students are not selected because of their commitment to work with or for the community; they are selected because of their academic background. We argued when we set up the program that we needed more lawyers so we could have eventually more judges, and we needed a critical mass of Black lawyers in this province. If the students going through law school are not from Nova Scotia we'll never acquire that critical mass, and we can't fulfill our original goals. Naturally the law school is jealous of its reputation and its graduates, and we are a small pool when you are looking at the numbers of people available to attend the law school and to fill, say, ten positions per year. There are not that many people in this area, so the calibre of the students may not be as high as the university would want, generally speaking. By opening it up, it then becomes a way to attract some of the better scholars across the country who happen to be African-descended people. I think the end is in sight for the idea that the program is the special preserve of Nova Scotia Blacks and Mi'kmaq.

Another issue is that although we have increased the number of Black students in the law schools, when they come out they primarily have gone to work for government, either for legal aid as part of the defence bar, or for prosecution services or the Department of Justice. There are a number of reasons for that. In our community we don't have a tradition of people being involved in law, or knowledge of the rigours of running a law practice. It is a business, a very ruthless, tough business. And we don't have mentors in our community to help out when you are coming out of law school. So for young Black law grads, the prospect of going into private practice, and the amount of money that has to be paid back to student loans and the amount of money you need to front your business is very intimidating. Without support it is not something that many Black lawyers want to take on. But if you go with the government, you've got a salary and a pension. Another thing is that a lot of the lawyers coming out of law school got their articles with government, because the bar society or the members of the bar were not that open to taking Black students. And when you see what has happened to some of the Black lawyers who have gone into private practice, government work seems a much better option. Of the handful of Black lawyers in the province before IBM started, at least half of them have been at some point under siege by the bar society. Now the question would certainly have to be asked, "Are Black lawyers more prone to be deviant, or more incompetent than their fellow members of the bar, or is it possible that Black lawyers, doing the same thing in the same fashion as white lawyers, are targeted?" My analysis would be that the Black lawyers faced a number of hurdles and difficulties that were political. First, most Black lawyers in private practice were in very small firms, either alone or with one other person, because the larger firms would not hire them. This made the Black lawyers more vulnerable. Secondly I do believe that the Black lawyers were targeted and treated more harshly than their white counterparts because of overt racism.

After I graduated I went to do my articles with my friend Jamie Armour, who was director of Legal Aid in Windsor. He invited me to join him, and this was a very good thing for me. I wanted to do Legal Aid in the first place, because that's where you get to help poor people who can't afford a high-priced lawyer. Also the Windsor Legal Aid office has responsibility for the Shubenacadie reserve, and I'd have a good opportunity to work with Natives as well as the Blacks in the Windsor region. And finally I could work with a good friend who was also a brilliant criminal lawyer. Jamie and I had been hunting and fishing buddies while he was a student at the Dal Law School. I had everything I could imagine.

In Shubenacadie I had a chance to observe firsthand the attitudes of the Natives and how they confront racism, which is different from Blacks. In the high school, for example, the white students would call the Mi'kmaqs "wagon burners" and other names like that. One day a younger Native boy was beaten up by several whites, and then after school some of the Native kids went to the whites who had done it, and there was a bust-up. The school then suspended all the Native kids who had been involved, but none of the whites. Furthermore one of the Native boys was charged by the RCMP. I was assigned to defend him. My first question was, why was the Native charged, and not any of the whites. I wanted to raise the issue of race. I was told in no uncertain terms that the issue was not racism, just a problem among schoolboys. I attempted, without success, to argue that the way the school dealt with it was racist, that the RCMP was racist in laying charges only against this boy, and the genesis of the whole thing was in a racist episode in the schoolyard. But the kid's mother insisted that my analysis was wrong, so I had to drop that argument. The kid himself and his buddies knew it was racism, but they refused to name it. On a couple of other occasions with obvious racial overtones I was told by Native clients not to raise it. I was very surprised. That year in Shubenacadie gave me a chance to learn a lot more about the Native community than I ever had before, even with my experience with Natives in TYP. There were also cases I had to deal with from Blacks in Windsor, but there was nothing really significant. Mostly it was petty crimes. This is not an urban environment, and the crimes reflect that, things like domestic violence, petty thefts, fights. There had never been a Black lawyer in Windsor before I came. As a professional I had a certain social position, but the white townspeople made it clear that I was not like them. Windsor was extremely segregated, rigidly stratified. In the downtown stores you wouldn't see more than maybe one Black person working there.

The experience in Windsor was exceptional, because of Jamie himself and because of the interaction I had with both Blacks and Natives that year. The judges I must say were very open and fair toward me. There was not one incident where I felt a judge was discriminating against me; in fact they were extremely helpful. The other lawyers were helpful as well. Though some of them were right-wing bigots, they were decent toward me. That time in Windsor is a year that I treasure. While I was doing my articles I had to apply for bar admission, and one of the questions on the form was "Have you ever been convicted of a criminal offence?" Now I had a conviction, but I had been pardoned so I didn't think I should have to put this in my application. I objected to this as being unconstitutional, in fact. But Jamie said to me, "Look, they already know about your conviction. The people reading your application were either defending you, prosecuting you, or judging you. You've got to pick your battles, and this isn't one of them." He was right, of course. Jamie was very wise.

After my admission to the bar I was offered a job by Dalhousie Legal Aid. They came to me; I didn't have to apply. They already knew me because I had been a student there for one of my summer terms. You could get 13 credits toward your degree by working there for the 13-week summer. Many of the professional staff were away, on holiday or whatever, so we students had long periods without supervision. We had to do things on our own. I was fortunate with the group of students I was working with. I learned a lot from them, and from the work we did. It was my best experience in law school. So now they are inviting me to join the Legal Aid Clinic full-time. They did a lot of family law and I knew I didn't want to do that, so we designed my job not only as a lawyer but as a community worker, and this suited me just fine.

My main responsibilities were to defend young offenders and to do community organizing. The Dalhousie Legal Aid Clinic at that time had a three-pronged approach to law. First, there were academic pursuits for the students who were attached there; second was the straight clinical practice of law, preparing court cases and so on; and third was law reform and community activism. In other words the Clinic's mandate was to participate in community development and law reform, and this was true from the time when it was set up. At that time we got block funding, from the Law Foundation, with an additional grant from Legal Aid and another grant from the university itself. Today the Clinic is funded by the cases it does. For example, if you have a youth court case it takes so many hours, and Dal Legal Aid bills Nova Scotia Legal Aid accordingly. So now the Clinic has to churn out cases in order to survive. Law reform and community engagement are no longer a part of their mandate. This all happened after I left, and I think it is too bad. I suspect it was a deliberate strategy to stifle the activism that had been very much a part of our activity.

I also had teaching responsibility for the law students attached to the Clinic. I did a seminar every week on racism and other contemporary issues like sexism. There were about a dozen students. Early in the term we were talking about poverty issues and how racial attitudes affect whether you are rich or poor. We had this one young woman from Newfoundland who sticks up her hand and says, "I know you're all going to laugh at me when I say this." I said, "No, no, we might not agree with you and we'll discuss what you say, but nobody's going to laugh at you." "Well," she said, "when I was growing up in my small town in Newfoundland, I thought all Black people were rich. All the Black people in our town were doctors in the hospital." Well we did have a little chuckle over that, and it gave us a great opportunity to examine how stereotypes come about. It was very useful, a meaningful illustration. I always tried to keep social issues in front of the students, to educate them to look at a legal problem as a reflection of a social problem. We tried to be broader in our approach to legal issues, for the problem is not just the crime itself. This was right up my alley. It suited me perfectly. I saw law as an extension of my political beliefs, a way of making some changes and challenging how things are done through the law. This was part of the continuum of my development, a natural progression from what I had always been doing, only now, as a lawyer, it gave me some legitimacy. It was just a different approach to putting change into effect. I had the opportunity to use the law as I thought it should be used, to develop community projects and to take up legal issues that were significant for the community and for society as a whole.

I was called to the bar in 1993, when I was working at Dal Legal Aid. It was an important year for me in terms of my career, but it was even more important in terms of my life because that's when Sharon and I got married. The newspaper ran a story: "The radical and the lovely banker wed in Tantallon." I first met Sharon many years before at the Lord Nelson Hotel in the Victory Lounge. A mutual friend introduced us, and we developed a very positive relationship. When Joan and I first separated in 1985, I camped in the ROPE office for a bit and then I moved in with my friend Bruce McCullough in Bedford. Sharon also lived in Bedford and so it was very close. It is important to state that I did not leave Joan for Sharon. Sharon had absolutely nothing to do with my separation from Joan. It was only when ROPE was ended in 1987 that I moved in with Sharon in her house. Sharon was a banker so she had her own independent career and wasn't relying on me for anything. When we lived in Bedford I had my own friends there. I liked to sail, and I had friends who had a sailboat. Then in 1989 we moved to Tantallon, St. Margaret's Bay, to a house owned by Sharon's parents. In fact it was the house where Sharon grew up. It was a beautiful spot. I'd look out my window and see a fox, and there would be a couple of deer. Or you look out the other side and you'd see the mackerel breaking on the surface of the water when it was mackerel season. I could drive home at the end of the day, dive off the wharf and go swimming and go fishing. The reason we moved there was because her father was sick and she wanted to move close to him, so she could assist her mother in looking after him.

We stayed in St Margaret's Bay all the time I was in law school and while I was doing my articles in Windsor. We had a good time out in St Margaret's Bay. It was a real community of people who were around the same age and we used to have these parties and go swimming in the bay. For my 50th birthday they had a big surprise party for me. When we came down the highway there was a big sign, "Nifty Nifty Burnley's Fifty." We had lots and lots of mussels, so we would have a party and you could go down in the bay and get mussels, and you go out on the bay and catch mackerel, and then you'd get the fresh corn from the farmers and you could feed 50 people for $10, because the mussels were free, the mackerel was free, and people would bring their own beer. You could have a big cook-out and it didn't cost you hardly any money. I certainly enjoyed living out in the Bay although it was difficult in so much as there are no Black people living there. Somebody shot my yellow lab with a .22 when I first moved in, somebody who apparently didn't want me living there. There was a certain harassment in the first little while.

I had some resistance from Sharon's father, who just didn't approve of his daughter living with a Black man. Sharon's mother on the other hand was one of the most loving people I've ever met. She later came to live with us in Halifax, for 13 years. She was just an absolutely beautiful person, totally non-judgmental. She had been a schoolteacher in a one-room schoolhouse in St. Margaret's Bay, very gentle person, never gossiped. When she died some of her former pupils came to the funeral. They had many fond memories of her. The two of them, the mother and father, lived up the hill, we lived down the hill. Our daughter Shalyn was running up and down between the houses, and Sharon's father thought that the sun rose and set on Shalyn. He was a bit of a contradiction, but he was old and that was his way. Sharon's brother Bob was a really good guy. He was like his mother, easy going and non-judgmental. When I was first going out with Sharon, he had his own apartment and I could go and stay with him there. And her younger brother Neil was also the same way. I must say Sharon's family all in all were very easy to get along with. Even her father for all of his ways didn't bother me much. I always teased and said I kept him alive for three years because he got such excitement out of insulting me. I gave him something to look forward to.

Our wedding was on Thanksgiving Weekend in 1993, while we were living in the old farm house. The wedding was on the property, outdoors. People came from all over, and wouldn't you know it, it rained. Our guests were wearing their rubber boots, and their slickers, and their outdoor gear, or some were in their high heels or whatever. The first idea was that I would arrive by ship, sailing up the harbour with a friend of mine in his boat. But the weather turned sour and we decided not to do that. So instead we just walked up the hill to where the ceremony was going to take place. I was wearing my African robes, a sort of a brown flowing robe with nice embroidery, and Sharon was wearing an embroidered white African-style outfit with a white headdress. Our daughter Shalyn was the bridesmaid. It was a civil wedding, performed by Bob Leavy, and we made it an African wedding. We had to jump the broom. Then the sun came out and it turned into a really beautiful day. A deer came bounding across the field while the ceremony was going on. We were being blessed by Mother Nature. Afterwards we had a dinner and party at the Fleet Club in Halifax for family and close friends, about 150 people altogether. My brother Roger was master of ceremonies, and we had a number of speeches. Then we had a really big party that anybody could come to at the Lord Nelson. The next day we just came back to Tantallon for our honeymoon, and Barry Stewart came with us. I spent the rest of my honeymoon going over the Black HERO Tapes with Jim Walker. Sharon and Shalyn and I lived on in the farm-house for a couple of months, and then in December 1993 we moved into Halifax, to a comfortable house on Romans Avenue.

Chapter Nine

INTO THE
COURTROOM

It would be fair to say that I'd had an ongoing issue with the police ever since Kwacha House, and my own attitudes and experiences were generally reflected throughout the Black community. My two biggest legal experiences, *R v. RDS* (scc, 1997) and *Campbell v. Jones and Derrick*, related specifically to my contention that the police were an occupying force in the Black community. That political position had not changed in 25 years. The difference was that now I was able to articulate a position that had legitimacy within the Canadian legal system. I had become part of the established system and as such I was gaining some kind of influence, certainly enough to be able to push a position and give it some validity because the courts ruled in my favour. In the 1950s Martin Luther King declared that he was "taking the struggle out of the courtroom and into the streets," referring to the long history of court battles waged by the NAACP against racial discrimination in the States. In a way I was reversing this process.

The case known as *RDS* began when I was just beginning my time as a staff lawyer at the Dalhousie Legal Aid Service. I was very new. A kid and his mother came in to see me, and it was arranged that I would represent the kid in court. He was charged with obstruction and assault against a police officer. He was known throughout the case by his initials because he was a juvenile, only 15. Since he is now an adult, and has become a personal friend of mine, I can give him his proper name: Rodney Small. As we were preparing for our court appearance there was no expectation that anything out of the ordinary would happen. It's hard to describe how "routine" it all was. The charges were straightforward, there were no witnesses to call, no experts. Bottom line was there were two versions of the story of what had happened; it would be up to the judge to make a decision over which story was more credible.

There were several postponements, all at the request of the police, before we finally got into court on December 2, 1994, over a year after the confrontation between RDS and the police, which occurred on October 17, 1993. As we entered the courtroom, and this was first time this had ever happened for me, I saw that the court clerk, the client, the lawyer and the judge were all Black! Only the prosecutor and the cop were white. My plan going in was to focus on the use of the term "non-white" in the call that went out over the police radio, leading up to the arrest of RDS. I always say to the community, "You're not a 'non' anything. Don't accept this negative definition. It makes white the norm." I wanted to get the police to stop using that over the radio, and I hoped this case might have that kind of influence. The incident itself was not so much in dispute, as I thought the facts were more or less the same.

I had interviewed RDS in advance, of course, but as it turned out that preparation left a lot to be desired. The cop comes to the stand first. The Crown thought they had a snap case, so they didn't call any other witnesses. Constable Donald Stienburg was riding in his patrol car when they get the call that some non-whites had stolen a van. Stienburg and his partner see some non-whites running through Uniacke Square. They separate and chase them, and Stienburg apprehends one of them. A crowd gathers at the scene of the arrest, and along comes RDS. He runs his bike into the cop, beats him on the chest, obstructs him, and so the cop arrests him. In my questioning I hit him with "non-white," trying to make a point. The kid they wanted could have been Chinese, or Native, or anything. This was not a valid description, and it showed a certain attitude on the part of the police by suggesting a negative identity for Black people. He answers that this is the usual terminology used by the Halifax police, nothing personal in it. Then my client goes to the witness box. He is riding along on his bike and he sees his cousin Nathaniel being arrested. He goes up to his cousin and says, "What's happening? Shall I call your mother?" The cop says, "Shut up or you'll be under arrest too." Then RDS says, "The next thing I know I'm in a chokehold and passing out!" This is the first time this has been mentioned that the cop put him in a chokehold. I drew him out on it, and the Crown realizes they've got a problem. The Crown was Rick Miller, from the North End of Halifax. He was pretty new to the game, I don't think much more experienced than I was, and a bit of a hawk. They expected this to be a slamdunk and didn't think they needed to bring out their heavy guns. RDS denies that he ran into the cop or hit him; he didn't even speak to the cop, only to his cousin. RDS is saying there were all these little kids who gathered around, seven or eight year olds. The cop had presented a picture of being intimidated by a crowd, but now I find out it's little kids. In my first examination of the cop I still thought it was adults in the crowd. As the description of the event gets filled out, we discover that the cop had the cousin in handcuffs at the time RDS rode up to them, that the cop put both RDS and Nathaniel (identified by the initials NR) in chokeholds, that this "intimidating" crowd was made up of little children, and this scene is so dangerous the cop calls for back-up. RDS was a skinny little guy, more like a 12-year-old, small for his age. His cousin was the size of a typical 14-year-old. The constable was a well-built six-footer. With his back-up they get RDS down to the station, run a check on him and discover he has no previous record, and then they hit him with three charges: assaulting Constable Stienburg in the execution of his duty, assaulting him with the intent to prevent the arrest of NR, and unlawfully resisting arrest. Well, this is over-charging to say the least, and I point this out in court.

The judge was Corrine Sparks, known to her friends as Connie, the first Black judge to be appointed in Nova Scotia and the first female Black judge anywhere in Canada.

She delivers an oral judgment and says while she doesn't believe everything she heard from the boy, she'd heard enough to raise a doubt as to his guilt, and this must be resolved in favour of the accused. Then Rick Miller, the inexperienced Crown, interrupts and asks her why a cop would lie in court. It's Stienburg's story that should be believed. Connie responds, as is shown in the transcript of the case: "I'm not saying that the constable misled the Court, although police officers have been known to do that in the past. And I'm not saying that the officer overreacted, but certainly police officers do overreact, particularly when they're dealing with non-white groups. That, to me, indicates a state of mind right there that is questionable." And then she adds, "I believe that probably the situation in this particular case is the case of a young police officer who overreacted. And I do accept the evidence of Mr. S that he was told to shut up or he would be under arrest. That seems to be in keeping with the prevalent order of the day." These few sentences caused all the trouble.

Constable Stienburg is upset by this decision calling his testimony into doubt. He goes out and calls his chief and his union, and they make a big fuss over the judge's remarks. He claims she acted with racial prejudice against a white police officer. Nobody expected it, not me and not Judge Sparks. So the

Crown files an appeal against the judgment, claiming that Connie's decision showed both actual and apprehended bias in favour of the accused and against the police officer because of his race. Connie Sparks realizes that she had better give a more complete explanation for her judgment, and she issues her written Supplementary Reasons in response to the claims made in the appeal. She does a great job, pointing out that the Crown had not brought any evidence to contradict RDS's testimony, that putting him in a chokehold was harsh and unnecessary, and that the Marshall Inquiry provided lots of evidence of police behaviour toward persons of colour. Now that was highly unusual, for a judge to add their reasons after the trial, and it just put more fuel on the fire. You've got all kinds of lawyers weighing in, legal opinions: should she have issued these Supplementary Reasons, can the appeal court consider these reasons along with the original decision and so on.

Obviously this appeal puts RDS back into jeopardy, so he has to be defended again. And Connie is in jeopardy too, as her professional integrity is being challenged. I put the law students at the Legal Clinic to work on background research. We left no stone unturned. We found there was no other similar case. Never in the history of Canada has there been a charge that a judge is racially biased, especially against the police. A lot of legal issues had to be thought about for the appeal. For example, we had to write a brief about whether a judge could make a supplemental judgment. It was a good thing I was at Dalhousie Legal Aid, as I had the kind of resources to pursue these issues. I had a lot of help not only from the students but from the faculty in the law school in preparing for the appeal case. It's April 18, 1995 before we get back into court. The Crown this time is Adrian C. Reid, a senior Crown and used to doing appeal work. He argued that Connie's decision was not based on the evidence that came forward at the trial, but purely on the fact that she was racially biased, that there was not just an "apprehension of bias" but *actual* bias displayed in the original judgment. The hearing was conducted before Chief Justice of Nova Scotia Constance Glube. I had high expectations of Justice Glube. She seemed to be a progressive person, and her own son had had some trouble with the police in the past. But this was not to be. First she excluded the information in Connie's Supplementary Reasons on the grounds that they contained material that had not been entered in evidence at the trial. The Marshall Inquiry, for example, with all its evidence about police misconduct, could not be considered. She said that Connie's decision up to the point where she declared that she had a reasonable doubt about RDS's guilt was fine, but when she added her remarks about the police, any "right-minded person" would find that she had shown "a reasonable apprehension of bias." So the charge of actual bias was dropped, but on the basis of the apprehension of bias, Constance Glube ordered a new trial "in front of a different trial judge." Since Connie was the only Black judge in the juvenile court, this meant RDS would be appearing before a white judge next time round.

The community was stirred up about this, because after all those years of Black people experiencing bias from police and courts, now, for the first time, a Black judge gets accused of racial bias. I knew absolutely that Glube had to be appealed further. The Crown says to me, "Don't worry about a new trial. The kid won't be in big trouble. We'll make a deal."

I say, "How can I make a deal, when Judge Sparks was right? Cops do overreact when dealing with Black kids." So I go to the Clinic and say I want to appeal Glube's decision. The Clinic says, "That will take a lot of resources." I almost lost my job on that one. It was a knock-down fight. I had the support of the law school, so the Clinic finally agreed to the appeal. Connie Sparks was out of the game at this point, unable to defend herself. There were no senior Black lawyers around in Halifax. Tony Ross had gone, Davies Bagambire had gone. People I could have turned to weren't there. I'm stuck with it. I was never the greatest scholar. I wouldn't pick me to argue such a case! But fortunately with serious help from the law school profs, especially Richard Devlin, Dianne Pothier and Carol Aylward, and from some of the Clinic students, we put together a case to carry to the Nova Scotia Court of Appeal. We argued that the test for a reasonable apprehension of bias had been too strictly interpreted by Justice Glube, and that Judge Sparks had been justified in considering the racial implications of the case in front of her. To ignore the race factor in a situation like that is not neutrality, but in fact perpetuates racial inequality by pretending it is not there. To eliminate racism, it has to be confronted directly, as Connie had done, and we argued that this is supported by the definition of equality rights in the Charter of Rights and Freedoms.

The appeal was heard by three justices, Freeman, Pugsley and Flinn, on October 13, 1995. They split two to one against us, meaning that RDS would have to be tried again on his original charges. Flinn and Pugsley concluded that the Charter issue could not be introduced, as it had not appeared in the previous trial, and that Connie Sparks's decision had demonstrated an apprehension of bias. Justice Freeman disagreed. He said it was proper to consider the racial issue in a case like this, and Connie had used her own "wisdom and experience" in assessing the evidence before her. He ruled that Connie's judgment should be restored, but he was outvoted. There was only one route to follow: appeal to the Supreme Court of Canada! So I say to the Clinic, "Now I want to appeal this decision. Justice Freeman did a very strong dissent. He gave me the arguments. He's a real scholar. All the legal precedents were laid out. All I have to do is argue what he argued." Again there's a battle, because of the cost in pursuing an appeal and because we now had lost twice on appeal and our prospect didn't look all that great. A lot of people I respected, even Jamie Armour, thought I was wrong to push this case, but eventually I got Dalhousie's support. We got a Court Challenges grant toward our expenses, and Dal put up the rest of the money.

I have to apply for leave to appeal, because there's no automatic right to go to the Supreme Court of Canada. We applied for leave on the grounds of national importance, to determine the threshold of bias for a judge, as that would affect every judge in Canada. The other issue we put forward is what right and under what circumstances can a judge rely on their own experience, because this is where it all came from. Justice Freeman gave me this inside track in his decision, and I knew the Supreme Court would have to take his dissent very seriously. We were successful, and once we had the leave, the issue becomes strategy. What are we going to argue? I met with the academics from the law school, and it was decided that we should make a Charter argument based on Section 7 (the principle of fundamental justice), Section 11(d) (right to a fair and public hearing) and Section 15(1) (the right to equality). But I wasn't comfortable arguing the Charter in this case. So they agreed Dianne Pothier would argue the Charter and I'd argue the rest of it.

I had to develop the argument, based on Freeman, that a judge not only could but *should* use their life experience to interpret the context of the case before them. I had to go to the law school to make the argument in front of the faculty and students, like a moot court. Because we were successful with Freeman, and because the Supreme Court agreed to hear us, obviously his argument had validity. I make my argument, and the profs start shooting me down. At the end of it all they basically say to me I'm all wrong. We'll lose if you argue that way in Ottawa. So I go back, and I consult with the students I had working with me, Vince Kazmierski, Lianne Lagroix and Bill Watts, but I couldn't see how I could change my argument. I got caught up in it. I didn't want to adopt the law school's argument, and they're telling me my argument is not good. We have one week to go before the Court. Nothing was working; I'm getting upset.

And now we've got interveners phoning us up, offering advice. The Legal Education and Action Fund (LEAF) joined with the National Organization of

Immigrant and Visible Minority Women of Canada (NOIVMWC) to success-fully apply for intervener status, as did the African Canadian Legal Clinic, the Afro-Canadian Caucus of Nova Scotia and the Congress of Black Women of Canada (together, the Coalition). The African Canadian Legal Clinic is saying we have to argue "judicial notice," that is, Connie was just taking judicial notice of the existence of racism, recognizing an obvious and undisputed fact, so she wasn't breaking with convention. I'm saying it's not that kind of case; we've got to argue that she was using her own experience as a Black person to frame her judgment, and this is a *break* with convention. Besides, Connie didn't claim to be taking judicial notice at the original trial. So now I've got the interveners telling me I'm all wrong. I get in a fight with the different interven-ers. It was an absolute mess.

They all disagree with the specifics of my argument. My position was that judicial notice was a loser, that the court would not broaden the case enough to take judicial notice of racism so we had to keep the issue narrowly focused on the events in Halifax and whether the judge could contextualize her com-ments. But with all these heavies against me I tried to change my opening oral remarks to see if I could accommodate the issues that had been raised by Dal profs and the others. By the time I left for Ottawa I had given in, and I included judicial notice in my opening argument. These people must know better than I do.

I get to Ottawa, and I find that Back people are coming from all over the country. This was the case of the century as far as they were concerned. RDS's mother was travelling with me, and my sister Lynn and my wife Sharon. I'm still troubling over my opening statement. What my advisers were saying just didn't work for me. I'm trying to make an argument I don't believe in. Lynn says, "Let's re-write your thing; you talk, we'll type like we always do." In the past she or another one of my sisters would frequently write up notes for me while I tossed around ideas, and then we could shape it into a speech. So we're in a B&B in Ottawa, and Lynn gets her union buddies to bring us computers and paper. Diane Kilby and Angela Payne, labour activists from PSAC, bring all the stuff. I have my students there, and I re-do the entire presentation. My students were very bright and were really into it. They knew what my previous arguments had been, and they would remind me of things. They were there when I presented to the faculty. I was on a roll. I could visualize the entire argument, re-adopting Freeman's judgment.

I'm nervous as hell getting ready to go into that courtroom on the morning of March 10, 1997. The most apprehensive period was walking through the parking lot to get to the door. Gordon Blackmore, one of my former students, now practising law in Ottawa, said, "You're the expert. You know all about racism, why are you uptight?" That gave me a lot when I was going in, a sense that people in the Black community understood. I probably knew more about racism than all those judges put together. I had to go around the back of the Supreme Court building, to the lawyers' entrance.

At the front entrance there were all these Black people lining up, two hours in advance, to make sure they got seats. What happened next was unknown to me at the time. None of our supporters understood how it works, so they are at the front of the line and they expect to be admitted. Then a bus arrives, or maybe two, filled with white law students, and they are ushered in ahead of the people already in line. My sister Lynn objects and says, "What's going on? We were here first." They explain: you have to have tickets. The students had been studying the case, and they arrived with their professor. Lynn says to her union friend, Diane, "You've got to talk to your people on that bus and get us those seats." Diane goes in, and comes out and says I've got three seats, or something like that. "Oh no," says Lynn, "That's not enough. I want them all, so go back and get more seats." Diane comes back out and says, "We got them all!" The students were moved to a room to watch on closed circuit. Only after all the Black people were seated were any others admitted.

Meanwhile I'm in the back getting dressed in my court robes. I felt really proud. I always believed being outside the system was the way to go. Now I am faced with the fact that I'm part of the system and I'm making the biggest argument of my life, inside the Supreme Court of Canada, and I really recognize that there is the weight of all of these Black people that is square on my shoulders. The argument that I am taking is not an argument about what I have done or about me or anything, but it is an argument that can make a difference in terms of the community. So when I put on those robes I realized that it was truly the end of an old era. It was a realization that I'm in it, and if it I'm in it I'm going to be one of the best in it.

So as I'm coming into court I see all these Black people, filling every available seat. I'm 20 feet high! One of the lawyers for the interveners, April Burey, was in a wheelchair, and nothing was set up to accommodate her. I was really upset for this disabled person, and so I'm moving chairs, rearranging things so her chair will fit. Dianne Pothier who was with me from Dalhousie, is almost blind, and she could use some help. While I'm trying to get all this settled, finding places for people to sit, in comes a judge. I'm not even in my place; I'm out in the aisle trying to help these people get settled in their seats. Three judges come in, and I go to move to my spot, and then another judge comes in, and another. I had no idea there were nine judges. I thought there were three, or maybe five. When they all get seated I'm thinking to myself, "Ain't this a bitch. The entire bench of the SCC is hearing this case!"

I was the first to be called upon. I had my text all ready. I spoke for three to five minutes before they started to pepper me with questions, and I never got back to the remarks I had prepared so carefully. The judges were trying to draw me out, and they were not hostile. The questioning is very intense but it was exactly as I thought it would be, and I was prepared for their questions. We had developed a game plan for all of the things I would need to know, and that was exactly the way it played out, exactly. The judges are well briefed; they know exactly what they are looking for. I felt that I was in a supportive environment, albeit one where I had to be sharp and on my toes. I knew that I had to have the right answers or I was toast, but it wasn't like they were trying to trick me; they were just coming up with these tough questions.

The emotional high point was when I would make a point, and I'd hear "Amen" coming from the public seats. Those folks acted Black in that court room. All the white jurists in their red robes, and you make a point and you hear "Yeah brother." At one point the clerk said, "Quiet or we will clear the court room." All those Black people were voicing their approval and disapproval, "Oh yeah. Tsk tsk tsk." It was so animated. A bunch of people in the courtroom and they were all of like mind and they were all there for support. Dressed to the nines, boy they came out in their finest. It was beautiful. Although the case is about an appeal for RDS, quite clearly what was on the line was Connie Sparks and her career, and whether she was correct in making a judgment that took into account her understanding of racism. That was the thing about this case that was so important, and that's what the judges were trying to determine with their questions. This young kid had no idea what was going on, no idea how significant this was, around this really simple thing of him confronting a cop. RDS, Rodney Small, he is the hero of this story, but the questions in court mostly related to how a judge can make decisions.

Dianne Pothier had much the same experience as I had, lots of questions and mostly to the point. On one occasion the Chief Justice is asking her about bringing outside awareness into a judgment. When he was a lawyer in Montreal, he says, the Chinese had a reputation for gambling. Would it be right for him to include that awareness if he was judging a case involving a Chinese charged with gambling? Not exactly the most relevant question in the circumstances of RDS. He made some other comments about other groups as well that could be seen as racial stereotypes. In fact a complaint was lodged against Chief Justice Lamer by the Chinese Canadian National Council, but because the remarks were "hypothetical" the complaint was dismissed. In any case he didn't seem entirely sympathetic to our arguments, but he was always respectful toward us. Yola Grant, who was there representing LEAF, also had a fair share of questions. The only person who was allowed to give her complete presentation without interruption was April Burey, the intervener from the Coalition, who made her statement from her wheelchair. The Crown at the Supreme Court hearing is Robert Lutes. He was very senior and also incredibly fair. He gave me so many tips on how to approach the case in going to the Supreme Court, some of the things to expect, what some of the rules were. Bob Lutes was my mentor in that case. He was what every lawyer would dream of being. I said to him once, "Bob, where are you going with your argument in the Supreme Court. Are you arguing actual bias?" He said, "You don't even need to worry about that. I would not make that argument in the Supreme Court." So he dropped the actual bias and argued for the apprehension of bias. He too had constant interruptions from the bench, and the sense I got was that he had less support than we did.

There was a lot of publicity about the fact that we were going to the Supreme Court of Canada; the press covered it well, nationally and locally. And then we had our day in court, and of course there is no decision that day, so it kind of dies. It is like you've done all of this work and everything is all complete and you sit and wait. It goes right off the public radar, and then six months later you get the word that the decision is coming down on such and such a day. And you've moved on to other things. I had gone out to B.C. for a fishing trip, and my Dal student Vince, who had been with me all along, sent a fax with the précis of the decision to my brother Roger's place in Vancouver. This was in September 1997. When I got home I had a chance to read the full decision, and was it ever complicated. It was interesting because the court was split in so many ways. There were four separate judgments. Out of the nine judges, basically six judges ruled that Connie was okay to say what she said, so that is the bottom line. We won six to three. But in the rulings of those six judges who said there was no apprehension of bias, only four said there was no problem with her decision; the other two went on to be critical of the judge but not critical enough. They said she almost crossed the line but didn't quite cross the line. The final three simply condemned Connie's decision. So the court was really split in terms of that judgment, but we did get the majority for our side. I'm sure people will be quoting those judgments in many future cases. In the final analysis, contextualized judging was endorsed by our highest court; a judge would be allowed, would be encouraged, to bring their life experience into their judgments. The existence of systemic racism was also acknowledged, without the formality of a judicial notice. My own strategy was more or less upheld.

What was most important for me was that, to my knowledge, it was the first case decided at the Supreme Court level where Black people had the chance to be totally involved all the way through the case, and where a Black person was actually able to argue it. In terms of image it was very important for the community, and their response was absolutely incredible. The other thing that was important was the community had a chance to see that they could protect one of their own. The idea of this was not the accused person, but the judge who made the comments, so if you talk about this case in many places it is called the Sparks case, because it was the judge really who was the centre of the controversy. And the community saw that the judge needed to be protected and the judge didn't do anything wrong. I think that the case had much greater relevance for community politics than it has had legal relevance. The case gets quoted quite often but not in bias cases. Only very rarely would the Crown argue that a judge is biased. But if bias ever becomes an issue, the threshold is enshrined in that case. Then again the idea of contextualized judging, that a judge has not only the right but the duty to look at the context, is used more and more. I was very conscious that those judges at the Supreme Court had to make one hell of a leap to accept sociological evidence, to be able to accept that the judge is not strictly objective. That is so far from what we have ever had before. In their *RDS* decision they are saying, "You are allowed to be subjective," when everything in the history of the judiciary insists that the judge is absolutely objective and colour blind, and we are arguing, "No, you cannot be colour blind. Put it all on the table where we can see." What this case does is it enshrines the role of a judge in a different way. It articulates it and it puts it into the judgment, that you can consider context that is subjective. That is a giant leap in terms of legal reasoning in our system.

Right in the middle of *RDS*, just as we were preparing for the first appeal before Chief Justice Glube, I got involved in the second biggest case of my legal career, and the most stressful case for me personally. Known as the Strip-Search Case, I was sued for defamation by a member of the Halifax police department. This case began on March 6, 1995, at St. Patrick's-Alexandra School. A university student was at the school to meet her mother, a teacher there, and she was waiting in a room where three young girls were doing some studying. The university student at one point went to the washroom, and when she returned she noticed that ten dollars was missing from her backpack. She accused the girls of taking it, and of course they denied it, so the university student reported it to her mother as an apparent theft. As it turned out there was already a cop at the school, Constable Carol Campbell, investigating a much bigger theft of $300 earlier in the day. Now, everyone in this story so far is Black, except Officer Campbell. The principal or vice-principal decided that these three young girls would be taken by the police officer into a separate room and questioned about the $10 that was missing. The police officer took the girls into this separate room which had windows low enough for young children to look through. The windows faced the hallway so anyone walking down the hall could see into this area where the police officer had these young girls. The hallway was quite busy and there were a number of students in the hallway. Also, a teacher was moving her class along the hallway just at that time. Officer Campbell decided that she was going to have to search the girls to find out who had the $10, and at that point the school official, a white male, said then he had better leave. So he knew or suspected a search was about to take place, and he implicitly condoned it by getting out of the way. Because the girls are juveniles they are known only by their initials, LS, J-LF and TV. Two of them were 12 and the other was 13 at the time of this incident.

The police officer frisked the girls, and when she didn't find anything she asked them to take down their pants. After they had taken down their outer layers of clothing, she then asked them to pull their panties away from their body to enable the officer to look down into their crotch area. One of the girls attempted to hide behind a screen or partition which was in the room. She indicated that a young boy was looking in the window while she was undressed and she was uncomfortable with removing her clothes in this very public area. Nevertheless the officer moved on to look in the girls' panties. She put on a pair of rubber gloves, and as she approached, one of the girls said, "I've got the money." Constable Campbell reached down between the girl's legs and took a bill that had been wedged in the girl's vagina. The one who had the money was LS, and she was charged with theft.

Upon learning about what had happened to their children, the mothers contacted the local media and stated that their children had been strip-searched by the Halifax police in their school. The media continued to refer to this incident as a "strip-search" and it was defined in that way prior to my interview with the mother of the child I eventually represented. This is crucial because it is the mothers who are pushing this thing forward. They are making it happen. The media go on this feeding frenzy. The story had been printed before the parents decided to get a lawyer. Apparently somebody said to them, "You'd better get a lawyer and sue these bastards." By the way, Patsy Barton, who was the teacher in the hallway, was not supportive of the children and the story they told of being strip-searched. Ms. Barton was a Black teacher, and she was later called by the police officer as a witness during our trial. So there is some dispute over what happened in that room, or at least over who could see what happened.

I was working for Dalhousie Legal Aid Service when I was approached by the parent of one of the girls. This woman was extremely distraught because she said that her daughter came home at lunchtime and told her about the police being at her school. The woman explained that her daughter was upset because she was treated in a way that made her uncomfortable. The woman decided that the police should have spoken to her before questioning her daughter or before they took her into a room by herself without supervision to interrogate her. The woman in speaking with me used the words "strip-search," and I too became concerned about the treatment that her daughter had received. When it became apparent that more than one child was involved, I contacted Anne Derrick to see if Anne would represent one or more of the girls. I couldn't take all of the girls because, first and foremost, I was only newly admitted to the bar, less than two years before, and secondly, the girls may have had a conflict with each other, so they needed separate representation. In the end Anne represented two of them, the one who was charged and one of the others.

I interviewed my client, who was I believe 13 at the time, and I determined that she indeed was treated in a discriminatory fashion. I believed that it would not have happened to a white kid or any kid for that matter living in a different community, a more affluent community. I spoke to Anne and we decided that we should have a unified response to our particular cases. I went to Anne because I knew her through our involvement in political activity around Halifax. She was a social activist who was involved with the Morgentaler case and the Junior Marshall case.

Anne and I filed two separate letters of complaint with the Halifax police department. In my letter I said there was a complete disregard for the privacy of the girls involved. They were instructed to remove their clothes in clear view of each other, in an unsecured area that was inappropriate for a strip-search. I added that they would not have been treated in the same manner if they were white and in a school with a different social and economic class of society. Anne's letter stressed that all our clients concurred with each other as to what happened, and the cases should all be dealt with together. She described the incident, where Constable Campbell searched LS by patting her down, including around her breasts with her shirt pulled partially up, and she was then required to take off her pants and other layers, including taking down her underwear. And Anne too insisted that race was a factor, and that white girls in a predominantly white school would not have been subject to the same treatment.

The parents involved in this case were extremely powerful, energetic, and committed to seeing justice. The parents were the catalyst for the movement that occurred. They were the ones who said, "We cannot allow these children to be treated with such disdain and disregard." The parents set the agenda that Anne Derrick and I followed. They wanted the community to be aware of how Black children were treated by the police, and they wanted the support of the community to fight for their children. The parents also wanted the larger community to know that their children were being discriminated against.

Anne and I felt that it was important to talk about the legality of what had happened to the children. We wanted to raise the issue with the public of the abuse of authority and the disregard the police officer showed for the civil and human rights of these children. And the parents wanted an opportunity to speak to the larger community through us as their representatives. So Anne and I decided to hold a press conference, and we issued a press release announcing that three young women had been strip-searched at St. Pat's-Alexandra School and we would provide the details at a public meeting on April 5, 1995.

The press conference was very interesting. It was held at a facility which had been a tavern in the past, known as Club 55, on Gottingen Street at the corner of Gerrish. Anne and I made our complaint letters public, and we took the position that these three girls were strip-searched because of their race and class, and that the police officer decided she did not need to be concerned about the rights of these children because they did not have affluent or educated parents to protect them. Anne stated clearly that what happened was a direct violation of the girls' constitutional rights. The press conference gave the parents an opportunity to speak out against the police for their actions.

There were cameras recording the press conference, and we were never able to determine who owned the cameras or who authorized them. The police had tapes of the press conference but they did not say who took the footage. The hall where the press conference was held was quite small. The people in the hall were known to us because they were either members of the community or representatives of the media. We were intrigued when we learned that the police could take pictures of the audience and of Anne and me, who were sitting in front of the audience, without anyone knowing they were being photographed. Most of the community groups in the area sent representatives to this press conference as support, and of course the police were there too. The community indicated their support of the young girls and was extremely critical of the police. I recall one Black person in the audience who stood up and started to be hostile toward the police. He did not break any laws so he could not be arrested, but the police who were present were quite agitated because this person was able to make negative statements about the police without being sanctioned in any way.

The press conference excited people in the community. They expressed their support for the children by phoning my office and stopping in to see the children's parents. The community was aware of who the children were although their names were not published in the newspaper.

The reaction of Carol Campbell was quite different. She left the city and went on vacation down south, I believe to Bermuda. The report in the newspaper indicated that she was suffering from a stressful reaction to being called a racist by Anne and myself. We did not at any time call Carol Campbell a racist. It was her interpretation of our position that led her to believe she was being called a racist. She stated that being called a racist was so traumatic, she could not fulfil her duties as a police officer, and it also had far-reaching results in her personal life. Meanwhile the police department conducted an internal investigation of the charges in our complaint, and they concluded that Campbell had failed to read the girls their rights, which supported our contention that the Charter had been violated, and she did not properly preserve the evidence she retrieved from ls. This amounted to "discreditable conduct."Following this, in September, the girls and their families sued the police department and the school board for the violation of their constitutional rights. Although Anne and I were not involved in this suit, it ended successfully and Campbell's behaviour was acknowledged as contrary to the girls' constitutional rights.

Imagine our surprise in October 1995 when Anne and I were informed that a lawsuit was pending against us, for allegedly slandering or defaming Carol Campbell. There was an offer presented to stop the defamation case if we would publicly apologize for calling Carol Campbell a racist. Included would be the cost of legal fees that we would be responsible for. We declined to accept the proposition put forward by Campbell's lawyer, George MacDonald. We could not apologize for calling her a racist when we had never done so. Campbell also sued the various media who had reported on the strip-search story and our press conference, claiming that they too had defamed her. Unlike ourselves, the media agreed to a settlement out of court for $114,500 in damages.

It was our belief that the issue was being pushed by the police union as a means of putting a muzzle on both Anne Derrick and myself. We were not intimidated by the actions of Campbell's lawyer, although the intention was to put a chill on us and any other lawyers who might contemplate challenging the police in a public forum. It was clear that there was an interest particularly in silencing Anne and myself because we were known to be verbal in our opposition to the police and civil authorities. Obviously Carol Campbell was not funding her own case and it was my belief that her case was funded by the police union, though it was not done openly and we had no proof of this. In *RDS* I was directly challenging the authority of the Halifax police department, and the judge in that case had made comments that were not flattering to the Halifax city police. The issue in that case was the authority and credibility of the police. In *Campbell*, which occurred two years after *RDS* began, the same issue was paramount. Both cases were constructed around a challenge to the authority of the police. Both cases involved Black youth. Both cases highlighted the discriminatory nature of the police department. The police had a vested interest in making sure that I, in particular, did not continue to raise these kinds of issues, and I'm sure an examination of Anne Derrick's cases and initiatives would certainly show that she also was confronting the police image and authority. In *RDS* you have a judge saying publicly, "Police officers are known to overreact particularly when dealing with," in her words, "non-white youth." So you have a judge acknowledging the difference between how they treat Black kids and how they treat the other kids, and then you have Officer Carol Campbell actually treating Black kids differently.

When we learned of the suit against us, I had students at Dalhousie Legal Aid research the case history of strip-searches. My students could not find any case where a child of 13 was strip-searched by the police, anywhere in the entire country. We knew this was a special case. Our formal response was to claim that our statements at the press conference were protected under "qualified privilege," they had been made "without malice," and as "matters of opinion they were fair comment of a matter of public interest." In other words even if we were mistaken, we had a right and a duty to criticize any suspected transgression in the justice system. We quoted the *Legal Ethics and Professional Conduct Handbook* for Nova Scotia, which contained the statement: "The lawyer should not hesitate to speak out against an injustice," and the police department itself had admitted that Campbell's conduct was "discreditable" and a constitutional violation. We were quite sure we were okay.

But the stress was severe. From 1995 through 1997, for two years, *RDS* is still in the courts and getting a lot of publicity. The Campbell case is also in the courts for those two years and it is getting publicity and it is not going away. And the pressure of being involved in those cases is extremely great on me. I can't speak for the pressure on Anne, but the isolation was incredible. The fact of the matter is, in *RDS* I had to fight with my colleagues at the university to get them to understand the need to take that case forward to the Supreme Court. They did not understand the need to fight that case when in fact the worst case scenario would be that the kid would get a suspended sentence, perhaps probation. So I had to convince my colleagues that this case was important for the Black community in general and Connie Sparks in particular. I didn't think even my own community really understood the significance of *RDS* and why we had to fight it. I had many, many people, including people who I respected and trusted, say to me, "It is not that important, let it go, you are getting stressed out over this thing." So it was very isolating. Then the Campbell case comes along before *RDS* is finished and I am going through the same kind of a thing. A lawyer, a member of the Bar Society, sent an email around to other members stating that the Society through our insurance should not pay for a defence for me and Anne Derrick because we had no right to hold a press conference and say what we said; it wasn't said in a court, it wasn't a legal forum, we took an opportunity to make these comments outside of a courtroom in a press conference, and they should not be forced to use their money as members of the Bar Society, to defend us. Basically the idea was that we are left-wing radicals that deserve what we get. This email went to all members of the Bar Society so even I got it. Again there was that feeling of isolation. I had no way of knowing how many members of the Bar Society agreed with that position. So every day when I had to go to work, go to the court, be involved with other lawyers, I didn't know whether they supported the position that we should have the right to fight this kind of case or whether we shouldn't, and I felt really insecure. Additionally we had a $5,000 deductible on our insurance, which meant that I was looking at potentially a $5,000 bill if there was an award against me, and if the Bar Society decided not to fund my defence I was looking at thousands and thousands of dollars in legal costs. The stress affected me to the point where it was almost impossible to work. I worried, I couldn't sleep, I couldn't concentrate. No one that I knew had ever been through anything like this, let alone going through it twice and have the same thing happening all the time. The isolation was absolutely debilitating. That was one bitch of a time. Even thinking about it years later, it is a very emotional. I'm not saying I did not have a number of sympathetic individuals who listened to me and lent their general support. Walter Borden, David Woods, Maxine Tynes, Gus Wedderburn, Clyde Bishop, Alonso Reddick: these people were all supportive and recognized that I was doing something significant for the community, even if we didn't always see eye to eye politically.

White authorities portray that there has been an affront to their dignity when they are challenged about their racist behaviour. The white authorities believe or send out the message that oppressed people have no right to question anything that they do or how they do it. This is what happened with Carol Campbell. "How dare you question what I do and how dare you draw a conclusion that what I have done is racist?" I received hate mail, hate telephone calls. That goes with the territory. I had a lot of experience dealing with the hatred that goes with being out front politically, but in this case I knew we were dealing with organized police, same as if we were dealing with organized crime. These guys knew their business and they weren't fooling around. They were out to crush us and they pulled out all the stops. People who are involved in dissent can expect to be attacked. You are attacked in your person, your finances are attacked, your freedom is attacked, and your ability to speak, your ability to express yourself, it is all under attack. An issue came up where I was asked to make public comment, but I was afraid to speak because I knew at that time I couldn't take any more, I couldn't handle more pressure, and so I refused to speak on something that before I would have been the first out there with my lips flapping. So they were successful in silencing me if only for a while. I'm trying to practise law under the ever-present threat of losing my house and everything. That affected me physically, and I ended up with a heart attack. I cannot say that my heart attack was a direct result of this, but quite clearly stress was the biggest factor. The Campbell case lasted for eight years, and that had an impact on me in terms of my health. Would I do it again? You bet your bottom dollar I would. It was worth every minute of it. It's a hell of a ride. When you can stick your head in the lion's mouth and hear him roar, there is no more excitement in this world of politics. It is the politics of survival for your community and change in your community.

The night I had my heart attack, I was with my secretary and I was doing a document for a woman who was in the hospital. It was a power of attorney, and my secretary was going to be a witness. After I left and got my secretary home, I was driving through the Halifax shopping centre and I experienced a real feeling of apprehension, an unexplained fear. I felt the sweat pop out of my forehead and the need to get to safety. I was actually speeding, I just had to get home. When I arrived home, Sharon and my sister Wilma were playing cards at the table and I went into my bedroom to look over my clothes that Sharon had put out, because I was leaving in the morning to go to Ottawa where I was scheduled to be the keynote speaker at the PSAC national conference. So I was looking at my clothes, to decide which ones I had to take, and I had two voices in my head. One voice was saying, "You are going to have a heart attack," and the other voice was saying, "Don't be so crazy, you are not a candidate for a heart attack." And the first voice said, "You are now having a heart attack and need to go to the hospital." And that was like a debate in my head. I have taken first aid and CPR and all of that, and I had none of the symptoms. I had no pain in my left hand, I had no pain in my left arm, I had no pain in my jaw or numbness, none of it. All I had was that real feeling that something was wrong in my body and it was really out of kilter. I said to Wilma and Sharon, I am going to the hospital. I called a taxi and went to the hospital. Sharon went with me. When I got to the hospital I still had no symptoms except I knew something was dreadfully wrong. Because of my age and the fact that I was a smoker, I think, they took me in and they wired me up and there was nothing wrong. They did blood tests, everything, still there was nothing wrong. So I told Sharon to go home because I would be home as soon as they finished this one test. I had been there for a few hours. There was still nothing wrong with all of the monitors, blood and everything, except that I knew. There was a certain weakness that had come over me. I said to the nurse, "Would you call my sister Marie, because there is something wrong." She brought me a phone and said, "Well, call yourself."

I noticed the time on a wall clock: three o'clock. I could feel myself starting to go into a spin or a spiral like falling down this tunnel. I could hear the bells go and all the alarms going and I could see myself doing this freefall, and the next thing I know there is a nurse standing there and there is all this action. And I said to her, "I guess I was in trouble, eh?" and she said, "Yeah you were." At that point I didn't know what had happened. And so they kind of got me stabilized, and my sister Marie arrives with the minister in tow. The nurse is there with me, and I looked at her, and said "Guess what?" and she said, "What?" I said, "Here I go again." And away I went, another heart attack, the monitor goes "Wheeee." So I had another one and they had to put the paddles to me twice to bring me back.

This little nurse from Cape Breton is watching over me. Of course I bond with her. She saved my life. So the doctor comes and picks up my chart and looks at it and he says, "I think we are going to do this, this and this." And the nurse steps right in front of him and says, "I don't think so, we've just got this patient stabilized and we aren't changing anything." She's standing up to the doctor like this and I looked at him and said, "Doctor guess what, I'm with the nurse." I think he had a sense he had better go along with this.

I was there for another couple hours and then they were going to take me out of emergency and put me up on the floor. They had me all wired up, and now they are going to unhook the wires and roll me away somewhere. And I'm thinking, "Oh no, you are not doing this to me. I like being wired up. You are not taking these monitors off me." They said I had to go, they had to take me to the intensive care unit. I said, "The only way I'm going anywhere is if she goes with me, if she takes me I'll go." So they made arrangements that she would take me. They get me upstairs to intensive care, and the nurse hands me over to the other nurses.

There are four intensive care beds in this area and the alarms are going all the time. So here I am, and you hear the alarm and you think that you are having another heart attack. You hear, "Beep, beep, beep" and you think, "Oh here I go again." It was very scary. The doctors are there and they have to determine what to do with me, so I eventually had to have a stress test. One of the nurses had schooled me. She told me, "If you do well on this stress test they will send you home." And one of the doctors had said that if I had to have a bypass they would send me home and then they would bring me back for the operation. And I thought, "I ain't leaving this hospital, there is no way." I had two heart attacks here, they haven't fixed me, and they are going to send me home? I don't think so, no way. Needless to say I didn't do very well on the stress test. So then they had to make a decision on what my priority was in terms of getting the operation. I got bumped two days in a row, but they didn't send me home and eventually I had the triple bypass. So I was in bad shape and in fact my heart was damaged so badly that it was less than half as much as a normal heart. The whole bottom half of my heart had been damaged beyond repair, so it was very serious. I still had a practice and I had to have someone come in and take over, and luckily there was a lawyer who was available and he took my caseload and worked with me, and I got through it.

When I was in the hospital the nurses told me they had to close the switch-board because there were so many calls coming in for me. It is not something I recall because obviously I didn't take the calls; it's just what they told me what happened. I don't know who called, why they would call, but certainly I felt the support of the community, and when I say "the community" I don't mean just the Black community. For all the years that I spent attacking white society as an institution, at the end of the day, when I was most vulnerable and at my sickest, the people who expressed sympathy and solidarity were people of every possible colour, religion and economic status you could ever believe. It just blew my mind. I could understand the Black community being concerned with my health, perhaps even the Aboriginal community being concerned, but in the white community for so many people to be concerned is amazing. I don't think it was about me personally. I think when I was sick the community wanted to send the message that they support the things that Rocky Jones was attempting to do. I'm sure many of them may not have even known me personally. There is support in this society for change, there is support in this society for dissent, there is support for the acknowledgement of the contradictions between rich and poor, Black and white, young and old. I think there is support for that and that is why I had so much concern when I got sick. That is just so fulfilling, uplifting, to know that that exists.

My sister Marie said to me after all of this happened, "You were saved," and I said, "Yes, I am very blessed." And she said, "What do you think of Jesus now?" and I said, "Why would you say that?" And she said, "You know you were saved, so now what do you say about Jesus, we were all praying for you." And I said, "Marie, there were so many people praying for me from different religions that I could not possibly say which religion saved me." I couldn't say that because I had Jewish people who sent me notes and called, prayed for me, and really meant it honestly. Different people were praying for me and it is a great feeling to know that you've got these people of different religions, different races, ages, sexes, whatever, that are praying for you. You can't just say that because you know someone was praying for me that it is the Christians that saved me. Maybe it was the Muslims that saved me, or maybe it was the Jews. Or maybe it was even that little nurse from Cape Breton.

This all happened in 1998. It was 2001 before Campbell's case against Jones and Derrick came to trial, beginning on April 3. The issue of race in the Campbell case comes to the forefront, right in the school when the children targeted are all Black. The press conference highlighted the fact that the kids were Black, the kids were poor and the kids were from a particular economically deprived neighbourhood. The racial dynamics again were front and centre of the case, just like in *RDS*. And in fact, it was the racial dynamic that was the genesis or the source of the defamation suit. Carol Campbell raised the issue of race; she made it central to her complaint.

The trial was a jury trial, very interesting because we participated in the selection of the seven-member jury. A majority of five would be enough to decide the case. We were trying to determine which jurors would be sympathetic to our position. We did this by looking at them. We should have had research done on each juror but we did not have the money or resources. We tried to select according to occupation, and in any event the people we selected collectively were from a variety of backgrounds. There was one person of colour on the jury and the male-female ratio was fairly even if I remember correctly. The jury was not very animated and it was difficult on a daily basis to try to read what they were thinking. We did determine that there were a couple of jurors who seemed to be interested in the case but that really did not tell us that much. When the trial began Carol Campbell took the stand and cried, and cried and cried. She gave the impression that she was a victim who had lost everything. She denied asking the girls to take down their pants, but she did admit that she pulled the girls leggings away from their body and looked down into their private area. She stated that to the best of her knowledge, no one could see into the room where she had the girls. She basically says she didn't do anything wrong. She just cried and cried. It was pathetic. To this day I can't see how a jury could convict on anything she said.

I was represented by Mick Ryan and Anne was represented by Bruce Outhouse. We attempted to present a case to show that we were very reasonable in our approach. Anne and I took the stand and we made the point that we never ever called her a racist. It wasn't part of anything that we said. They introduced the tapes of the press conference, but they couldn't say who had taken them. We knew it was a spy. Somehow they had a police officer with a hidden camera. I still don't know how they did it. Obviously they were shooting the audience to see who was there and what position people had, so they were likely shooting private conversations too. It was a real undercover operation and they had to have more than one camera. The press conference tapes were used to show that Anne and I deliberately put this issue of race and class in the media. Ultimately my lawyer argued that although we said the children were strip-searched because of their race and their class, we did not go on to say that Carol Campbell was racist. The Campbell lawyers called the Black school teacher, Patsy Barton, as a witness. They used her to suggest that the children were not of good moral standing. She was also used to question whether or not I provided positive leadership in the community. Interestingly, she was one of the participants who regularly attended the functions put on at Club Kwacha. It was also interesting when you looked at the gallery. The public were seated behind our team if they supported us, and on the other side of the court room if they supported Carol Campbell. The Carol Campbell legal team usually had one or two Black people sitting behind them.

Campbell's lawyers argued that my record showed that I was prone to fight the establishment. They pointed out that on many occasions I was in conflict with the police and indeed had done a number of police complaints. In fact, I had done more police complaints than maybe any other practising lawyer. They used this as an indication that I had a propensity to dislike the police and my attack on Carol Campbell's actions was just another example of my displeasure with the police.

At one point George MacDonald turned to the jury and he said, and I quote from the trial transcript:

"Aren't you tired of people who will not take responsibility for what they do? Who are always taking the position that it's somebody else's fault? Or that racism and discrimination are at the heart of every interaction that goes wrong between those in authority and those of minorities? Every time something goes wrong, it's because of race or discrimination. It can never be just the fact that we have a difference of opinion, you did something wrong, it's always race. Aren't you tired of that?"

When I was called I said, "Someone strip-searched three children, and I'm on trial? What's wrong with this picture?" Campbell's lawyers argued that the jury should send a message, and they should determine the amount of the damages. It worked.

The evidence, if that's what you call it, went on for 16 days, and then there were four more days of submissions by the lawyers. Judge Moir advised the jury that the defence of "qualified privilege," which we had argued, was not applicable. The jury deliberated for another two and half days. I believe the jury wanted to teach a lesson to the militant, short-haired, lesbian-looking Anne Derrick, who challenged the system and authority. They wanted to put her in her place. Similarly they wanted to send a message about these Black militants who dared challenge the system and take on authority. They wanted to punish us. In my opinion the facts of the case and the decision the jury made didn't add up. The jury convicted us, and I think it was not because of who we were as individuals but because of what we represented. Both Anne and I represented a challenge to the police, and that jury wanted to send the message that that kind of action is not acceptable. The jury determined an award which was the highest award ever given in a defamation suit in Canada: $240,000! And this did not include the costs we were liable for, which was another $75,000. Altogether $315,000! Looking objectively at what Carol Campbell lost, if indeed she lost anything, she certainly did not lose any money in salary whatsoever. She was paid for the time she was off work and she was paid for the time that she attended trials. She was held in high regard by members of the police fraternity because in fact the police showed their support for her every day by showing up in the courtroom and sitting behind her. There is no possible loss that Carol Campbell suffered within her work place. So without a loss to her reputation and without a loss financially from her employment, what was the basis for the award being the largest in the history of Canada? Again, in my opinion, it was simply because the jury wanted to punish us and send a message, and it was totally irrational if you consider the facts and evidence. We had been watching that jury, and we believed that they were on our side. That jury came in smiling and looking at us like we were doing okay. I saw one of the jurors leave the courtroom after that verdict in tears. And I know that juror did not support the decision. After we were found guilty, our lawyers announced that we would appeal, and made an application to the court to allow the appeal to proceed before anything was paid to Carol Campbell. The court allowed that nothing was to be paid until after the appeal process was fully completed.

The reaction to the verdict was interesting. Paul Fromm, a notorious right-winger, praised the jury's verdict. He claimed that "professional anti-racists have a field day lying about and defaming those concerned about immigration or other politically incorrect issues," and he called the Campbell episode "a story that can give white Canadians encouragement. A white Canadian police officer was awarded $240,000 from a Nova Scotia jury for defamation from remarks made by professional whiners Anne Derrick (lesbian activist) and Rocky Jones (Black activist), who falsely accused her of racism." Even Walter Thompson, a director of the Nova Scotia Civil Liberties Association, was quoted as saying that "people's reputations are important…. The size of the award sends a strong message about the degree to which the jury regarded the matter as being injurious to the police officer." The local press was split. There were members of the press corps who understood what was going on and there were others who more or less followed the police line. But the issue was raised in the letters to the editor, in editorials, by commentators in the newspaper. It was a fact that this judgment sent a chill throughout the community, and it was questioned. Steve Kimber, Parker Donham, Joan Jones and Charles Saunders all wrote criticisms of the judgment, and there was a community rally organized in our support at the Workers' Health and Safety Centre. I remember talking to Anne at that point, and I asked her if she was finished with the case, and she said "Absolutely not." She was going to fight and see this case through to the end. And our supporters, who came day in, day out, Anne's family, my family, friends, they indicated that we should continue. We had some amazing support. Anne was extremely strong even though it was taking a toll on her too. We also had members of the Bar Society who were just rabid. We get hit for $240,000, and that is going to come out of their fees and they would have had to make a special assessment on every lawyer in the province to pay for this. So we weren't the most favourite two lawyers.

The basic terms of our insurance were that if it were found that we were indeed targeting this person with forethought and malice, and that we really wanted to do something harmful, then the insurance would not pay. And given this verdict, it was very dangerous for us because, in essence, the jury is finding that there was malice, or else they wouldn't have banged us the way they did. So we have the jury saying that it was deliberate and we maligned Carol Campbell and we called her a racist. Fortunately for us, the bar insurance did not buy into that, and to their great credit they supported us. Even when members of the Nova Scotia Bar Society turned against us, and there was that email and the sentiment that the Bar Society shouldn't have to pay for Anne and me, the insurance people of the Nova Scotia Bar Society stuck by us 100%. Before they arrived at this decision I was extremely nervous. I didn't have any money to pay this kind of fine; I would have lost my house, I would have lost everything. But I still would not apologize and get out of it. I could have apologized and that is what they wanted. They wanted us to capitulate, they wanted to see us grovel, they wanted to show that if you stand up to the police and authority you get crushed. That is all they wanted. The people behind Carol Campbell did not care about the money; they were after the opportunity to crush Anne Derrick and Rocky Jones, and they would have given up all of that money just to see us publicly apologize and say that we were wrong about the police. At any stage all the way through, that is what they wanted, the apology.

There was a downside risk to appealing the jury decision. The justices in the Court of Appeal could determine that we *had* acted with malice, in which case the insurance would have been withdrawn and Anne and I would be liable for the jury award plus the additional costs of the appeal. But we were in so deep, we had been at it for so long, and we felt so strongly that we represented our clients openly and fairly to the best of our ability and within the spirit of what it means to be a barrister and solicitor in this country. Although the jury convicted us, we still believed that we were right. The appeal of the jury deci-sion was important for several reasons. We were able to say to the police, "No we are not going to cave in, even if it costs us everything we own." They could not intimidate us that way. And it was important in the community because people could see that we were still prepared to fight even though we had been slammed so hard. The appeal was important for us personally because it still gave us hope that we could get out from under the economic ruin that we were facing. Also the position we took could be justified if we were successful on appeal, maintaining that we did not do anything wrong. We simply stated the truth. So in that sense the appeal was critically important. The appeal meant that we had a chance to contest the heavy-handed way the jury dealt with us. We were concerned about what could happen if the court did say that we acted with malice, but even with that concern we wanted to appeal. We wanted to take the chance that we would be vindicated, and we believed that so strongly that we weren't going to give up.

Our appeal came to the court on June 10 and 11, 2002. Our main argu-ment was that we enjoyed qualified privilege as lawyers and that we were justi-fied in making our fair comment about the events at the school back in March 1995. We also challenged the amount of the award assigned by the jury. The decision, which didn't arrive until October 24, was split two to one, just like in *RDS* at this same court, but this time it was in our favour. The majority decision was written by Justice Elizabeth Roscoe, and Chief Justice Glube concurred. They decided that what Campbell had done did fit the definition of a strip-search and that it was our responsibility as lawyers to "speak out against injustice." Justice Roscoe described the errors Campbell committed in subjecting the girls to "intrusive personal searches," ignoring "their personal dignity and privacy." They were not advised of their rights to counsel, and their families were not contacted. "The Charter rights of three young girls were violated." Roscoe explained that the term "strip-search" was being widely used in the media even before we took up the case, and our press conference was "an occasion of qualified privilege" because we, the appellants, "in accordance with the principles of their professional ethics, had a duty to speak about the events at the school, the complaints filed against the respondent, and the Charter breaches they reasonably understood had taken place."

We were totally vindicated in a ringing statement from the court: "If con-stitutional rights are to have any meaning, they must surely include the free-dom of persons whose Charter guarantees have been deliberately violated by officials of state agencies, to cry out loud and long against their transgressors

Dalhousie Law School, 1992, Rocky the Valedictorian.

in the public forum, and in the case of children and others less capable of articulation of the issues, to have their advocates cry out on their behalf." The third member of the Court of Appeal, Justice Saunders, admitted that Constable Campbell "made a serious error in judgment" for which she had been disciplined by the Halifax Police Department, but he still concluded that the officer had been defamed by our statements at the press conference and she deserved the compensation awarded by the jury. But two to one is a victory! The jury award was overturned. The Appeal Court understood our argument, understood our position and understood the law, and ruled in our favour. It was an incredible relief. The most important thing about the Appeal Court decision was the message to all of the naysayers and all of the people in our profession who had turned against us, that the highest level of court in our jurisdiction was saying to them that we were right. It wasn't just some of our friends or community activists; this was the Court of Appeal of Nova Scotia declaring we were right.

But it wasn't time to celebrate yet. Our opponents advised us that they were applying for leave to appeal to the Supreme Court of Canada. We had been slammed so hard that we weren't about to be too self-assured that it was going to stay in our favour. We had been optimistic when we went into trial, we were optimistic after we picked the jury, we were optimistic throughout the trial. We didn't think we had a slamdunk but certainly the way the evidence was and the way everything was going, deep down inside we did not expect to lose, and then once we had lost we didn't expect the amount of money that the jury awarded against us. So having gone through that experience and been so wrong about the outcome, at the next level we couldn't guess what was going to happen. We were pretty gun shy. Then, finally, after almost eight years of struggle and anguish, the Supreme Court of Canada denied their leave to appeal. It was over. Our friend Jackie Barkley held a celebratory party at her house.

I must say that working with Anne on this particular case was a real pleasure. She is very professional, but she was also extremely committed. She had a lot of personal reasons to say, "Okay let's throw in the towel and keep on going, give the woman her apology and get back to work." And never once did she waiver, not in speaking to me, not once did she even question if we should continue. She was so committed and on-side, though I kept asking her, because for me the stakes were so high, "Are you still with me?" And at every stage, at every step, Anne Derrick would say, "We are in this together and we are going to see it through, and that is what we are doing." And now

Anne is herself a judge, in the Provincial Court. Anne was someone who had made a very good reputation in the legal community. She was known to be a scholar, she had the experience necessary to be appointed to the bench, and it would be an appointment that the government could make without playing favourites to one of their own. Anne was not a known government supporter, so it was a good appointment. Anne was the lefty appointed to the bench. And she has been doing a good job since she has been there. There is another way of looking at her appointment, if I wanted to be cynical. Anne was a thorn in the side of the establishment, very much so, and to appoint her a judge means that she could not be an advocate in the same way. So they removed her as a spokesperson for the women's movement, and for a lot of things that Anne was previously involved in that she couldn't do as a judge. Despite my own victories in the courtroom, I'd have to say that I do remain cynical about our justice system. Still, I have never regretted my turn into the law, and my attempts to use the courtroom to bring change to our society. Sometimes it works.

Chapter Ten

CITIZEN JONES

I had always been active in the community, even when I was attending law school. One of those affairs was a challenge we raised against Parks Canada for their policy about hiring students to work at the Citadel in the summertime. Many years before this the ACLM had renamed the fort Maroon Hill, and we had a big march with all kinds of people to recognize the Maroons and their involvement with the Citadel. The people at Parks argued that in 1749 there were no Black people in the military, so to have Black students on display for the tourists would be historically inaccurate and against their professional standards. We argued that the Maroons were organized as military units, and if they wanted to they could use Black kids to portray Maroons. In any case we didn't think a past injustice should be perpetuated in a present injustice, which would definitely be a misuse of history. Davies Bagambire, an African lawyer then practising in Halifax, joined with me in heading up this challenge, and I also have to give credit to Skip States. When we were turned down we went to the Human Rights Commission, then led by our old friend Bridge Pachai. He said that because it was a federal property there was nothing he or the provincial authorities could do about it. Although Parks never actually conceded, at least not to us, they did quietly begin to hire Black kids and they still are today. And an issue of the Nova Scotia tourism magazine had a cover photo of a Black man in a military outfit, a Highlander no less.

The Citadel problem never attracted a lot of attention within the Black community. More significant was the launching of the James R. Johnston Chair in Black Canadian Studies, which began formally in 1991. There was talk of this sort of thing in the NBCC for some years, with Dorothy Wills and

Howard McCurdy involved in the discussions. At Dalhousie itself Fred Wien, a white prof in the School of Social Work, did a study on the employment of Blacks and other minorities at Dalhousie called *Opinions from the Centre*. I was still at TYP then, and I was among the people consulted. Fred's report showed that there was considerable discrimination, and in his conclusion he had the notion of a Black Studies program. Long before it was formalized there were discussions about establishing an academic chair, and along with Howard McCurdy we raised it with Jerry Wiener, the minister responsible for the Ethnic Studies program in the Mulroney government. The government agreed in principle, but we had to get the university to buy into it and we had to raise our own money without tapping into Dalhousie's traditional fundraising base. Donnie Oliver took on the responsibility of finding new money for the project. I wrote a position paper expanding on the idea, and a committee in the university was formed, chaired by Fred Wien and Judy Fingard, who was then Dean of Graduate Studies. Alumni were approached across the country and even into the States to attract funding for this initiative. Fred Wien and Judy Fingard called together an advisory meeting to discuss some of the details: Should it be a visiting position or a full-time tenured chair? Should community outreach be included in the job description? What qualifications were we looking for? Should it be reserved exclusively for a Black academic? It was an interesting committee, chaired by two white academics, and there was a white observer from the Secretary of State, Judy Young, who was there to explain the Ethnic Studies chairs then being established by the federal government. Jim Walker was the only other white person, included because of his academic interests. Most of the Black people were non-academics. Howard McCurdy was there of course, and Dorothy Wills, Rita Devereaux from Vision TV, Esmeralda Thornhill from the Human Rights Commission in Quebec, a lot of others. Members of the public, all of them Black to my recollection, were admitted to listen to the deliberations. Up to that point there was a lot of community involvement.

The Johnston chair was a chance for Dalhousie University to actually get into the community. The first thing about the chair was that the person appointed had to be a recognized scholar with good international credentials. We were also hoping that it could be a local person, and that person had to be Black. There was some considerable discussion over this last point, but the committee reached consensus. One person we hoped would apply was Peter Paris, because he had Nova Scotia roots and we saw this as desirable at least for the first person to get the chair. It would have been nice to have someone who had a direct connection to Nova Scotia and who also had that international experience and reputation. We also thought of George Elliott Clarke, who was Nova Scotian and beginning to make a name for himself in his discipline and obviously involved in the academic community. There was interest in Howard McCurdy, because Howard was a Canadian with a reputation in his field, biology, and was also known to have an interest in the community and in community development. So our hope was that we could take this combination of academic excellence with commitment to community involvement to excite people in the community about the potential of attending university, making it clear that we could accomplish as scholars the same as whites. The person holding the chair would be a real role model with their hands in the community and a prestigious academic record. We were looking for someone who could attract graduate students and build up a critical mass of scholarship in Black Canadian Studies.

When we started with this committee, we thought that we were the decision-makers. But that was not to be. Exactly as happened with the TYP community advisory committee, the university used the community locally and nationally to develop the concept and gain support for it, and then when it was time to implement the concept the university took the power away from the community. The community participants did not have a say over who was to be appointed. So I took no part, and could take no part, in the hiring of Esmeralda Thornhill as the first occupant of the James R. Johnston Chair in Black Canadian Studies. She was appointed through the law school. When the chair was being developed there was a lot of jockeying for position in different faculties. The law school was interested because it would be a prestigious position and James Robinson Johnston was the first Nova Scotian of African descent to graduate from the Dalhousie Law School. The School of Social Work was interested, and so was the Faculty of Arts. The Faculty of Law seems to have had the sway with the committee, whichever committee it was, and so they were successful in getting the appointment of someone with a legal background. But Esmeralda, though she did have a PhD at least, was not an academic. She came from a human rights commission and had no extensive record of scholarship and publication, no stable of graduate students following her. She did lectures in the community, but the chair's mandate for the community aspect of the program was never developed.

The community itself never embraced the chair the way we were anticipating. So this appointment didn't deliver on either community or scholarship. Until the appointment of Afua Cooper, in my opinion, the chair did not succeed in fulfilling the original intentions. When Esmeralda's term was finished the chair moved from law to social work, and the person they hired, David Devine, didn't even have a PhD and was not Canadian, so the distance from scholarship and local community was greater than ever. I have no intimate details on what went on, because the role of the original community people had been completely diminished and the advisory committee was not even called together to be informed, let alone to participate. The people making the appointment of David Devine must have known that if we're going to attract graduate students and stimulate original research, the person in the chair would need a PhD. So by not hiring someone with a PhD, was the university in some way trying to scuttle the program? I hate to think it's possible that a university would purposely jettison one of its own programs. How can you attract graduate students if you don't have the qualifications to supervise them? Both Esmeralda and David did organize conferences that brought different scholars to Halifax and no doubt fostered some scholarship that would be useful to academics and to the community, but the chair did not become that intended bridge between the university and the community.

I was much more directly involved, and more satisfied, with the People's Summit in June 1995. Canada was hosting the G7 Summit in Halifax, so we organized a parallel, alternative set of meetings called the People's Summit. Every time the G7/G8 meets, the people of the host country organize this alternative forum to present different speakers and theories that challenge the assumptions of the World Bank and the International Monetary Fund as the right way to do everything. A number of organizations interested in these topics came together to prepare the opposition to the mainstream Summit, and I was elected as chair of the organizing committee. Then, because this was considered onerous and time-consuming for one person, we elected Paulette Sadoway as co-chair. We had to put together an organizational structure and invite speakers from around the world and arrange the venues for the events. We had funding from a wide variety of sources and we got free use of several venues at St. Mary's, Dalhousie, the Halifax Commons and other outdoor locations. We had a great volunteer group and we were very well organized. We had enough money to hire Colleen Ashworth full-time. Colleen of course is very experienced with community organizations, so that was of immense help to us. This was my first position at an international conference of that magnitude. It was huge, thousands of people. Besides these high profile speakers we also held demonstrations. We were really disciplined in the way it was organized, and we avoided any direct contact with the VIPs. In fact they would cordon off parts of the city to keep demonstrators away. Naturally, the local police were not totally in charge of security. We also had the FBI, the CIA, the German secret police, the RCMP. The different G7 leaders send in their own henchmen to make sure they're not going to get assassinated. We had advance meetings with the police; they were very nice but very clear: here is where you cannot go. When you think of the violence that has occurred at some other international gatherings, like Seattle, Vancouver and so on, ours was remarkably peaceful. We made it a festive occasion. Although we had serious discussions and speakers, we balanced that with a festival atmosphere, including families. We were encouraging people to bring their children, and many did so. The whole of Halifax was excited and happy. We didn't have an invasion of anarchists, and there was no pepper spray. And we were blessed with good weather.

We held workshops on almost everything imaginable. World economics and the exploitation of the Global South was perhaps the biggest topic. Repaying loans and even interest on loans was bankrupting many countries, so debt relief was constantly being considered in our discussions. There were workshops on establishing cooperatives and funding for small groups. The environment was another big issue. Today if you are discussing the environment you would have to include global warming, but then it was more the waste of resources and pollution that were attracting attention. The anti-war movement had a lot of influence during the People's Summit, discussing the arms race and how to achieve disarmament.

I particularly wanted to include the Black community as a focus for our discussions. Eddie Carvery was already camped out at the Africville site, using the world's attention on the Summit to publicize the destruction of Africville and the claim for compensation. So Africville offered us a very real issue, and we had a march from downtown out to Africville and back. A full morning session was devoted to that topic. The press was giving us pretty good play, explaining to the general community and, in fact, to people all over the G7 countries, what our concerns were. I think the People's Summit had a lot of momentum, toward things like debt relief and micro-credit as a means of trying to develop economic opportunities in poor countries. It may have had an impact on the eventual compensation for Africville; it certainly helped to keep the issue alive. When I look back on it I have to feel that it was one of the highlights of my life as a community organizer. And I have to remember that *RDS* was still going on, and the Campbell case began just a few months before the Summit. I wonder why it took me to 1998 to have a heart attack!

Sometimes it's frustrating trying to be a good citizen. I was invited to join the Employment Equity Committee, made up of people who were all lawyers. It was chaired by Douglas Ruck. The bar society had a representative on the committee, and the law school was represented by Carol Aylward. The government had a representative as well. I guess I was considered a community representative. We began by looking at hiring practices in law firms, and in particular what was happening with the Black students who came through the IBM program, and we moved out from there. This was one of the hardest-working committees that I was ever involved with. Meetings were often early in the morning, and we did a lot of research on different policies that could improve the employment status of Black people in this province. We looked at contract compliance, we looked at quotas, we looked at what was happening in other jurisdictions. It was a real thorough job. I was an advocate for contract compliance. I argued, and I still think, that the government should show leadership in its own employment practices and have special hiring and training programs. We put pressure on government to increase numbers in the civil service. The government in turn says the jobs are open, but they're not getting the applicants or there is nobody trained to take the position. So therefore they're not discriminating; the ones who are applying are not the ones we need.

As an example from the private sector, the hotel industry was under pressure to hire Black people to work in a managerial capacity. The industry basically said, "We don't have qualified Black people coming forward to take any of these jobs." The truth of the matter is that we don't have very many people trained in the hospitality industry at any level other than cleaning staff. So nothing will ever change. If it's left alone the industry can always say, "We are open, you bring us somebody and we will hire, but until then don't blame us." There was a job fair held in Halifax for the hotel industry. It was reported in the media that for all of the jobs that are offered, 50% of them will not be filled. They can only fill 50% of the jobs and there's stiff competition amongst the hospitality industry for qualified staff. These are not minimum wage-level jobs; they're higher than that, and they can't find workers. And Black people can't take advantage of it because they don't have the skills.

In order to overcome that problem we've got to have special training programs to give people the skills and credentials that are necessary for these jobs, both public sector and private, and we must specifically target particular occupations and be prepared to fully fund Black students so they can become qualified. The government can then say, "We want to buy 20 widgets and

230 Burnley "Rocky" Jones – Revolutionary

we will accept bids from any firm that agrees to hire a percentage of their workforce from certain designated groups. If you want to do business with the government, this is the percentage and this is the level they've got to be working at." Then the industry would hire those people in order to get the contract. The government has to put up money to provide the training. The government has studies to forecast labour needs. Based on that labour market information there should be special incentives to enable people from the African Canadian community to take that training, and the employer should be required to hire them in order to get the contracts. That's one way we can change what's happening. The government doesn't want contract compliance because it takes a lot of work just setting it up. I don't think it would have any negative impact on the government in the end in terms of the services they get. I don't think it would hurt industry because industry will be getting trained people if the government were putting up the training. These were the kind of remedies that were being discussed in the Employment Equity Committee. At the end of the day the provincial government did not implement any of our recommendations, and they were supported by the Barristers society in this. Our committee report was simply neglected. It was a lot of work and a lot of good policies were put forward, but nothing became of it.

There are a few other groups that I became involved with that have been important. The Court Challenges program was one of the organizations that I felt was beneficial to the Canadian Black community in particular and the Aboriginal and francophone communities as well. The Court Challenges program contributed funding to most of the race-based cases in Canada, including *RDS*. I was on the national board of Court Challenges for a number of years, right after *RDS* in fact. It was a very exciting organization because we debated the direction that the legal community and government were going in, and we made presentations to government and funded cases to challenge government policies. Court Challenges was the way that community groups could affect government initiatives and policies. There were certain amounts available for certain initiatives. For instance Court Challenges would pay $5,000 for you to develop a framework to put in a proposal to do a Section 15 challenge. That $5,000 would enable you to do some research and put your facts together. Then it would make $50,000 available for Section 15 challenges in court, and if I remember correctly $100,000 for an appeal to the Supreme Court of Canada. It had different levels of funding, but most importantly it had a body of information available to people who were doing legal work. If you wanted to know what was happening with language rights, Aboriginal rights, Section 15 jurisprudence, Court Challenges had that information and made it available and helped to organize the legal cases. Court Challenges also commissioned reviews of different decisions, so that the legal commentary on different aspects of the Charter was funded by them. It was a very fulfilling organization to be involved in. In Court Challenges I gained knowledge and understanding of things that I don't think I would have had otherwise. As an example, in Court Challenges we had discussions about transgendered people. I had no idea what transgendered was. There was another lawyer there from rural New Brunswick, and she didn't know what a transgendered person was either. But through Court Challenges we had people who explained it and who in the debates began to make us aware of many different people in our society, and what the gay and lesbian community were saying and why, and what their histories were. The people involved in that program were from those different communities. I'm proud to have been involved in that program for quite some time. I condemn the Harper government for destroying the program and cutting its funding. It was a very important program for Canada.

Another program I was involved in over this period of time, that is during the Campbell case, was the Canadian Broadcast Standards Council. This is a national organization that has a mandate to govern broadcasters. It is a self-regulating body that's made up of the broadcast industry, which in essence is the industry regulating itself. But they have people representing the community and I was one for the Atlantic region. I see the Council as a social agency, an agency that receives complaints from the public and generally monitors industry standards. The Council members have an opportunity to comment on what the standards should be, and that can have a tremendous impact on our society and the kind of information and entertainment that is available. There was one occasion where I was involved in the resolution of a complaint concerning a radio station that had offended a person or persons in the community. As a result the station was reprimanded and they had to amend their policy. All of my experience in dealing with youth and prisoners and Black people and Aboriginal people, all of that background became useful in participating in the discussion as to what the standard should be in the community. So I saw it as a way to continue to use the things I've learned by being a volunteer or political activist, and that's an ongoing part of my life.

I was being kept pretty busy in my role as Citizen Jones, and it was taking time away from my legal work. After *RDS* was successfully concluded, I left Dal Legal Aid and took a job as a staff lawyer for the Canadian Union of Public Employees, from 1997 to 1999, and then I opened my own firm: B.A.

"Rocky" Jones and Associates. I put in the "Associates" in case my firm should ever expand. My CUPE connection led to my appointment to the Highway Workers Board. Highway workers are part of CUPE, but they are not allowed to strike. Instead they have arbitration, and the Board deals with anything that cannot be settled by arbitration. When I was a member the chair was Susan Ashley. She could appoint an arbitrator, and if necessary the Board would meet to hear appeals from the arbitrator's decision. In addition the Board generally oversees the Highway Workers Collective Bargaining Act. The union has the right to appoint someone to this Board and so does the employer, which is the government. I was the highway workers' representative. I saw this as important because it was a recognition of my commitment to workers, and it was also a recognition that the workers would value my legal expertise. This was very satisfying for me. You work all these years to get people to understand that this is where I'm coming from, and the highway workers say, "Hey, this is our representative to the Board." Besides my constant concern for Black community affairs, the condition of workers has always been a priority for me. The Board gave me a practical opportunity to contribute to furthering the cause of our working people in Nova Scotia.

There were a couple of other community commitments, all of them overlapping in time, all of them considered important, but none of them contributing to the bottom line. One of them was the board for the G.I. Smith scholarships. I had myself been a recipient of a G.I. Smith scholarship while I was a student at the Dal law school. This was an interesting experience because in Truro, where I grew up, G.I. Smith is a very big thing, and he was a Tory. Another member of the board was John Buchanan, and the honorary chair was Robert Stanfield. Need I say more? Here I am sitting as a director of the G.I. Smith board, surrounded by the biggest Tory names in the province! Who would ever have thought that the Tories would ask me to sit on any kind of a board? Actually I regarded it as an honour and I took it seriously. They presumably recognized that I could make effective decisions, and I could influence who would be the recipients of the scholarship.

And then there was the Parks Canada Community Committee. I believe this was an initiative of Sheila Copps when she was a federal minister, and the idea was to diversify the Historic Sites and Monuments by recommending the names of people, places and events from different minority communities to be honoured as historically significant for Canada. Our provincial committee was called together by Ron MacDonald and Skip States, from Parks Canada, and it included people from different parts of Nova Scotia and one member from away, Jim Walker. George Elliott Clarke sent several written submissions. The committee was a lively mix of academics and community people. Our concern was primarily to identify Black historical contributions. We met out at the Black Cultural Centre, and at our first meeting I was elected chair. We had some very good discussions, and passed recommendations to the Board in Ottawa, which would commission research and make final decisions. One particular discussion related to the absence of any monument to the enslavement of African and African-descended people in Canada. In Ontario a plaque had been set up commemorating the abolition of slavery in Upper Canada in 1793, but we reasoned that this moment could not be understood without acknowledging those who had been enslaved in the first place. We recommended that a plaque should be placed prominently at the harbour in Halifax, where there were sales of enslaved Black people right from the founding of this city in 1749. I'm not sure if this recommendation was adopted and awaiting execution, or perhaps is still under consideration, but certainly no plaque was ever erected. We also discussed things like the Black Loyalist Heritage site in Birchtown, recommending federal funding for their proposed interpretation centre, and we argued firmly that the Reverend Richard Preston's work in founding the African Baptist Association, along with his anti-slavery and other community work, must be accepted as being of national historical significance. This was successful, and Richard Preston now resides in the gallery of Canadian history.

In 2002 the Johnston Chair, Esmeralda Thornhill, hosted a useful and interesting conference on reparations, and I was invited to speak. My approach was to raise a series of rhetorical and legal questions which could complicate the demand for reparations unless they are answered fully and convincingly. There are legal, political, and social implications in the idea of reparations. I've always believed that we deserve to be repaid for the work put into the development of this society by our ancestors, and for the fact that they were unpaid or underpaid. We had participated in the society without being able to benefit equally from the society. In the first instance we have to ask, "What was the crime? We're going to demand repayment for what?" I think there's a real difficulty in defining what is the crime. Was the crime that we were enslaved? If that is the definition, then what liability do we have for participating in it? Is it that the Europeans came to Africa and enslaved African people and took them away, and they are 100% to blame for it? Or if there's collusion by our African ancestors, what responsibility do they have in participating in the original crime? So it is not quite so cut and dried as to say we should be compensated strictly for slavery. Not only do I need to look at what was the crime, I have to look at when was the crime committed? How far back do we go when we define the crime that was committed? If we begin with the establishment of Black communities in Canada, there certainly is an argument that the prior slave experience in the American colonies and the United States before people arrived here shaped the people who came and denied them education, land, equality and so on. There has to be some way to tie in that experience prior to the arrival in Canada, and then who is responsible? If we say we are going back to the slave society and that's what reparation deals with, and we live in Canada, are we going to say to the Canadian government, "We're seeking reparations for what happened to our ancestors and we're asking you as the Canadian government to go back beyond when you had any responsibility for us?" I would argue it's impossible. If we are going to confine our request for compensation to the Canadian government, surely we can only ask for reparations or compensation for anything the Canadian government itself had an involvement in.

Another issue is whether the crime has ended? We're talking about a system of exploitation that has its origins in Africa through the theft of the African person, is continuing through organized slavery in America, and continues to be exploitative in Canada, where the people are denied benefits and paid different wages and not given the same land grants. The impact of that continues today where you have a school system that does not respond to the needs of Black children, you have segregated communities that are not part of the economic mainstream of society, and where you have Black tradespeople who are essentially disenfranchised or cut out of their trade. Not only are we looking at what was the crime, when was the crime, how far back do we go, but has the crime ended? And I say "No!" We then have to examine who were the perpetrators of the crime because it has to be framed in that way. I think we have to separate government from industry and from the populace in general. On one hand the government perpetrates the crime and sets up the legal justification for the continuation of the crime, but the businesses, the churches, the society that works within the framework of that government, they are also perpetrating the crime. So they cannot say, "We don't have any responsibility as we are simply the descendants of a person who ran a store. We've been here since the 1700s, we are white but we have never owned slaves. We don't see why our tax dollars should be used to pay you because your ancestors were exploited by government or exploited by some particular white racist employer, when we did not do anything or our ancestors did not do anything to you." My answer would be that although they may not be the direct perpetrators of the crime, they are beneficiaries of the system that creates the crime. If the society in general benefitted because of the exploitation of the Black slaves or Black labour, then even though you're not the perpetrator of the crime, you benefitted from the crime and therefore should be part of the payback and the reparations. We've got to examine not only who were the perpetrators but who were the beneficiaries.

We must address also what was the benefit? If we couch this in strictly economic terms, does the benefit accrue only to those who are economically in a position where they are favoured economically? For instance there are whites whose families go back to the genesis of Canada who are as poor or even poorer than most Blacks. Certainly we couldn't argue that they received any more economic benefit than the Black person who lives next door to them, who is also poor and may be married to members of their family. So the benefit cannot be just framed in terms of economics. You have to look at benefits in terms of social benefits, as opposed to or including economic benefits. One benefit you receive is safety. You can be in Montréal and not worry about being beaten up by police because of your race. You have the benefit of being able to apply for and get a job at the fire department because of your race. You have the benefit of going to the school in your community because of your race. So all of these things that are connected to race and racism are benefits and liabilities. If one person is disadvantaged, it follows that someone else has been advantaged. Reparations has to address this issue, that there is a benefit that is connected strictly to race that is not necessarily only economic. That analysis leads to the conclusion that the overall society benefits or has benefitted from that kind of exploitation.

In terms of reparations and a lawsuit, what was of interest to me was who do we sue? Do we sue all levels of government or do we sue the provincial government of Nova Scotia? All levels of government were complicit in the exploitation, but who can afford to pay? When you look at taking someone to court, it's okay to get a judgment on someone who has no money, but it doesn't do any good. You want to go after the bucks and the bucks really are with the federal government. That leads me to the question of what bodies have jurisdiction over what we define as the crime? We've got to find a way of defining this kind of exploitation both as economic exploitation and social exploitation, in such a way that we can fit it into some type of jurisdictional model. Can it come under the jurisdiction of the Supreme Court of Canada, and if so under what body of law? Are we saying that this is of a criminal nature, so therefore we're going to find the section of the Criminal Code that can handle it? Are we going to say that it's a crime of equity that's not codified, and we'll go back to the British common law to say that we've been exploited and taken advantage of and we're looking for a redress based on equity? Equity is not written down; it's floating out there in space somewhere and it's just the belief that in the British system everything has to be fair. If we could frame our reparations in terms of equity we could say it was not fair: they enslaved us, they took advantage of us, everyone else benefitted, we did not benefit, we lost on it. Then we have to ask, is there a limitation period? Do we back ourselves into a corner by framing something in a way that then gives rise to limitation because no one knows or ought to have known that the crime was committed a couple of hundred years ago?

In my talk for the conference I was putting together a case for reparations and how you would do it and what you would have to be really concerned about. And then I thought, what kind of evidence would you really have to present? I'm a Black man living in Nova Scotia. To say that I should benefit from any reparations, what evidence would I have to show that this crime was perpetrated against my relatives? And secondly, if I say it's ongoing, what evidence would I have to show that I personally am suffering because of this ongoing crime? Or can we say this is a class action, and then we produce evidence that as a class our people were treated in a particular way that unfairly disadvantaged them, and therefore as a class we should be compensated? There is no lack of evidence that Black people in this province and this country have been severely disadvantaged because of their race. Compensation would only and could only be to the group, and not to individuals. Governments would say African Canadians as a class were exploited, we're going to put X dollars into a fund that can be accessed by the African Canadian community, and no individual can make a claim. I don't think in our claim we would even look at anything in terms of the individual. I think our reparations must be as a class, and the benefits have to come to the community as a whole. In looking at which court to bring our case to, we could involve the United Nations. This exploitation in fact is a crime against humanity, and the court that would have the overriding jurisdiction is the United Nations. The benefit of that would be that we would have a court that wouldn't be making the decision about themselves.

I can't say I worked out a strategy, or considered all the possibilities, and I can't say my rhetorical questions were answered at the conference, but it was a very good conference. We had some excellent discussions, and the best thing was that there were a lot of local people there. People came all decked out, some in African garb. It was very colourful. People from Halifax became excited about the idea of reparations. Usually in Halifax when you talk of reparations you are talking about Africville, so I tied Africville into my talk and the discussion afterwards. It was good because people who were not academics were comfortable asking questions and participating. I think it was a consciousness-raising experience for many people. We considered the various other reparations agreements, especially the Japanese Canadians, and Japanese Americans, above all, not to mention the Native land settlements, and compensation for Jews because of the Holocaust. Look at all this money that's gone out, millions of dollars. We don't figure in it at all, yet we had all those millions of people stolen from Africa. There are on-going discussions, of course, and the African Canadian Legal Clinic, among others, is doing some research. Just before our conference there was the World Conference Against Racism in Durban, South Africa, where reparations was a major topic. So the troops are mobilizing, and I'm confident an answer will be found.

It was not long after this that the U.N. Special Rapporteur on Contemporary Forms of Racism, a man from Senegal named Doudou Diéne, came to Halifax to write a report on Africville's claim to compensation. Before his arrival I had several meetings with Denise Allen, nicknamed Tinky, who was giving a report to him on behalf of the Africville Genealogical Society. She asked me if I would help her prepare her position paper, which was presented to Mr. Diéne and later published as "Africville: The case for compensation, exposing all aspects of racism in Nova Scotia." The Special Rapporteur met with a group of us out at the site of the Nova Scotia Home for Colored Children. I gave a presentation there on September 20, 2003, using some of the information I had prepared for the 2002 conference on reparations. The Rapporteur was open and asked a lot of questions about Nova Scotia. He readily accepted the fact that racism was prevalent here and that it had had a negative impact on the Black community. It was exciting to see someone of his stature, coming from the United Nations, and actually listening to what we had to say. I had the confidence that he would report what we said openly and truthfully. In my remarks I said I wanted to highlight three of the objectives of the World Conference Against Racism, the Durban Conference in 2001. The objectives of that conference were to increase the level of awareness about the scourge of racism and racial discrimination; to review the political, historical, economical, social, cultural and other factors leading to racism and racial discrimination; and to formulate concrete recommendations to further action-oriented national, regional and international measures aimed at combating all forms of racial discrimination. Using this as my opening, I said that the awareness of the scourge of racism in Canada as it relates to African-descended people is almost nonexistent. The popular history of Canada neglects the fact that we've been here since 1604 and we've been part of the development of this country since the Europeans began their conquest of this land. To understand our present problems and dilemmas one must have an awareness of our history and appreciate how racism and racial discrimination created almost insurmountable obstacles for our people just to survive. Canada was a slave society until the Imperial Emancipation Act of 1833, which abolished slavery in Britain and all of its territories. African-descended people were used to toil the land, labour on the public works, and as keepers or caretakers of Europeans' children and elderly. We maintained this subservient position in Canadian society after slavery was abolished, when we became a source of cheap but readily available labour. Racism kept us in this place. Racism, rooted in slavery, colonialism and white supremacy, is a fundamental aspect of Canadian history. This racism had a devastating effect on our people economically, politically, personally, culturally and socially. There must be a redress of this grievance. Canadian society, the beneficiary of our exploitation, must pay compensation for what has been done to us. My remarks were general, while Tinky was specifically addressing the case for Africville. It showed the things that have been done in the Black community to get these high powered, important people to pay attention to us. Mr. Diéne's report did include all these points. He recommended compensation for Africville and eventually they got it, though not exactly what they had been asking for. As for the more general argument about "all aspects of racism in Nova Scotia," we're still waiting for the response from Canadian governments.

So accomplishments have been made by our community and we have shown what we can do, but lots of issues remain. Our society has not been restructured. There are challenges that can inspire other citizens to step up and carry on the struggle. We have a community that is going through some really difficult times. The community itself is breaking down, and the response has to be to build the community back up, the community as a community. Look at the number of our young people turning to crime. You can't just count the number of criminal charges or court cases and say, "Look it is on the increase," because that would not account for racial profiling, false charges and abuse of power by police. What I'm talking about is the drugs, the pimping and prostitution, the assaults. Our children, that is some of our children, seem to have lost respect for themselves and for their parents and for the community. They don't believe they have a future and they don't believe their life is worth much. There is nothing to stop them from being involved in crime and violence. With the destruction of the Black community and the takeover by the state, the result is the alienation of these children from their family and from their community. The families don't have the same influence over the children and the children don't have the sense that they are valued.

One underlying issue is the extent of unemployment among Black people, and not just the youngsters. We have families that are going three generations on welfare, and to qualify for welfare they have to live a certain way and perhaps even lie about certain things: who lives in the house, who is visiting the house, what's going on in the house. They have to be prepared to lie or cheat because that is what determines whether they get the welfare cheque, whether they keep their house even. There is a depressing tendency for these kids to drop out of school before they finish high school, and all they would qualify for is minimum wage jobs or welfare, or they can turn to crime. You hate to see these children destroyed when you know it's not their fault. They didn't chart their own course. They are not in control. So what we have to do is take control, and let these kids take control. That's why we need strong organizations. We cannot afford to have "gatekeepers" who do the government's bidding. Governments should be responsive and supportive of community initiatives; that's their proper role. Instead, we have them dictating what our needs are supposed to be. We cannot afford to have organizations that will not confront government. We cannot afford to have hand-picked government-sponsored leadership that won't have progressive programming and take on the varied issues that force these young kids into desperation and often crime and dealing dope. What if, in your community, there are no jobs, or people are not going to hire you even at minimum wage because Black people don't control the jobs or own the businesses? What are your options when there's nothing that can help you out of a bad situation except crime or welfare?

The Black United Front began with such hope and idealism, but it went down the path of government dependency and eventually it disappeared because it had long outlived its value to the community. If we want to address the social issues facing our community and our young people today, we have to construct organizations that are really and truly in the hands of the people and dedicated to the interests of the people. If you don't seize and hold power effectively, then the long-term transformation of the social problem is stymied. The institutions that do exist continue to support the kinds of social policies and political programs that are not helpful. They are not building a sense of community that would make our youngsters proud to participate, for the benefit of everyone and not just for themselves as individuals. From a historical point of view, the message is that you need wholesale change, fundamental structural change. Messing around with partial reforms won't do anything except delay the solution. This is the critical lesson, I would say, of my lifetime as a community activist. As the saying goes, "Freedom is a constant struggle."

Chapter Eleven

SENIOR STATESMAN

The discussions among Rocky, George Elliott Clarke and myself (Jim Walker) continued until February 2013, but the time period we were discussing ended in 2003. This meant there was about a ten-year gap that was not covered with Rocky's own anecdotes and reminiscences, and thus it is not possible to continue this narrative in his voice. Instead, I am offering an overview of those years, based on interviews with Rocky's friends and family, newspaper accounts and my own awareness of what was going on in his life through our regular visits, emails and telephone conversations. The material is organized thematically in a generally chronological order, dealing with his social and recreational life, his law practice, his community activities, the honours he received, the many significant speeches he delivered in his later years, his declining health, and his final days toward his passing in July 2013.

Rocky obviously worked hard and gave his everything to every task and project. But despite all his activities and accomplishments, Rocky was not a person who kept his nose to the grindstone. Every Monday night, with only emergency exceptions, he played pool with a group of friends, and on Thursday nights he played poker, often in Truro at the home of Bill Yarn or Kevin Canes. His earlier life as a "card shark" notwithstanding, some of his poker buddies declare that he was in fact a "reckless" player who would make wild and inappropriate bets and often lost his stake. Other nights would find him at Bearly's House of Blues and Ribs or some other Halifax evening spot, enjoying a few "wets" with his friends, and on a Saturday afternoon taking in the live music at Your Father's Moustache.

But his greatest love was to get outdoors and hunt or fish. Rocky waxed poetically about his favourite fishing spot, the Forks Pool on the Margaree River. Fall offered the best salmon fishing, he reported, and in the spring you get sea trout and salmon. As Rocky put it, "You can do anything on the Margaree," swimming, tubing, just meditating on the beauty of nature. "The fall colours on the Margaree cannot be surpassed," he claimed. "You have the mountains in the background, sandstone, and it's very pastoral because you have cow pastures running down almost all the way to the river in some places. There is a gentle quality about the river. If you are in a pool on the Margaree and someone else comes in, you are obligated to move along at a nice slow pace, so that the other person can step in behind you. It is called rotating a pool. You can't go and get one spot and keep it for yourself. That is a tradition that is guarded extremely jealously." Many rivers in Nova Scotia get run-off from agriculture, and the water can become muddy. But the highlands of the Margaree Valley remain intact, so you still get clean, cold water running down from the mountains and the river is always clear. It's also a good location for the older fisherman. "In a lot of places you can fish right from shore without wading any further than your ankles, so it allows people who are starting to get frail to fly fish for huge salmon."

Rocky's experience while fishing was almost spiritual. "When you are on the river you can hear things, things you cannot normally hear. You can hear the birds, you hear the leaves, you hear little animals scurrying, you can hear a lot. You hear subtle changes, you can hear a squirrel who starts to chatter and you know there is something or someone coming, or there is something wrong with his world. A lot of times when you are on the river you hear a fish move, you hear it break the surface and you turn and you can see that ring in the water where that fish was so you know where you are going to fish. Your hearing becomes acute and you see things that you are not conscious of seeing. You see the change in the water with the wind that is shifting and even though the wind seems to be blowing the same on you, you can see on the water that there are different swirls and different patterns. You can see in the bottom where the fish are or where they should be, and you can see where the water is coming down and where the feed would be going for the fish, so you can see where the food channels are and where a fish would go if it wanted to feed. In those choice spots there is lots of feed and that is where the big fish are, because they are going to chase out any of the little fish. They are going to dominate in that area, so if you can read the river, then you can catch the big ones.

"When you are fishing a river, you have got to be able to see the trees, because that will determine where you will fish. Sometimes there is space, and you can back cast, you can let your line go behind you, you are not worried about catching up on anything. But at other times there are trees and you've got to put it in your mind, there is a tree just to the left and back of me so when I'm going to back cast I'm going to cast back to the right to miss that tree. And that has got to be a part of what you see when you look at the water. You just don't keep looking at it, it is part of your evaluation of that particular time. You've got to see the obstacles that are in the water and some of them are hidden, and sometimes you can see that the water is going to bubble up. The water may be coming and cresting and bubbling here so there is an obstacle in front of it, but you've got to be aware that the obstacle isn't exactly right where the bubble is, it is a different spot a bit further ahead, and when you are going down a river reading the water is maybe the most important part. Whether you are wading or canoeing or boating on moving water you've got to be able to see the danger before you get there. You can't wait until the last minute. You've got to see down the river and you've got to see the obstacles and you've got to see the channels. And you've got to continually make decisions, based on what it is you are doing and what you want to do and recognize the dangers that are in the decision. The danger is always with you, it changes from situation to situation. You've got to make a decision whether you are going to accept a certain amount of risk to do something, or whether the risk is too high and you have to back off. That is what you see when you are on the river.

"But what you feel is maybe even more important because when you are out on the river, you can feel scared because you cannot compete. You cannot take on Mother Nature, you'd get whipped; you have to feel how to become one. You've got to feel how you become part of the nature and the river, because it is the only way to survive. You can try to fight it, but you don't have the strength, so you must go along with it, but you just don't go passively along, you have to be part of it. At the same time once you have the confidence to know you are part of it, then you relax. It is one of those times that you do get a chance to think, because when you are out there you are alone in a boat or sitting on the shore or you are throwing a fly or casting a lure, you do get a chance to think, and you are not wearing a headset listening to music. There are not the distractions that you have in an urban office setting, they aren't there, you are just there and it is a great time to see realistically where you are at or what you have to do or how to look at different problems. It is a great place and a great time to solve problems or make decisions."

Although we planned to give Rocky an opportunity to make similar meditations on hunting, our sessions ended too soon. But hunting and fishing combined in his life as sublime pleasures. And he took it very seriously, as I can attest from my one duck-hunting trip with him, in the fall of 1968. There is a brief reference to this trip in Chapter 7, in the context of establishing the Transition Year Program at Dalhousie. As mentioned, this "had" to be a genuine wilderness experience, no tent, just build a lean-to, start a fire and cook up some ducks. In the morning, after our long, cold, sleepless, but conversationally fruitful night, I expected to light a fire for warmth. It was still dark. "No no," said Rocky, "the ducks will see the smoke and you'll scare them off." Then he took a handful of cold ashes from last night's fire and started rubbing it in my face. "What are you doing?" I protested. "Well, when the sun rises it will reflect off your white face, and scare off the ducks. That," he explained after a pause, "is why Black people make the best duck hunters." We set up our blind on shore and settled in to wait for some fearless ducks. Nothing was happening, so I took out a cigarette (we were both smokers at the time) but before I could light it he was tossing water in my face. "No no you can't smoke, you will scare off the ducks!" As we sat there I became aware that our shore was tidal, and the water at our feet was up to our knees. No ducks were in sight, so I clambered out of our blind onto some dry land behind. "No no," it's Rocky again, "you will scare off the ducks." Two days later I did go home with four dead ducks, which my wife Stephanie threw in the freezer where they languished until we committed them to the garbage a year later.

Fortunately, Rocky usually went hunting and fishing with friends who shared his enthusiasm and his expertise. In recent years a pattern evolved: in the fall Rocky, his friend Hughie Grant and various others would gather at Bookie Wood's place in Truro on a Saturday and go hunting for ducks or pheasants, sometimes rabbits, at night have a poker game or go to a tavern, returning to the chase on Sunday. No lean-tos or blackened faces. The season begins in Colchester County on October 1 and in Annapolis County on November 1, so there was a complete autumn of hunting. Sometimes with different people, Rocky would hunt in different areas for different game, including deer, availing himself of just about every weekend when he was not committed elsewhere. More adventurous were his summer fishing trips to Newfoundland, usually with Bookie and Bill Yarn, and sometimes they would hook up with local fishermen. All three of the regulars obtained their Nova Scotia fishing guide licences after taking a course in Truro about a decade before Rocky's death. Then, through an interprovincial agreement, they were able to get a Newfoundland licence as well. This meant that they no longer had to hire a guide during their Newfoundland trips and they could charge a guide

King of all he surveys, Rocky the Outdoor Enthusiast.

fee to any other people who came along with them. Under the regulations there had to be one guide on duty at all times. This meant that two of them could fish, while the other served as guide. But once upon a time Rocky, who was supposed to be the guide on duty, casually threw in a line and hooked a trout. It turned out that a pair of Newfoundland Rangers was watching them from the bushes, and Rocky was fined for fishing while guiding. They had already returned home to Nova Scotia when their case came up. They had agreed to a plea bargain of a fine of $500, which the three would share, but when the sentence came down it included not only the fine but the loss of his guide licence. This happened about four years before he died. He was, Bookie says, very discouraged by this episode and never applied for renewal of his Newfoundland licence, though he did join his pals for their annual fishing trip until the very end.

Another annual event that Rocky never missed was the Black Golf Tournament in Truro, during the first weekend in August. It was a huge home-coming, with old friends like Dougie Collins returning from their lives in other places as far away as B.C. and the Caribbean. Rocky was less interested in the golf than in the social events, including a ballgame of oldtimers versus the youngsters, a late-night party and a dance. As the social event of the year, for secular African Nova Scotians the Golf weekend has replaced the African United Baptist Association weekend, which also happens each August. In addition there was the annual Atlantic Salmon Federation Dinner, usually held at a large Halifax hotel or the Casino, the Woodcock Dinner, a fundraising event for the Woodcock Society and its efforts for improving the environment for woodcocks, the Turkey Dinner, similarly dedicated to the welfare of wild turkeys, and the Ducks Unlimited Dinner. In between there would be smaller "Fishermen's Dinners" at the home of Hugh McKervill. This was a culture that Rocky lived to the full.

Meanwhile, of course, there was a living to be earned and causes to be fought. In 1997 he launched his own firm, B.A. "Rocky" Jones and Associates, and his case-load included in particular criminal law, human rights, labour and employment, and real estate, though he never turned away a needy client whatever the issue. His wife Sharon's contribution to the daily operation of the law practice was invaluable. An experienced banker, Sharon kept the trust accounts in order and wrote reports concerning them to the Bar Society, she handled the paper work for buying, selling and refinancing houses and commercial properties, she trained the clerical staff and generally oversaw the office. This was the "bread and butter" of the firm. Because of his CUPE

connections Rocky frequently received cases from union locals, mostly dealing with complaints between employers and employees. His criminal cases,
though numerous, generated very little income because his clients were almost
invariably poor and he forgave them not only for his own fees but for any
expenses he undertook on their behalf. Among lawyers who had won stel-
lar victories at the Supreme Court of Canada and the Nova Scotia Court of
Appeal, Rocky Jones was surely among the most poorly paid! One cause that
occupied much of his time and effort, both before and after his retirement
from the official bar, was the Sydney Tar Ponds. The coke ovens, where coal
was "cooked" to remove chemicals and impurities preparatory to use in the
manufacture of steel in the Sydney plant, produced an effluent that ran into
a nearby creek and then into the harbour. Eventually this process resulted in
what became known as the Tar Ponds, which oozed toxic materials into the
air and water and affected the health and lives of Sydney residents. Rocky was
enlisted by a group of homeowners along Frederick Street to represent them
in their fight for clean-up and compensation. The clean-up campaign was ultimately successful, though the struggle for compensation was continuing at the
time of his death. He often mentioned how much he valued his acquaintance
with Elizabeth May during the Tar Ponds fight.

The Tar Ponds blended into a major concern for Rocky during his final
decade: environmental racism. This term identifies the longstanding practice,
particularly in Nova Scotia, of situating dumps, incinerators, sewage and other
polluting materials in the neighbourhood of communities populated primarily
by Blacks and First Nations, and generally by poor people with insufficient
means to fight back. As long ago as 1996 a Dalhousie University study reported
that over 30% of all African Nova Scotians lived within a five-kilometre radius
of a waste dump, and this percentage has been increasing ever since. A case in
point is the small Black community of Lincolnville in Guysborough County,
where a concerted "Save Lincolnville" campaign was initiated to halt the construction of a landfill intended to handle waste from 17 municipalities. A
research study known as the "ENRICH Project" (Environmental Noxiousness,
Racial Inequities and Community Health), led by Dalhousie Professor Ingrid
Waldron, is gathering evidence on the health effects of this kind of site, and
a documentary film *In Whose Back Yard?* was released shortly after Rocky's
death. He had participated in the "Save Lincolnville" protest and had helped
to popularize the term "environmental racism," which is an effective naming-
framing device more powerful than simply complaining about a dump being
located in your back yard. By emphasizing the racist undertones, this term

serves to link communities fighting unwanted pollution into a network that attacks the concept rather than individual instances, and it potentially wins broader public support through its revelation of the discriminatory aspect of pubic waste disposal. The term embraces any environmental threats, including unwanted intrusions such as flooding or wind farms. Interestingly, Rocky's sister Lynn has become an outstanding spokesperson against environmental racism, as part of the ENRICH group. And his good friend Lenore Zann, NDP MLA for Truro, introduced a private member's bill in the Nova Scotia legislature in 2015 to address environmental racism through a panel of government officials and private citizens, including African Canadians, to conduct a province-wide consultation and produce recommendations to overcome this apparently deliberate contamination, or certainly vicious disregard, of disadvantaged communities.

Lenore Zann was also one of the people who encouraged Rocky to re-engage with the NDP. Although he had never quit the party, he had dropped all leadership positions. Lenore returned to Truro in 2007 after a career as an actress, and in 2009 she was elected as Truro's first New Democratic MLA. Through a friendship between their mothers, teachers in the same Truro school, Rocky became acquainted with Lenore and, with sister Lynn (herself a former candidate in Halifax), campaigned energetically on Lenore's behalf. She attributes her win, in part at least, to the efforts of Rocky and Lynn and their Truro connections. Although Alexa McDonough had retired from active politics she too campaigned for Lenore, and in this way Rocky and Alexa re-established a warm relationship. He became a member of the executive of the Truro NDP riding association and then of the provincial council, when another old friend, Joy Woolfrey, who was herself a member of the provincial executive, organized his nomination papers for the executive of the party. He again became an enthusiastic New Democrat and for his contributions to the party he was honoured with a lifetime membership in the Nova Scotia NDP.

Rocky's greatest institutional involvement in his later years was with a new Black organization known as Ujamaa. The term comes from the Swahili word for "socialism," given special meaning by Julius Nyerere when he was leader of Tanganyika/Tanzania in the early 1960s. "Ujamaa" was always translated as "African Socialism," an Africentric program for social advancement and economic sustainability. The Halifax organization that adopted the name sought racial equality through capacity-building in the Black communities to provide employment that would compensate for the continuing loss of their land.

Carolann Wright-Parks, once a student in the Dalhousie TYP, director of the Community Economic Development and Strategic Engagement for the Regional Development Authority, had convened community roundtables in 2006 to discuss priorities and discovered a demand for an organization that would sustain the identity and legacy of the province's Black communities. She involved Rocky, who became co-chair and then chair of the Reference Group, which evolved into the Ujamaa Council. The Council has members from every part of Nova Scotia and includes a strong youth component, partly a result of Rocky's personal recruiting. In a speech in New Glasgow just a month before his death Rocky explained the history and functioning of Ujamaa. It began in 2007, he said, and was deliberately building slowly in order to avoid the problems that had faced BUF in the 1960s. Ujamaa would accept no government funding, allowing them to criticize the government without fearing budget repercussions. "We are not an elitist group," he told his all-Black audience, "we speak for the community." Personal membership was $5, and at the time they had only $751 in the Ujamaa bank account. But despite its modest resources Ujamaa became an outspoken advocate for issues related to Black community advancement. "There's nothing wrong with the young people themselves, the problem is with an education system that does not serve the needs of Black people, and the absence of employment opportunities," Rocky insisted. "No wonder our youth are unemployed." The issues were essentially the same as they had been in 1968–69, and Ujamaa was intended to be the community force that BUF could and should have been.

In addition to advocating the build-up of local infrastructure and training facilities, Ujamaa has been taking positions on issues of immediate public concern. Right up until July 2013 Rocky was the chief spokesperson on most of these issues, and he became identified as the Black community's representative voice demanding attention to matters of equality, justice and self-determination. One of those issues, and one that gained Rocky nationwide media attention, grew from the Africville Heritage Trust and the curator it hired in 2011 to oversee construction of the Seaview African United Baptist Church and its interpretation centre. The replica church and centre were to present the history of Africville, surely Canada's most famous Black community, from its early nineteenth-century beginnings, including its confiscation and destruction in the 1960s. The Africville Genealogical Society had fought for many years for compensation, finally resulting in 2010 in an official apology, return of land on which part of the community once stood, and funding of $3 million for the construction project. No individual compensation was awarded to the dislocated parties, and this constitutes a continuing struggle for many

Africville survivors, to whom Rocky provided legal counsel. The cash award was placed in a trust, whose officers were to hire a curator. Without what Rocky considered sufficient consultation the Africville Trust announced that they had hired one Carole Nixon, recently an Anglican priest in Shelburne and, most ominously, a white woman. Rocky immediately objected, and because his objection was interpreted as a reaction to Nixon being white, a media frenzy broke out. Rocky insisted that he was protesting against the apparently secretive hiring process, and he pressed the case that because Africville was of importance to all African Nova Scotians the search should have been wide and public. An explosive all-Black meeting, attended by "hundreds" according to press reports, was addressed by Rocky, but Nixon had already been hired. While this controversy was churning, Rocky and some others received anonymously a large brown envelope containing highly injurious allegations about Nixon. According to the information, she had been fired from her four previous positions, or left them under some sort of cloud, and had been accused of misusing her employers' funds for personal benefit. The Africville Trust job offer was consequently withdrawn, but not before causing a division among the Black leadership. Irvine Carvery, for example, the long-serving head of the Africville Genealogical Society and member of the Trust, resigned from the Ujamaa Council, in whose name Rocky had been making his public criticisms. Until the revelations against Nixon, Irvine had defended her as the most qualified applicant. Rocky continued to insist that his attack was not aimed at Nixon or the Trust but purely at the hiring procedure, an echo of his reaction to the 1968 appointment of Marvin Schiff as the Nova Scotia Human Rights Commissioner. Rocky and Irvine had been friends for decades, since Irvine was one of the charter students in the TYP in 1970, and they remained so despite this disagreement. In January 2012 the Trust hired a new executive director, Sunday Miller, an African Nova Scotian, and in 2014 Canada Post issued two stamps commemorating the history of Africville.

Another controversial, and divisive, cause adopted by Ujamaa under Rocky's leadership was the quest for compensation for about 150 former residents of the Nova Scotia Home for Colored Children who had been physically, sexually or psychologically abused while living there. Rocky was calling for a government inquiry into the allegations, not only to support a pending class-action lawsuit but to reveal the racism inherent in the Home's management. The then-NDP government declined to conduct an inquiry, leading former MP for Halifax West Gordon Earle to resign from the party. Rocky was openly critical of the government but decided not to resign his party membership in the hope of winning over Premier Darrell Dexter. In this he was unsuccessful, and it was left to the next premier, Liberal Stephen McNeil, to take up this cause.

Even more divisive in terms of Black community relationships was the Council on African Canadian Education (CACE) and its battle against the naming of the Delmore Buddy Daye Africentric Learning Institute. Again Ujamaa, and Rocky Jones, featured prominently in the controversy. The complexities of this confrontation have been the subject of several court cases and appeals, though Rocky's core position was apparent and consistent. After an incident in Cole Harbour between Black and white youths in 1993, the provincial government set up an inquiry that recommended the establishment of CACE to promote research and policy development for African Canadian education programs and to advise the Department of Education. The government assigned a $2.2 million budget for its activities. CACE created the Africentric Learning Institute to deliver their programs, hired Delvina Bernard as director and registered their name with the Registry of Joint Stock Companies. Rocky was supportive of CACE and the Institute, and his daughter, Tracey Jones-Grant, was at one time chair of the Council and a member of the Institute board. The controversy arose when the provincial government funded a new association, the Delmore Buddy Daye Africentric Learning Institute, named after Rocky's old friend Buddy Daye and the father of his close friend and associate Gilbert Daye. CACE took legal action, ultimately successful, on the ground that the new Institute's name would cause confusion with their Institute. Consequently, it was renamed the Delmore Buddy Daye Learning Institute, though its programs remained focused on African Nova Scotian education. Rocky's position was two-pronged. First, he objected that the Buddy Daye Institute was initiated by the Department of Education and would be subject to government control, and in fact he suspected that its purpose was to subvert the original Institute, whose pronouncements were interpreted as becoming more radical. This was probably Rocky's most longstanding political position. Secondly, he felt that any institute serving the entire community should not be identified with a particular person, even Buddy Daye. He argued for a more generic title, as would be consistent with the community's tradition, and agreed with Delvina Bernard's statement: "This is about self-determination. We have the power and the right to name ourselves and define ourselves, and you don't get to pick who our heroes are." Though it won the court battle, the original Institute was starved for funds and lost both staff and programs. Because the provincial government (then NDP-led) was involved, there were New Democratic Party splits and family and friendship consequences over this dispute, which Rocky felt were unnecessary and simply another demonstration of government interference in Black community affairs.

Another issue taken up by Rocky, through Ujamaa, was the battle between North End Halifax residents and City Council over the conversion of the former St. Patrick's-Alexandra School to commercial purposes. The school had been closed due to a decline in the local student population, and according to Halifax's own policy the space was required to be offered first to a non-profit group. Nevertheless, a private developer was awarded ownership of the property for a price of $3 million, a decision challenged by the North Central Community Council Association on behalf of the Richard Preston Centre for Excellence, the North End Community Health Centre and the Micmac Native Friendship Centre. The Rev. Rhonda Britton of the Cornwallis Street Baptist Church led the community campaign, with Rocky's fervent support. After several appeals to the courts, with varying results, the developer prevailed in the Nova Scotia Court of Appeal and leave to appeal to the Supreme Court of Canada was denied, leaving the developer victorious. While the case was still proceeding through the Nova Scotia courts, and at a stage when the developer was winning, Rocky called the situation "a crying shame" and "a disgrace." He asked a Halifax audience to "feel my passion on this issue" and pronounced that the episode showed "just how far we have not come." The developer's intention was to construct high-end condominiums on the site of the former schools, a kind of gentrification that Rocky had always opposed. Rather than displacing Black communities and their facilities, Rocky had consistently argued in favour of strengthening them in their traditional locations. Just as he had fought, and won, against the development of Creighton Street into high-rise apartments (described in Chapter 4), he threw his considerable rhetorical skills into keeping St. Pat's-Alexandra in community control. Although he did not live to see the final result, this time his side did not win.

Apart from these highly public activities, Ujamaa holds meetings with the Halifax municipality and the provincial African Nova Scotian ministry to lobby for community issues, and continues to conduct Dialogue Lounges, semi-structured conversations over community matters such as racism in the workplace. It also resurrected the practice of holding Black Family Meetings, chaired by Rocky until his death, to allow open discussion on any situation that would benefit from community participation. It was after his death that his daughter Shalyn "Folami" Jones opened the Kwacha House Café, dominated visually by a portrait of Rocky, with facilities for public meetings and an atmosphere that encourages discussion along the lines of the original Kwacha

House of the 1960s. Kwacha House Café has partnered with Ujamaa and with Solidarity Halifax, which is not identified as a Black association, to create a website called "Working While Black in Nova Scotia." Launched in December 2014, "Working While Black" raises awareness of employment and other discrimination in Halifax, and helps validate the personal stories of Black Nova Scotians who have experienced racism at work. The website also lists resources so that participants can find the appropriate assistance, either government or private, where available. It is a worthy successor to Rocky the Community Activist.

In contrast to his earlier identification as an outsider, a disturber of communal order and an irritant in the side of the establishment, by his final decade Rocky was being regarded as a senior statesman and a wise commentator. Public institutions took note of him and awards began to rain upon him. One, of which he declared himself particularly proud, was an honorary doctorate of laws from the University of Guelph in 2004. The nomination was initiated by Rocky's old friend Stan Barrett, a former CUSO volunteer and Dalhousie grad student, and at the time a professor of anthropology at Guelph. Stan recruited John Baigent, George Elliott Clarke and Jim Walker to provide supporting letters, and the university's Board of Governors approved the nomination. Fittingly, the university chancellor bestowing the degree was the Honourable Lincoln Alexander, former lieutenant governor of Ontario, former federal cabinet minister and a revered pioneer in breaking barriers for African Canadians. In his remarks to the Convocation, Alexander referred to Rocky's time "in the trenches," once deemed conspiratorial and now recognized as an outstanding contribution to Canadian life.

Later that same year Gilbert Daye, on behalf of the Delmore Buddy Daye Foundation, organized the Rocky Jones Appreciation Night to give the people of Halifax an opportunity to acknowledge Rocky's enduring contributions to their city and province. Hundreds of people, of all colours and political persuasions, attended the dinner and dance at St. Antonio's Olympic Centre on November 20, 2004. The two speakers who were brought "from away," George Elliott Clarke and Jim Walker, extolled Rocky's public achievements, peppered to be sure with personal anecdotes intended to be amusing. Hugh McKervill told stories about their fishing adventures, Bookie presented Rocky with a sculpture of the head of a fox, Sylvia Hamilton, appropriately, sent a video tribute, Michelle Williams brought greetings from the Dalhousie IBM program, and Gilbert, chairing the event, announced that Rocky was the first recipient of the Buddy Daye Community Service Award. Rocky's comment was that he felt he had attended his own funeral, though privately he admitted to being "humbled and honoured," not to mention "surprised," by all this attention and gratitude.

The honours continued. In 2008 he received the Canada Democracy 250 Medal from the Province of Nova Scotia, commemorating the 250th anniversary of the first representative government in Canada, located in Nova Scotia, and in 2010 the Order of Nova Scotia, the highest possible provincial honour. His home town gave him the Truro Apex Community Award, presented during the Black Golf Tournament weekend. Another well-attended public event was held in the Music Room in Halifax's North End in March 2011, "The Blues Night for Rocky Jones," featuring local talent both Black and white, acknowledging not only Rocky's public accomplishments but his lifelong appreciation for blues music. Posthumously he received the Lorne Clark Access to Justice Award, named for a former Chief Justice of the Nova Scotia Court of Appeal, the Justice Award from the Multi-Ethnic Sports Hall of Fame, his portrait has been installed in the Indigenous Blacks and Mi'kmaqs Program at Dalhousie, and the Nova Scotia Human Rights Commission named its annual award after Rocky. Not bad for a kid from the Marsh! Rocky the Revolutionary produced a revolution after all; his outsider analyses and tactics have finally penetrated the establishment he provoked so insistently all his life.

Honours and recognition did not still his urgency to promote justice and equality. Indicative of his status as senior statesman, Rocky was invited to address prestigious gatherings where he was enabled to explore publicly the issues that had been closest to his heart for decades. A few examples follow, from his final two years. Videos of most can be found through putting his name into an internet browser. In January 2012 he gave the inaugural lecture, entitled "The Struggle for Human and Civil Rights by African Nova Scotians," in the Johnston Chair Distinguished Lecture Series. The next month Rocky and I jointly delivered a keynote address, "Black Power, Community Politics and the Promise of Multiculturalism in Canada," to an international conference on multiculturalism at the University of Matanzas in Cuba. In July that same year, he gave a TEDx Talk, "Breaking Down Social Barriers," in St. John's. The following January, he spoke at St. Francis Xavier University on Martin Luther King Jr. Day, a special occasion for Rocky as he was introduced by his son Augy, head coach of women's basketball at the university. Another Dalhousie lecture, "Racism, Privilege and Power," took place in February 2013. Not all his speaking engagements were held at institutions of higher learning. Also in February 2013 Rocky spoke to the pupils at Hubbards Public

University of Guelph, 2004, Honorary Doctorate — George Elliott Clarke, Rocky, Stan Barrett, John Baigent, Jim Walker.

School, where the children sat on the floor of the gym and listened intently to Rocky tell the story of the African Nova Scotian community. The questioning went on beyond their lunch-hour. My favourite question came from a boy of about eight or nine, who asked Rocky if he had ever been a slave. He smiled and answered patiently, explaining the history of Black enslavement in Nova Scotia and elsewhere.

There was a general pattern to most of these public-speaking engagements. He would often begin with a reference to a current issue, such as St. Pat's-Alexandra School or the Home for Colored Children. When appropriate he would offer some local commentary, for example, in his talk at St. F.X. he criticized the relationship between the university and the surrounding Black communities. The Coady Institute had projects around the world, he pointed out, yet it neglected impoverished groups in its own neighbourhood. Next would come a description of what it was like to grow up Black in Nova Scotia. This involved a loving account of his family and the community on the Marsh, and he would stress in particular the role of women in maintaining the community's traditions and sense of identity, and their encouragement for their children to obtain an education. The core of many of Rocky's addresses was an overview of Black history in the province. From the time of the Black

Loyalists, he would argue, Black labour has been exploited for the benefit of the mainstream economy. When speaking to a white or mixed audience, he would conclude that therefore his white listeners had themselves gained advantages from Black oppression, and it was time to confront the attitudes and institutions that were historically embedded in the provincial culture. "The benefits you enjoy, you enjoy because we've been exploited," he said at Dalhousie in February 2013. After all this history, after years of contributing to their larger society, not only economically but militarily and culturally, Blacks were still deprived and neglected. He also used the historical overview, especially for Black audiences, to argue that African Nova Scotians are a *people*: their ancestors arrived in groups, they gained their strength from their community, they developed their own churches and other associations and institutions, they had to look inwardly to each other for their support. They have generations invested in the soil of Nova Scotia and must be considered indigenous, while still being a part of the global African Diaspora, and from these sources African Nova Scotians derive their unique identity.

Rocky liked to insert an account of the 1960s into his speeches, with its new and revolutionary analysis of racism as a systemic rather than an individual problem. Because of its roots in the peace movement, the Canadian campaign for civil and human rights differed from the American civil rights movement, which was occurring at the same time, though eventually Black Power won adherents on both sides of the border, a concept he interpreted as Black self-confidence and self-determination. He often claimed that he was most proud of his role in creating and then sustaining the Transition Year Program at Dalhousie, for he felt it had the greatest impact of any program or issue with which he had been associated. But the changes effected in the sixties and seventies still left Black communities impoverished, still seeking equality, still separated, still under-educated, under-privileged and under-employed. He would lament the crime and violence that feature in many Black communities, and explain that because Black people regard the police as an occupying force, there to contain rather than protect them, they don't trust the police and are not inclined to cooperate with them or inform on local violators. But this current situation of the Black people of Nova Scotia was not simply something to regret: it was a challenge, it was the new cause for the new generation, and everyone in his audiences, regardless of colour, would be called upon to answer the question "What can *we* do? Where do *I* participate?"

Rocky set himself, or accepted, a gruelling schedule even after his law practice was theoretically abandoned. He was called upon frequently to speak to assorted meetings. He continued to advise people, for free, on legal matters. He was a volunteer with heart patients in the hospital every Wednesday afternoon. As was his lifelong habit, he continued to give his all to every endeavour, and it took its toll on his health. His major heart attack and triple-bypass operation are described in Chapter 9. Afterwards he tried to go for a walk every day with his Labrador retrievers, often in Point Pleasant Park with his friend Bob Russell. He went three times a week to the Pulmonary Gym. He did not, however, seriously care for his health. When told by his doctor to give up cigarettes, he switched to smoking cigars! More heart problems followed. He had three stints inserted in 2006, he received a pacemaker, he had more operations. In addition, he'd had a jaw problem for many years that would flare up and cause considerable pain. It derived, apparently, from the altercation in the Prizefighters Club in 1968, described in Chapter 5, when a gunstock hit him in the face. A tumour developed, and finally the jaw had to be re-built, using bones taken from elsewhere in his body. This required two separate operations, and in the meantime his mouth was wired shut and he could only get his nourishment through a straw. He was prescribed painkillers, but generally avoided them because they made him feel foggy and he preferred to keep his mind alert.

Around Christmastime 2010 he took his daughter Shalyn and her three kids to a swimming pool in Dartmouth. Perhaps it was the shock of the cold water that caused his difficulty; some of his internal equipment failed, he sank to the bottom and Shalyn had to pull him to safety because he was too big for the lifeguard to manage. On that occasion he was ordered not to drive a car. I was coming to Halifax to speak at Pier 21 a few weeks later, and he explained on the phone that he would not be able to pick me up at the airport as he usually did. When I arrived in the Halifax airport there was Rocky. "How did you get here?" I asked. "I drove," he replied. "But I thought you weren't allowed to drive." "Well, the doctor told me not to, but they didn't take away my licence so I figured it was safe to drive a little bit." To me, this epitomized his attitude, both his sense of duty to care for a friend and his inclination to risk his health, or at least to disobey his doctor.

Another illustrative anecdote occurred during our visit to Cuba in 2012. Rocky and I had planned (i.e., talked about) going to Cuba for decades. Then an opportunity seemed within grasp. Professor Augie Fleras of the University of Waterloo drew our attention to a conference on Canadian Studies at the University of Matanzas that was to occur in February 2011, so we submitted a proposal and it was accepted. But after his swimming-pool incident he was not allowed to travel, so we sent our regrets to the conference organizer, Professor Emilio Rodriguez Barroso. Emilio replied with an irresistible invitation: if we could come the following year, in February 2012, his university would pick up all our expenses — travel, accommodations, food and drink — for two whole weeks, and the conference would be organized around our presentation as a keynote address. We spent a few days in September 2011 organizing our talk, and in February 2012 off we went to Cuba. One evening as we were walking along a darkened path he stepped on a stick that flipped up and cut his shin. He washed it off, but after a day or two it was apparent that it had become infected. He went to the Foreigners' Health Clinic in Varadero, was put on an antibiotic, told to keep his leg up, and no swimming and no alcohol. And we were oceanside with all expenses paid! Rocky's decision came as no surprise. "Well, I'll just swim and drink a little bit." This was Rocky to the proverbial "T."

His health continued to deteriorate. Shalyn, who had moved back to Halifax from Toronto with her children, became his primary health provider, monitoring his blood pressure, arranging his medications, fashioning blister packs. Staying home more, he became increasingly attached to his grandchildren. He took them fishing, he took them to their basketball games and generally doted on them in a way he had not behaved with his own children. Shalyn reports that it was "beautiful" watching him settle into a more sedentary life, more, that is, than ever before but still filled with enough activity for any "normal" person — speaking, volunteering, organizing, pursuing every cause that affected his dedication to justice and equality. And, from time to time, working on our book. George, Rocky and I had arranged a two-week period in July 2013 when we would go over our recorded sessions, fill in gaps and bring the story up to date. My wife Stephanie's family owns a cottage in Muskoka, and our plan was to spend the time there. No telephone, no television, no distractions. It turned out that George was unable to come, but Rocky would so I bought his airline ticket for July 17. He phoned me that very morning and said he was in the waiting room at the hospital and could not come to Ontario after all. He did return home, but it was clear that he was in trouble. On July 26 I telephoned him to commemorate Cuba's National Day, and we talked half-seriously about another trip down there. He sounded very weak and tired. He said "I want to finish the book before I croak." I think he knew what was coming.

After our conversation he called Bookie and asked him to set up a poker game for that night, a Friday. Usually they gathered on Thursdays, but Bookie put together a group of men, Bill Yarn, Kevin Canes, Con Geddes, Gary Geddes, Don Matlinson, and they played at Bookie's house until 2 a.m., with Danny Gilbert watching but not playing. Usually they would quit at midnight, but Rocky insisted on extending their game. "He was playing with abandon," Bill says, and in fact Rocky lost $200 to Bill that night. Rocky stayed at Bookie's overnight, and early on Saturday morning they went fishing on Folly Lake. They caught some bass and trout, and by mid-afternoon Rocky was feeling tired. He had forgotten to take his pills with him to Truro. Sharon put them on the bus for express delivery but they didn't get there until Saturday afternoon, so he missed his morning dose. After a break he wanted to return to the fishing, but his buddies dissuaded him. He and Bookie dropped by the Black Golf Tournament dance that evening, though apparently they did not go in, just visiting outside with friends. Rocky had done just about everything he ever wanted to do in the previous 24 hours.

On Sunday, July 28, Rocky drove back to Halifax. After dinner he watched *Just for Laughs* with his grandchildren. He appeared to be behaving strangely, almost incoherent, so the family called 911. The paramedics took him to the hospital, and en route he suffered cardiac arrest. Because this caused a delay, Rocky's daughters, Tracey, Casey and Shalyn, along with Sharon, actually arrived at the hospital before the ambulance. From the Emergency waiting room, Sharon could hear them performing CPR on Rocky. He was put into an induced coma, intended to still his organs and allow a recovery. He never emerged from that coma, passing away at about 9 p.m. on Monday the 29th. The official cause of death was "organ failure."

The reaction was immediate and enormous. Within an hour of the family's announcement the Halifax CBC was broadcasting the news, and the next day the CBC *National* had an extended clip, including archival film footage, commemorating Rocky's public career. People were interviewed for their reaction; many declared that Rocky had "changed their lives." Adulatory obituaries appeared in the *Globe and Mail* and many other newspapers across the country, where "Rocky the Revolutionary," the "fierce champion of racial equality and justice," was often emphasized, and "larger than life" was a frequent descriptive. George wrote an elegiac poem, published in the *Chronicle Herald* and reproduced in the Afterword of this book. There was a visitation at the Atlantic Funeral Home in Halifax on August 6, with Rocky garbed in full ceremonial African dress, and the funeral service was held at the Colchester Community Funeral Home on Willow Street in Truro on August 8, with hundreds of friends and family filling the chapel and spilling into the corridors. Again the

African theme was present, with the procession led by African drummers who also offered an African libation. There were Aboriginal prayers and the burning of sweetgrass. All his children, Tracey, Casey, Agassou, Patrice, Shaka and Shalyn, spoke movingly, his niece the Rev. Denise Gillard invoked a meditation, and his friends Dougie Collins and Jim Walker gave the eulogies. The celebration continued at the Royal Canadian Legion in Truro. A more public memorial, "Remembering Rocky," occurred in October at the Rebecca Cohn Auditorium at Dalhousie, chaired by Walter Borden, with over three hours of music and with speeches from former lieutenant governor Mayann Francis, former minister Percy Paris, Judge Connie Sparks, friends Bookie Wood and John Baigent, family members and other friends and dignitaries, and a poem sent by George was read by Walter. The Senior Statesman was well and truly laid to rest.

Rocky concluded his July 2012 TEDx Talk with the comment: "I've had a pretty good life." No one could disagree.

Afterword

HONOURING
— NO, *UNDERSTANDING* —
THAT JONES MAN

by George Elliott Clarke

When Burnley Allan "Rocky" Jones somehow died, I mean, proved actually mortal, aged 71, on July 29, 2013, he became *instantaneously* deathless, for all us who believe — who trust — in some divine ideal dubbed *Justice*. Even so, I was shocked — terrifyingly saddened — by that news. His passing was expected; he was mortally ill; it had to happen. But the fact struck a blow.

Two years after his decease, I feel our loss is profoundly harsh. I look around; I see that Africadia (African Nova Scotia, y'all) remains headless and paralyzed. I see that progressive folks are asked to sink their hopes in one political party, which is well-meaning, has some good people, but is — since 2013 — uncertain about the virtues of democratic socialism, of public spending, of popular agitation for positive change. I see that the Occident is in turmoil over radical Islam and seemingly oblivious to our own roles as *meddlers* (see the Iraq Invasion of 2003) which spawned this trigger-happy *Malice*. I see that the First Black President of the United States (or first U.S. President "who happens to be Black") feels empowered to *drone everywhere*, but is quite powerless to stop blank-faced cops from shooting down unarmed — and more-or-less innocent — Black youths and men and women in the streets. I see that the globalist *moneyed* feel so comfy (despite crashing the world economy in 2007–09) that they dictate cavalierly to democracies (as in Greece) and employ *their* bought police to eye every keystroke on *your* keyboard or keypad.

I begin with this overview because I'm damned sure that Dr. Burnley Allan "Rocky" Jones, ONS, LL.B., LL.D. (HON.), would have. He was a thorough, true-blue (Black) Bluenoser outta Truro — rural, even backwoods — Nova Scotia. But he was never a stick-in-the-mud, never a rube, never a hick. He was an angler, a hunter, a salmon man, a deer man; he could pitch a tent and never mind the mosquitoes; roll out a sleeping bag and wave off the black flies. But he was also cosmopolitan, an adventurer. True: His stage was "only" North America, with the Caribbean at hand, not Africa, not Europa, not Asia. But his thought was universal, his outreach was to the world; his compass was his passion and his atlas was all of history.

Rocky resembled Malcolm X in this way; he was a tall, autodidact, organic, orally-oriented intellectual, with a world-view that was informed by history, but never limited by borders or by schools. He was able to think clearly and afresh about "local" issues in Halifax, or in Nova Scotia, or in Canada, but he always saw their connectedness to international or extraterritorial plights, and he tried hard to make his audiences — the *people(s)* he sought to lead — understand these *linkages too....*

Look up Rocky's speeches, videos; compare em with the X-Man: They offer the same plain talk, the same sharp interrogations, the same rhetorical suave, the same *zinging* pizzazz and joy in *debate.*

He was a double "O" — not in the James Bond-assassin sense, but as a dude who was simultaneously Orator and Organizer. Yet, he's not known for any particular speech — not like Martin Luther King's "Dream," or X's "The Ballot or the Bullet," or even Barack Obama's "A More Perfect Union." As far as I know, Rocky's raps aren't circulated or memorized or quoted as much as are the works of these African American contemporaries. Rocky's importance lies not as much in what he said as in what he did: Create coalitions and found institutions. In this sense, he's a "Black Scotian" version of Monsignor Moses Coady, who made speeches and wrote poetry, but is best remembered for his Antigonish Movement, which shepherded poor farmers, fishers, and miners into credit unions and co-operatives, with a strong dollop of adult education — "pedagogy of the oppressed" — as a spur. Crucially, Rocky took up Coady's example: Help the people gain institutions that can empower them, educate them, and lead them to greater prosperity.

Naturally, Rocky's insurgencies, his shake-up of low-down matters, are founded on material — brute — facts. He didn't need to be a Baptist (Christian) to see the need for *Liberation*; he was a Black man; that was enough. He didn't need to be Marxist/Maoist either; he'd felt racism in junior high; racism in the pool hall; racism in the army; racism even in the courts of law he was privileged to navigate late, late, late, in his chosen career as devil-may-care firebrand, as don't-give-a-damn tribune, as an essential agitator from the roots.

His politics owed more to Niccolò di Bernardo dei Machiavelli (cut with Moses Coady) than to Malcolm X or Marcus Garvey or Martin Luther King or Mao Zedong: A lot more. That's because he didn't identify one's suffering of oppression as being merely a function of one's class, gender, "race," ethnicity, language, religion, and/or sexual orientation. No, he saw it as a matter of *Power* — wielded by elites against their thralls, the "lesser-than." The *Power* could be *White Anti-Social(ist) Plutocrats* (WASP); or it could be *Black Religious Overlords* (BRO); or it could be *Anglo Privileged Elites* (APE); or it could be *Masculinist Authoritarian Heterosexual Imperialists* (MAHI); etc. The *beauty* of such a diversified analysis of the ways of masters and minions is that it is flexible, forensic, real, and *not* theoretical gobbledygook. It also means that Rocky was seldom the captive of any hidebound, lockjaw-producing set of protocols.

Rocky saw, then, that only empowered persons can be *effectively* — for instance — racist. An alienated, incestuous Klansman might hate Blacks, but his hatred is nearly neuter, for it lacks institutional definition, funding, and force. However, take that same man and put a paycheque in his pocket, a badge on his chest, and a gun in his hand, and now he is *legally* licensed to jail bodies and take lives, with a smile if he wishes, and likely with impunity.

In addition, from the time that, as a teen, he was prevented from playing pool with other "sharks" just because he was a "Negro," but was still told that he could stay and watch the white *guys* shoot, Rocky figured out that Canuck racism is different — *deviant*, really — in comparison with the American "norm." In Truro, in Nova Scotia, in Canada, racists don't show up with white sheets and burning crosses (*usually*), but with apologies, almost humble, for whatever discrimination you *think* you're experiencing. Even weirder, the segregation or second-class treatment gets masked as *politesse*: "You really prefer to be a maid, cook, porter, or shoeshine boy, doncha?" The arch *niceness* of Canadian racism makes it hard to detect and hard to fight. You can get your back up and get in someone's face, but then he or she will say, "Hey, it's just a misunderstanding. What's your problem?" Rocky "got" this nuance about *some* snow-job, upper-crust Canucks; how they like to do *Oppression* with photo-ops and *no-hard-feelings*....

Yet another difference between U.S.A. Negrophobia and the True North version is that "our" racism is more elitist. What I mean — and what Rocky knew — is that, while grassroots Black folks can be trampled upon, the hardy "flowers" among the "weeds" might, in fact, get plucked up *and displayed as an example of* the good futures awaiting those weeds *that can be relabelled as* respectable "flowers." Because America is a Republic, white folks "*en masse*" can practice racism against most Blacks; however, Canada is based upon European notions of privilege; thus, the "better class" of Blacks can achieve *noblesse oblige* elevation — just simple-simple *Respect*, even if *most* Black people — like *most* Indigenous citizens — suffer racism and *racisme*.

Canadian racism is European; it's indirect. In the Republic, the battle lines are clearly drawn and long defined. But Canadians prefer to discriminate invisibly — like letting out a silent fart. Our racism is based on the elitism of this *Monarchy* (lest we forget): Some people are just naturally better than others — *supposedly*: So, Anglophones lord it over Francophones; Protestants pretend they're better than Catholics; Gentiles play superior to Jews; Settlers oppress First Nations; men suppress women; the middle-class ride rough-shod over the poor; whites act like they're better than Blacks, etc.

In any event, in his journey from "Sapper Apprentice Jones" to Dr. Jones, ONS, LL.B., LL.D. (HON.), however, Rocky doesn't usually directly *confront* the powerful; rather, he *negotiates* openings that can lead to empowerment of the marginalized. Like Malcolm X — and like Pierre Elliott Trudeau — Rocky is not *generally* a leader of sit-ins or marches or occupations-of-premises. Instead, he is a negotiator; he offers the oppressed an analysis; they act upon it; he then confronts "the Man," "the Establishment," the "Power Structure," and demands meaningful concessions. He is not cynical in doing so, but wise. Rocky knew his Frederick Douglass — "Power concedes nothing without a demand," and, like the Abolitionists of yore, he chose to position himself to make the *Demands*, and that strategy did not mandate rotting in jail *or* wasting precious activist dollars on bail.

(Intriguingly, while King sought to actualize favourable U.S. Supreme Court rulings by creating a Movement that took to the streets, Rocky ended up doing the opposite: Taking street-borne protest and moving it into the Supreme Court of Canada or the Nova Scotian courts for jurists' debates and judgments. One way to understand his Supreme Court of Canada "laureate-ship": Rocky and his team asked nine Canadian "Supremes" to consider — by extension — Black folk wisdom and lived experience as having a potentially just influence in judicial meditation. That 6/9 agreed was an implicit validation that the context of "race" cannot always be evacuated, not even in supposedly *"raceless"* Canada….)

Step back now and study the 1960s radicals: Those who won the Vietnam *Peace*. How many of them founded useful institutions? The Black Panthers exist as nostalgia, as T-shirts and bumper stickers. MLK is dead; as is Malcolm; as is *Marcus*. Even Castro's Cuba is — like Mao's China — subject now to bankrupting, boom-and-bust *Speculation*. Not even Barack Obama — as a Saul Alinsky acolyte — has forged any social-change infrastructure in Chicago. *Shame*. But, *friends*, in Nova Scotia in particular, Rocky has left keystones — so to speak — that are milestones: the Human Rights Commission, the Transition Year Program for Blacks and Natives, the Indigenous Black and Mi'kmaq Law Program, the James R. Johnston Chair in Black Studies, plus the intellectual legacy that is The (Africadian) Cultural Renaissance. Then there are the spin-offs: Cultural Awareness Youth Group, Africville Genealogical Society, Black Educators Association, Association of Black Social Workers, Black Artists Association of Nova Scotia, Society for the Preservation and Protection of Black Culture in Nova Scotia. Gee! *Can I get an Amen?*

Another of Rocky's institutional offspring, the Black United Front of Nova Scotia, is long defunct. However, through its decades of operation, 1969–96, it became the Black community *"training centre"* wherein many social workers, journalists, and activists apprenticed. While its inception was radical, it slowly morphed from being a government-funded, anti-racism, and pro-Black-rights organization to becoming, instead, the Black adjunct to the provincial government's social-services department.

Add to the above, Rocky's *promotion* of the NDP to Africadians, plus the introduction of a Black-identified seat in the N.S. legislature, plus Rocky's support to People's Summit (1995) social activists and social workers, and one begins to see that little progress — in "race relations" (the euphemism for white supremacy and coloured folks' *acquiescence*) — happened in Nova Scotia that did not have Burnley's imprimatur…. Absolutely.

Indeed, when we hang the sixties tabloid tag, "Rocky the Revolutionary," on our champ — the people's champ, we need to define what we mean by "revolutionary." If we mean, "speaking *Truth* to *Power*," well, yes, the tag fits. If we mean, educating folks about the reasons for their oppression (poverty, illiteracy, marginalization) and then promoting ways to make (peaceful) change, then, yes, Rocky was revolutionary. But I think the noun makes most sense if we view Rocky as a catalyst, as a firebrand, keeping in mind Mao Zedong's notion, *circa* 1930, that "a single spark can start a prairie fire." In other words,

Rocky was a roots man, radically able to organize grass-roots, and then provide the spark that could set up — *not* a mass movement — but a would-be vision-ary, catalytic organization, to help preserve people's rights or provide them with enhanced opportunity.

Rocky knew Stokely Carmichael when he was Stokely Carmichael (not yet Kwame Turé) and had just co-authored *Black Power: The Politics of Liberation in America* (1967), a blueprint for Black populist agency. Informed by this book, but also by 1960s student, anti-Vietnam War mobilization, Rocky adapted and adopted the lingo and agit-prop of everyone from King to Carmichael to the Black Panther Party for Self-Defense, so as to rally Africadians and allies to push for systemic change economically, politically, and culturally. He did stand out as *the* revolutionary, as Canada's very own Black Radical, what, with the natty Afro, the Black-power raised fist, the dark-chocolate-velvet skin tone, the tenor-trending voice (gravel at base, reedy at the top), the turtleneck sweaters, the dark sunglasses, the medallions, the dazzling shoes, the correct slogans, the ever-present cigarettes, the politic wit. Nor was it all just chic, tele-genic pose, just slick packaging for primetime eyes and ears. Really, he was an insurgent public intellectual, using sound bytes to urge Afro-Canadians, Black Canadians, Africadians, West Indians, Africans, to unite with the like-minded and the good-hearted, to shake "loose change" from government budgets and create institutions or programs that would foster real change at the neigh-bourhood level. His "Black Power" was usually cosmopolitan in essence and internationalist in scope. He could bar whites from "Black Family Meetings," for purposes of enacting communal solidarity, but he was, nevertheless, in tacit dissent from Carmichael, radically open to inter-racial coalition, simply because, in Nova Scotia, the Black population base could not sustain long-term solo and/or segregated activism.

Yet, just as Malcolm X almost singlehandedly changed the minds of "American Negroes," to remind them that they were "Afro-Americans," with an African context to their identity, so did Rocky perform the same brain surgery for Africadians. Yes, we were influenced, anyway, by the oratory rising up from stereos and radios and TVs, but Rocky was the local exponent, the down-home proponent, of the mental shift essential to transform "Coloured Nova Scotians" into "Black Nova Scotians" and, eventually, into African Nova Scotians. This change was not cosmetic. Funkadelic proclaimed in 1970, *Free Your Mind ... and Your Ass Will Follow*: Thus, to alter the self-identification of the people, to bid them re-imagine themselves as positive representations of a decolonizing Africa, was to effect a cultural liberation *en route*, Rocky must have hoped, to economic independence with social equality. This was a big deal, "a sea change"; a lot of "Coloured Scotians" felt threatened by the notion that they could be "Black"; they associated the noun with Panthers and with pale cops shooting Panthers dead. That they did morph, agonizingly slowly, from "Coloured" to "Black" to "African" is likely Rocky's most subtle and most significant *Triumph*.

Nevertheless, it's an important dimension of the man, the revolutionary-without-a-conk, to realize that, while he was a "Soul Man," a "Soul Brother," slappin five and, at times, rappin jive, he was also a Bluenoser "buddy" — rank-and-file — to the apolitical pub brawlers and the *laid-back poker players* and the tense, but patient hunters. These are the "boys" he hung out with when he wasn't necessarily shaking up Establishments or getting ready to argue a case in court. These *Lumpenproletarians* — I mean, boyz-in-the-hood or Newfs-*off*-the-Rock or the ex-crooks-goin-straight helped keep Rocky "grounded," sensitive to the inchoate issues in policing or community politics or in socio-cultural debate. In this way, too, he resembles X, who was Muslim and thus resolutely separate from most (Christian) African Americans, but who was beloved and influential, partly because he maintained his "street cred" by keeping in touch with the "Commons."

But the outdoorsman aspect of Rocky conjures up a connection to Canada's 15th prime minister, namely, Pierre Elliott Trudeau, who was — like Rocky — a traveller in backwoods, a backpacker and canoeist, who could give an intellectually solid discourse on world affairs, federal-provincial relations, and/or the Constitution, and then vanish into forest, to commune with the spirits and re-establish his equilibrium. There's something of this Rousseauvian "Noble Savage" imagery at play in Rocky's self-display too: The organic intellectual who once had to burrow into a pile of buffalo manure to keep from freezing to death in a terrible, Washington State winter…. The story is comic, but also plays up Rocky's quick thinking and resourcefulness. I'm reminded again of Trudeau's stories of dodging bullets in Chinese fog or spouting French poetry at would-be bandits in Iraq; his tales also emphasize his wit and ability to improvise. I've gotta note here too the striking correspondence — at the level of metaphor — between buckskin-jacket Trudeau "fathering" the Charter of Rights and Freedoms and buckskin-jacket Rocky using that same Charter to defend the rights of justices to apply personal experience to contextualize their written judgments. It makes sense that Rocky was on a fishing trip when he learned of the success of his *1995* Supreme Court of Canada star-turn….

Then again, Rocky was comfy in the Great White North's Great Outdoors;

he rocked the plaid jacket, the fisherman's hip-waders, the hunter's knife and gun. The Black Panther Party grabbed headlines by telling Black Americans to get Black Power (*pace* Mao) by grabbing guns. But, for Rocky, the gun wasn't an agit-prop prop; it was the real deal: Not for shooting Ku Klux Klan clowns, but for shooting game.

Unlike Trudeau, though, Rocky didn't employ a Grey Owl / "Noble Savage" front — as an adjunct to his popular appeal. He was deeply — *impassionedly* — troubled by Canada's historical enmity for Indigenous Peoples. Comin from Truro's Marsh, next door to a Mi'kmaw Reserve, and bein part-Native in his own descent, Rocky was always aware of the particularly pernicious racism that the First Nations endure from the Canadian *State*. Although he acknowledges frustrations in his efforts to collaborate with the fiercely distinct and proud Mi'kmaw Nation, it is also true that many of the institutions that he championed — Transition Year Program and the Indigenous Black and Mi'kmaq Law Program — address fundamentally the joint needs of similarly marginalized peoples to acquire access to middle-class-cementing university educations. This is not to deny the primary difference between Africadians and Indigenous Peoples: The latter have a primordial relationship to the Canadian State — nay, the Crown — that Africadians do not. No matter: Whatever the stresses that Rocky encountered in his more-or-less successful efforts to unite the communities on shared issues, it is a poignant memory for me that, at his wake, there was both African drumming and Mi'kmaw chanting, and that *The Man* himself, garbed in an African robe in his casket, held an eagle feather in one clenched fist.

A DRAFT ELEGY
FOR B.A. (ROCKY) JONES

à la manière d'Yevgeny Yevtushenko

by George Elliott Clarke

I.

I don't want to write this elegy —
not for Rocky —
not for Burnley Allan Jones —
because no coffin can frame him,
no words can take his measure;
he doth orbit beyond obituaries....

But he was unprecedented *Excellence*,
outta all Nova Scotia:
He lit up even daylight like a flare
because he had game, had flair,
like a copper black flame —
irrefutably black —
the brilliant epitome of never diminished blackness....

Spy him spookin the T.V.:
Shaft gone intellectual.

The very air got impregnated with his black leather —
never scruffy —

but indelible, chic —
suitable to a scientist of speech
as bright and biting as a knife —
heroic chrome,
dazzling, sure, but no mere accessory.

Check:
When Rocky had to stand up for *Justice* —
or had to stand up for us —
Black (*et*) Mi'kmaq —
Africadian —
he showed the poise
and took the pose
of a hammer quick to strike.

Don't deem his bravado merely pantherish!
His stride was lightning tearing cross our eyes,
and his rappin struck us upside the head
with thunderous shocks:

Dude unleashed zingers and zest —
sound bites with teeth —
and handsome laughter —
vivid, ferocious.

The chap was earthy
and down-to-earth,
plain-spoken because
lying is an abuse of *Time*.

Rocky's talk shot straight stereo to our ears.
He demanded that we demand
that *Law* act *Righteous* by us.

He couldn't bring any routine medicine:
He saw that he had to fumigate
every sanctimonious cranny
of every legislature and every church.

Job 1 for him?
Discombobulate the Oppressor!

He took home the Order of Nova Scotia
for trying to end the disorder of Nova Scotia —
all the discord and disaster of Bluenose racism.

So Rocky stood his ground —
on sand or flinty soil.
Never a bystander,
he helped us to "overstand" —
right outstandingly.

Helplessly joyous in his hope for us,
he taught that *Hope* is a catalyst:
(For the hopeless, *can-do*'s got *done-in*.)

Rocky brought no fleeting gifts —
he was solid-state,
down with the People.
He was the true do-gooder,
rowdy, with steady nerves.

Admit that he was scintillating —
and terrifyingly tall.
Casual in his languid nobility,
but ready to produce *Wit*
and induce *Delight*,
Rocky would step into a room,
and all the gravity therein
would prove specific to him.

He was like inimitable poetry,
perfect in any translation.

Never any atrocious, politic rhetoric,
his talk leafed through intangible but priceless volumes.

Nor would he hobnob with snobs —
the guys with button-down degrees

and pointless appointments.
Rocky liked folks to prove as factual —
as sweet-and-sour, Chinese takeout.

Comin to us live from Truro,
proud outta Truro,
he was never confused —
and not one bit foolish.
Rocky knew the bite of *Keith's** ale
and the kick of a rifle,
and the dip of a fishing line.

We can name the sell-outs:
They don't *represent*;
they *front.*
Those are dollar signs that were their eyes.
These bourgeois coddle *Injustice,*
relax, collect brand-name luxuries —
Gucci this, *Versace* that.
They claim that they're "on fire,"
but all they are is piss with a temperature.
No one can place Rocky in such company.
He never dealt with any stuck-up culture —
no Parliament Hill or Beverley Hills airs.
He couldn't fit in
with the 'in' crowd.
He was too good an outsider,
because he cometh out the Marsh.

I began this poor elegy apologizing,
dreading this writing.
I still do.
But *Poetry* revives the cemetery'd,
and survives the cemetery....

II.

As I write, I see the man himself.
Rocky could rock a top hat
while rockin a canoe;
I spy the "subversive" out there,
anglin a line and hook
through a river's dangerous chuckles.
Later, he drowns a cold beer in his belly,
then fires up a trout,
enjoying ale and fish
in the intrepid cold of dusk,
a fitting finish
to a day of thought and talk and laughter —
the dividing line of his face.

Rocky could whistle up
a salt moon, a sugar moon,
a moon as weightless as milkweed fluff,
and he knew how trout look up
at shaken up stars.

(He heard *Nature* as *Spiritual* because —
To listen,
One must be silent.)

Misfortune's medals are tears.
Our eyes have minted them
and must mint them still.

But Rocky would have us spend
our silver tears and diamond sweat

in the struggle

to make money worthless —

compared with breath.

* Correct pronunciation: Keats.

Acronyms

ACLM	Afro-Canadian Liberation Movement
AUBA	African United Baptist Association
AWOL	absent without leave
BUF	Black United Front of Nova Scotia
CACE	Council on African Canadian Education
cap	Cultural Awareness Program
CB	confined to barracks
CBC	Canadian Broadcasting Corporation
CCF	Co-operative Commonwealth Federation
CO	commissioned officer
CORE	Congress of Racial Equality
CUCND	Combined Universities Campaign for Nuclear Disarmament
CUPE	Canadian Union of Public Employees
CUSO	Canadian University Service Overseas
CYC	Company of Young Canadians
DRUM	Detroit Revolutionary Union Movement
ENRICH	Environmental Noxiousness, Racial Inequities and Community Health
FESTAC	World Festival of Black Arts and Culture
HERO	Historical Educational Research Organization
IBM	Indigenous Blacks and Micmacs Program
LEAF	Legal Education and Action Fund
LIP	Local Initiatives Program
MLA	Member of the Legislative Assembly
NAACP	National Association for the Advancement of Colored People (USA)
NBCC	National Black Coalition of Canada
NCO	non-commisioned officer
*NDP	New Democratic Party
NHL	National Hockey League
NOIVMWC	National Organization of Immigrant and Visible Minority Women of Canada
NSAACP	Nova Scotia Association for the Advancement of Colored People
OFY	Opportunities for Youth
OISE	Ontario Intitute for Studies in Education
PSAC	Public Service Alliance of Canada
ROPE	Real Opportunities for Prisoner Employment
SCC	Supreme Court of Canada
SCLC	Southern Christian Leadership Conference
SCM	Student Christian Movement
sds	Students for a Democratic Society
SNAFU	Situation Normal All Fucked Up
SNAP	Scotia Nonviolent Action Project
SNCC	Student Nonviolent Coordinating Committee
SSHRC	Social Sciences and Humanities Research Council
SUPA	Student Union for Peace Action
TNVA	Toronto Negro Veterans' Association
TYP	Transition Year Program
UNIA	Universal Negro Improvement Association
UPEI	University of Prince Edward Island
VD	venereal disease (sexually transmitted infection)
VOW	Voice of Women
WIF	West Indian Federation